# *Reader's Choice*  International Edition

# Reader's Choice

## International Edition  Book 2

**E. Margaret Baudoin**
**Ellen S. Bober**
**Mark A. Clarke**
**Barbara K. Dobson**
**Sandra Silberstein**

*Developed under the auspices
of the English Language Institute
at the University of Michigan*

*Revised by*

**Mark A. Clarke**
*University of Colorado at Denver*

**Barbara K. Dobson**
*University of Michigan*

**Sandra Silberstein**
*University of Washington*

*Ann Arbor*
THE UNIVERSITY OF MICHIGAN PRESS

# Acknowledgments

We thank the many teachers who, over the years, have provided insights and suggestions for revision. To the roll call from the previous edition, we add the following names and apologize for any omissions: Sally Alexander, Kathryn Allahyari, Carol Deselams, Patricia A. Carrell, Joan Eisterhold, Pat Grogan, Liz Hamp-Lyons, Linda Hillman, Sara Klinghammer, Cherie Lenz-Hackett, Ellen Lipp, Daphne Mackey, Sharon Myers, Marnie Ramker, Sam Shepherd, Jerry Stanfield, Marianne Wieferich, Kay Winfield. We are grateful to our colleagues and to the dynamic context of TESOL reading pedagogy and research. Similarly, we continue to benefit from the contributions of our coauthors on the first edition, Margaret Baudoin Metzinger and Ellen Bober.

Special thanks to research assistants Elisabeth Mitchell, University of Washington, and Kathy Riley, University of Colorado at Denver, and to our colleagues at the University of Michigan Press.

Finally, we once again thank our families for continued support and patience toward a task that, no doubt, they hoped they had seen the last of.

Denver, Detroit, Seattle, June 1987

The successful completion of *Reader's Choice* is the result of the cooperation, confidence, and endurance of many people. The authors greatly appreciate the contributions of the individuals listed below. It is impossible to overestimate the importance of their efforts in helping us meet deadlines, their insights during classroom testing, and their encouragement through critique and rewrite sessions.

Heartfelt thanks, therefore to:

H. Douglas Brown, director of the English Language Institute (ELI), University of Michigan, whose assistance ranged from personal and professional advice to administrative and financial support. Professor Brown has consistently encouraged creativity and innovation at the ELI. His continued support of *Readers' Choice* ensured its successful completion.

Eleanor Foster, ELI administrative assistant and her capable secretarial and production staff: Elaine Allen, Ginny Barnett, Shelly Cole, Gail Curtis, Lynne Davis, Sue Feldstein, Martha Graham, Donna Head, Barbara Kerwin, Debbie Milly, Lisa Neff, Cathy Pappas, and Louisa Plyler.

George E. Luther and Roderick D. Fraser, ELI administrators, whose efforts made possible financial support and the classroom testing of *Reader's Choice*.

David P. Harris, director of the American Language Institute, Georgetown University; ELI authors Joan Morley and Mary Lawrence; Betsy Soden, ELI lecturer and reading coordinator; Carlos A. Yorio, professor of Linguistics, Toronto University—colleagues in English as a second language (ESL) whose critiques of early drafts proved invaluable.

ESL teachers whose patient and skillful use of the materials through numerous stages of development made detailed revisions and improvements possible—Honor Griffith and Lynne Kurylo of the University of Toronto; Betsy Berriman, Cristin Carpenter, Eve Daniels, Susan Dycus, Adelaide Heyde, Wayne Lord, Michele McCullough, Nancy Morrison, Syd Rand, and John Schafer of the English Language Institute.

And finally, thank you to Mario, Patricia, Tom, and Doug, friends and family for their patience and support; our parents and children, for whose pride and enthusiasm we are grateful; our students, whose insightful suggestions made revisions possible; and all the teachers and staff of the English Language Institute for providing an atmosphere which nurtures innovative teaching and creative materials development.

The authors wish to gratefully acknowledge grants from the English Language Institute and *Language Learning*, which provided funds for released time for several of the authors, and for secretarial and production assistance.

Ann Arbor, June 1977

*Grateful acknowledgment is made to the following for permission to reprint previously published material.*

Aldine de Gruyter for "The Changing Family," an adaptation of "Historical Perspectives on the Development of the Family and Parent-Child Interactions" by Maris Vinovskis. Reprinted with permission, from: Jane B. Lancaster, Jeanne Altmann, Alice S. Rossi, and Lonnie R. Sherrod, Editors, *Parenting Across the Life Span* (New York: Aldine de Gruyter). Copyright © 1987 by the Social Science Research Council. "The Changing Family" first appeared in *LSA* magazine.

American Automobile Association for Nashville map and for portions of Kentucky/Tennessee map and accompanying index, legend, and Driving Distances Chart. © AAA—Reproduced by permission.

*Ann Arbor News* for "Pockety Women Unite?" by Jane Myers, Staff Reporter, *Ann Arbor News*, September 22, 1975.

Associated Press for "Parents Seeking Cool Classroom for Son."

Beacon Press for adapted excerpts from *Deception Detection* by Jeffrey Schrank. Copyright © 1975 by Jeffrey Schrank. Reprinted by permission of Beacon Press.

Christian Science Publishing Society for adapted version of *"Non-Smoker's Lib."* Shout heard 'round the world 'Don't puff on me' by Clayton Jones, July 3 1975, © 1975 The Christian Science Publishing Society; and for "Unfolding Bud" by Naoshi Koriyama, © 1957 The Christian Science Publishing Society. Reprinted by permission from *The Christian Science Monitor*. All rights reserved.

William Collins and World Publishing Company, Inc., for material from *Webster's New World Dictionary*, College Edition, copyright © 1966 by The World Publishing Company. With permission.

*Detroit Free Press* for material from "The Calendar," *Detroit Free Press*, April 4, 1976.

*Encyclopaedia Britannica* for material adapted from "Jenner, Edward" in *Encyclopaedia Britannica*, 15th edition (1986), 6:530.

Farrar, Straus and Giroux, Inc., and Brandt and Brandt for "The Lottery" from *The Lottery* by Shirley Jackson. Copyright © 1948, 1949 by Shirley Jackson. Copyright renewed © 1976, 1977 by Laurence Hyman, Barry Hyman, Mrs. Sarah Webster, and Mrs. Joanne Schnurer. "The Lottery" originally appeared in the *New Yorker*. Reprinted by permission of Farrar, Straus and Giroux, Inc.

Features and News Service for adaptation of "How Do You Handle Everyday Stress?" by Dr. Syvil Marquit and Marilyn Lane.

Grolier for "Addams, Jane," "Austen, Jane," "Dionne Quintuplets," "Curie, Pierre and Marie," and "Eddy, Mary Baker." Reprinted with permission of *The Encyclopedia Americana*, © 1983, by Grolier Inc.

Harcourt Brace Jovanovich for "Fueled" from *Serve Me a Slice of Moon*, copyright © 1965 by Marcie Hans; and for "American Values in Education" excerpted from *American Civics*, Second Edition, by William H. Hartley and William S. Vincent, copyright © 1974 by Harcourt Brace Jovanovich, Inc. Reprinted by permission of Harcourt Brace Jovanovich, Inc.

HarperCollins Publishers and William Heineman Limited for excerpts adapted from *Cheaper by the Dozen*, by Frank Gilbreth, Jr., and Ernestine Gilbreth Carey. Copyright 1948, © 1963 by Frank B. Gilbreth, Jr., and Ernestine Gilbreth Carey. Reprinted by permission of HarperCollins Publishers and William Heineman Ltd.

HarperCollins Publishers and Tavistock Publications for excerpts from "The Milgram Experiment," adapted from "Blind Obedience to Authority" from *Psychology: The Frontiers of Behavior* by Ronald E. Smith, Irwin G. Sarason, and Barbara R. Sarason, copyright © 1978 by Ronald E. Smith; and for table, figure, and excerpt from *Obedience to Authority* by Stanley Milgram, copyright © 1974 by Stanley Milgram. Reprinted by permission of HarperCollins Publishers and Tavistock Ltd.

Harper's Magazine Company for "The Odds for Long Life" by Robert Collins. Copyright © 1973 by *Harper's* Magazine. Reprinted from the May, 1973, issue by special permission.

Houghton Mifflin Company for material from *The American Heritage Dictionary of the English Language*. Copyright © 1969, 1970, 1971, 1973, 1975, 1976, Houghton Mifflin Company. Reprinted by permission from *The American Heritage Dictionary of the English Language*.

Houghton Mifflin Company and George Weidenfeld and Nicholson Ltd. for an adapted excerpt from *In the Shadow of Man* by Jane van Lawick-Goodall. Copyright © 1971 by Hugo and Jane van Lawick-Goodall. Reprinted by permission of Houghton Mifflin Company. All rights reserved.

King Features for two "Sally Forth" cartoons. Reprinted with special permission of King Features Syndicate, Inc.

*Ladies' Home Journal* for "Why We Laugh" by Janet Spencer, *Ladies' Home Journal*, November, 1974.

Liveright Publishing Corporation for "in Just-" which is reprinted from *Tulips & Chimneys* by E. E. Cummings, edited by George James Firmage, by permission of Liveright Publishing Corporation. Copyright 1923, 1925 and renewed 1951, 1953 by E. E. Cummings. Copyright © 1973, 1976 by The Trustees for the E. E. Cummings Trust. Copyright © 1973, 1976 by George James Firmage.

Harold Matson Company for "The Chaser" by John Collier. Copyright 1940, © renewed 1968 by John Collier. Reprinted by permission of Harold Matson Company, Inc.

Michigan Daily for selected advertisements from the classified section, *Michigan Daily*, November 19, 1976.

Harry Miles Muheim for "The Dusty Drawer" by Harry Miles Muheim. Copyright © 1969 by Harry Miles Muheim. Published in *Alfred Hitchcock Presents a Month of Mystery*, copyright © 1969 by Random House, Inc. Reprinted by permission of the author.

New Directions Publishing Corporation and Carcanet Press Ltd. for "This is Just to Say" by William Carlos Williams, from *Collected Poems, Volume I: 1909–1939*, Copyright 1938 by New Directions Publishing Corporation.

Newspaper Enterprise Association for "Quick Reference Index," "Waterfalls," and "Years of Life Expectancy" from *The World Almanac and Book of Facts*, 1987 edition, copyright © Newspaper Enterprise Association, Inc. 1986, New York, NY 10166.

*Newsweek* for adaptations of the following articles: "A Burning Issue on the Job and Off" by Ian M. Rolland and Bernard J. Dushman, copyright 1986, Newsweek, Inc.; "Sonar for the Blind" by Matt Clark and Susan Agrest, copyright © 1975 by Newsweek, Inc.; "Graveyard of the Atlantic," copyright © 1974 by Newsweek, Inc.; and "Conjugal Prep," copyright © 1975 by Newsweek, Inc. All rights reserved. Reprinted by permission.

*New York Times* for "Major Personality Study Finds That Traits Are Mostly Inherited" by Daniel Goleman, *New York Times*, December 2, 1986, copyright © 1986 by The New York Times Company; and for "Japanese Style in Decision-Making" by Yoshio Terasawa, *New York Times*, May 12, 1974, copyright © 1974 by The New York Times Company. Reprinted by permission.

W. W. Norton and The Bodley Head for material reprinted from *The City* by John V. Lindsay by permission of W. W. Norton & Company, Inc. Copyright © 1969, 1970 by W. W. Norton & Company, Inc.

Opera Mundi, Inc., for "Class Day," "Ruth's Birthday," "The Ex-Wife Murder," "Case 463," "Murder on Board," "Death in the Mountains," "Case #194," and "The Break" from *Minute Mysteries* by Austin Ripley.

Overseas Development Council for material from "The Sacred Rac" by Patricia Hughes, in *Focusing on Global Poverty and Development* by Jayne C. Millar (Washington, D.C.: Overseas Development Council, 1974), pp. 357-58. Reprinted by permission.

Random House for an adaptation of "The Midnight Visitor." Copyright 1939 and renewed 1967 by Robert Arthur. Reprinted from *Mystery More Mystery* by Robert Arthur, by permission of Random House, Inc.

Random House and William Morris Agency for adapted excerpts from *Iberia* by James Michener. Copyright © 1968 by James Michener. Reprinted by permission of Random House, Inc., and by permission of William Morris Agency, Inc., on behalf of the author.

Marian Reiner for "How to Eat a Poem" from *Jamboree: Rhymes for All Times* by Eve Merriam. Copyright © 1962, 1964, 1966, 1973, 1984 by Eve Merriam. All rights reserved. Reprinted by permission of Marian Reiner for the author.

Robert Ritter for "Graveyard of the Atlantic" illustration.

Melvin Schnapper for "Your Actions Speak Louder . . . ," *Peace Corps: The Volunteer*, June, 1969.

*Science News* for the following articles: "The Trouble State of Calculus," April 5, 1986; "People in Americas before Last Ice Age?" June 28, 1986; and "Babies Sound Off: The Power of Babble," June 21, 1986. Reprinted with permission from *Science News*, the weekly newsmagazine of science, copyright 1986 by Science Service, Inc.

*Smithsonian* for "Summits of Yore: Promises, Promises, and a Deal or Two," *Smithsonian*, September 1986.

Sterling Publishing Company and Guinness Superlatives Ltd. for material from the *Guinness Book of Records*, copyright © 1975 by Sterling Publishing Company, Inc., N.Y. 10016.

May Swenson for the following poems: "By Morning," "Living Tenderly," and "Southbound on the Freeway," by May Swenson. Used by permission of the author from *Poems to Solve*, copyright © 1966 by May Swenson.

Universal Press Syndicate for "Love Handles" and "Doonesbury" cartoons. Love Handles copyright 1987 Universal Press Syndicate. Doonesbury copyright 1987 G. B. Trudeau. Reprinted with permission of Universal Press Syndicate. All rights reserved.

*U.S. News and World Report* for pictogram from "The Global Community: On the Way to 9 Billion," copyright 1983 U.S. News & World Report, reprinted from issue of April 9, 1983; for "The Stork Has a Busier Time, but—" copyright 1982 U.S. News & World Report, reprinted from issue of November 29, 1982; and for "Crowded Earth—Billions More Coming," copyright 1974 U.S. News & World Report, reprinted from issue of October 21, 1974.

Viking Penguin and Granada Publishing for adapted excerpts from *My Family and Other Animals* by Gerald Durrell. Copyright © 1956 by Gerald M. Durrell. All rights reserved. Reprinted by permission of Viking Penguin Inc. and Granada Publishing Ltd.

Washington Post Syndicate for "Happy Customers Matter of Honor among Japanese," © The Washington Post.

Wesleyan University Press for "Looking in the Album" by Vern Rutsala. Copyright © 1964 by Vern Rutsala. Reprinted from *The Window* by permission of Wesleyan University Press.

*Every effort has been made to trace the ownership of all copyrighted material in this book and to obtain permission for its use.*

# Contents

# Preface to the International Edition

Like the first edition of *Reader's Choice*, this revised volume is designed to provide students practice in a range of problem-solving tasks in the context of a wide variety of readings. It is based on the premise that reading is an interactive process in which readers use information from the text and their own background knowledge in order for communication to take place. The exercises in *Reader's Choice* provide practice in using both text-based knowledge and the background information of the reader. Skills units introduce and provide practice in text-based information processing. Opportunities for discussion before and after reading selections, and the focus on critical reading, require that students bring their background knowledge to bear during the entire reading process. These activities are designed to create independent readers who actively make decisions about how and what they will read, choosing strategies appropriate to their goals for a particular reading task. Teachers and students are encouraged to use the book flexibly, selecting and ordering activities to match the requirements of specific situations.

In revising, our intent has been to retain the basic format of the textbook while making explicit much that was previously implicit:

1. In the first edition, discourse-level practice of reading strategies occurred exclusively in the reading selection units. To provide additional, explicit practice, discourse-level exercises have been added to the skills units. Along with discourse-level Vocabulary from Context exercises, we have added a Discourse Focus to each skills unit. These exercises provide focused practice in skimming and scanning; reading carefully, and drawing inferences from, mysteries; and forming predictions about expository prose.

2. To facilitate introductory discussion and development of background knowledge, we precede reading selections with the introductory section, Before You Begin.

3. To facilitate use of the book in integrated reading/writing programs, we have added a composition focus for each reading selection. These are listed on the Contents page.

4. We have added example vocabulary items to our Stems and Affixes exercises and provided additional, contextualized practice.

5. In the Paragraph Reading: Main Idea exercises, we have added open-ended items that supplement the multiple-choice format by providing students opportunities to summarize the main ideas in their own words.

In addition, the book has been updated:

1. Much of the nonprose material has been updated or replaced.

2. Where a controversy documented in readings in the original edition has continued, we have added additional readings. This allows students to explore an issue over time, to compare and contrast different perspectives on the issue, and to build background knowledge through "narrow reading." We have adopted this strategy for the topics of population growth (Unit 2) and Japan (Unit 4).

3. Finally, new reading topics have been added. Series of selections have been added in the area of poetry (Unit 4).

For a more comprehensive discussion of the text, we strongly recommend that teachers and students work through the detailed introduction that follows.

Additionally, note that among the Longer Reading units, the selection from *Future Shock* has been replaced by a unit on psychology.

# Introduction

## *To Students and Teachers*

*Reader's Choice* is a reading textbook for students of English as a second or foreign language. The authors of *Reader's Choice* believe that reading is an active, problem-solving process. This book is based on the theory that proficient reading requires the coordination of a number of skills. Proficient reading depends on the reader's ability to select the proper skills or strategies to solve each reading problem. Efficient readers determine beforehand why they are reading a particular selection and they decide which strategies and skills they will use to achieve their goals. They develop expectations about the kinds of information they will find in a passage and read to determine if their expectations are correct. The exercises and readings in *Reader's Choice* will help students to become independent, efficient readers.

When you look at the Contents page you will notice that there are three kinds of units in *Reader's Choice*. The odd-numbered units (1 through 5) contain skills exercises. These exercises give students intensive practice in developing their ability to obtain the maximum amount of information from a reading selection using the minimum number of language clues. The even-numbered units (2 through 6) contain reading selections that give students the opportunity to use the skills they have learned, to interact with and evaluate the ideas of texts. Finally, Units 7 and 8 consist of longer, more complex reading selections.

Basic language and reading skills are introduced in early units and reinforced throughout the book. The large number of exercises gives students the opportunity for repeated practice. Students should not be discouraged if they do not finish each exercise, if they have trouble answering specific questions, or if they do not understand everything in a particular reading. The purpose of the tasks in *Reader's Choice* is to help students improve their problem-solving skills. For this reason, the process of attempting to answer a question is often as important as the answer itself.

*Reader's Choice* contains exercises that give students practice in both language and reading skills. In this Introduction we will first provide a description of language skills exercises followed by a description of the reading skills work contained in the book.

## Language Skills Exercises

### *Word Study Exercises*

Upon encountering an unfamiliar word in a passage there are several strategies readers can use to determine the message of the author. First, they can continue reading, realizing that often a single word will not prevent understanding of the general meaning of a selection. If further reading does not solve the problem, readers can use one or more of three basic skills to arrive at an understanding of the unfamiliar word. They can use context clues to see if surrounding words and grammatical structures provide information about the unknown word. They can use word analysis to see if understanding the parts of the word leads to an understanding of the word. Or they can use a dictionary to find an appropriate definition. *Reader's Choice* contains numerous exercises that provide practice in these three skills.

#### *Word Study: Vocabulary from Context*
Guessing the meaning of an unfamiliar word from context clues involves using the following kinds of information:
  *a*) knowledge of the topic about which you are reading
  *b*) knowledge of the meanings of the other words in the sentence (or paragraph) in which the word occurs
  *c*) knowledge of the grammatical structure of the sentences in which the word occurs
Exercises that provide practice in this skill are called Vocabulary from Context exercises.

When these exercises appear in skills units, their purpose is to provide students with practice in guessing the meaning of unfamiliar words using context clues. Students should not necessarily try to learn the meanings of the vocabulary items in these exercises. The Vocabulary from Context exercises that appear with reading selections have a different purpose. Generally these exercises should be done before a reading selection is begun and uses as an introduction to the reading. The vocabulary items have been chosen for three reasons:

    *a*) because they are fairly common, and therefore useful for students to learn

    *b*) because they are important for an understanding of the passage

    *c*) because their meanings are not easily available from the context in the selection

### Word Study: Stems and Affixes

Another way to discover the meanings of unfamiliar vocabulary items is to use word analysis, that is, to use knowledge of the meanings of the parts of a word. Many English words have been formed by combining parts of older English, Greek, and Latin words. For instance, the word bicycle is formed from the parts *bi,* meaning two, and *cycle,* meaning round or wheel. Often knowledge of the meanings of these word parts can help the reader to guess the meaning of an unfamiliar word. Exercises providing practice in this skill occur at regular intervals throughout the book. An introduction to stems and affixes appears in Appendix C along with a list of all of the stems and affixes that appear in these exercises and all those that appear in Books 1 and 2.

### Word Study: Dictionary Use

Sometimes the meaning of a single word is essential to an understanding of the total meaning of a selection. If context clues and word analysis do not provide enough information, it will be necessary to use a dictionary. We believe that advanced students should use an English/English dictionary. An introduction to dictionary use is provided in Appendix B. Dictionary Study exercises that accompany some of the reading selections require students to use the context of an unfamiliar vocabulary item to find an appropriate definition of these items from the dictionary entries provided.

## Sentence Study Exercises

Sometimes comprehension of an entire passage requires the understanding of a single sentence. Sentence Study exercises give students practice in analyzing the structure of sentences to determine the relationships of ideas within a sentence. Students are presented with a complicated sentence followed by tasks that require them to analyze the sentence for its meaning. Often the student is required to use the available information to draw inferences about the author's message. An introduction to sentence study is provided in Appendix D.

## Paragraph Reading and Paragraph Analysis Exercises

These exercises give students practice in understanding how the arrangement of ideas affects the overall meaning of a passage. Some of the paragraph exercises are designed to provide practice in discovering the general message. Students are required to determine the main idea of a passage: that is, the idea which is the most important, around which the paragraph is organized. Other paragraph exercises are meant to provide practice in careful, detailed reading. Students are required not only to find the main idea of a passage, but also to guess vocabulary meanings of words from context, to answer questions about specific details in the paragraph, and to draw conclusions based on their understanding of the passage. Introductions to paragraph exercises are provided in Appendix E (Main Idea), Appendix F (Restatement and Inference), and Appendix G (Reading for Full Understanding).

## Discourse Focus

Effective reading requires the ability to select skills and strategies appropriate to a specific reading task. The reading process involves using information from the full text and information from the world in order to interpret a passage. Readers use this information to make predictions about what they will find in a text, and to decide how they will read. Sometimes we need to read quickly to obtain only a general idea of a text; at other times we read carefully, drawing inferences about the intent of the author. Discourse-level activities provide systematic practice of these various approaches to reading. These reading skills are described in more detail in the discussion that follows.

### Nonprose Reading

Throughout *Reader's Choice* students are presented with nonprose selections (such as a bus schedule and a road map) so that they can practice using their skills to read material that is not arranged in sentences and paragraphs. It is important to remember that the same problem-solving skills are used to read both prose and nonprose material.

## Reading Skills Exercises

Students will need to use all of their language skills in order to understand the reading selections in *Reader's Choice*. The book contains many types of selections on a wide variety of topics. These selections provide practice in using different reading strategies to comprehend texts. They also give students practice in four basic reading skills: skimming, scanning, reading for thorough comprehension, and critical reading.

### Skimming

Skimming is quick reading for the general idea(s) of a passage. This kind of rapid reading is appropriate when trying to decide if careful reading would be desirable or when there is not time to read something carefully. An introduction to skimming is provided in Appendix I.

### Scanning

Like skimming, scanning is also quick reading. However, in this case the search is more focused. To scan is to read quickly in order to locate specific information. When you read to find a particular date, name, or number, you are scanning. An introduction to scanning is provided in Appendix H.

### Reading for Thorough Comprehension

Reading for thorough comprehension is careful reading in order to understand the total meaning of the passage. At this level of comprehension the reader is able to summarize the author's ideas but has not yet made a critical evaluation of those ideas.

### Critical Reading

Critical reading involves making judgments about what one reads. This kind of reading requires posing and answering questions such as *Does my own experience support that of the author? Do I share the author's point of view? Am I convinced by the author's arguments and evidence?* To a certain extent, of course, we are always doing this, but the critical reading activities in *Reader's Choice* focus specifically on improving this skill.

Systematic use of the exercises and readings in *Reader's Choice* will give students practice in the basic language and reading skills necessary to become proficient readers. Additional suggestions for the use of *Reader's Choice* in a classroom setting are included in the section To the Teacher.

# To the Teacher

It is impossible to outline one best way to use a textbook; there are as many ways to use *Reader's Choice* as there are creative teachers. However, based on the experiences of teachers and students who have worked with *Reader's Choice,* we provide the following suggestions to facilitate classroom use. First, we outline general guidelines for the teaching of reading; second, we provide hints for teaching specific exercises and readings in the book; and finally, we suggest a sample lesson plan.

## General Guidelines

The ultimate goal of *Reader's Choice* is to produce independent readers who are able to determine their own goals for a reading task, then use the appropriate skills and strategies to reach those goals. For this reason, we believe the best learning environment is one in which all individuals—students and teachers—participate in the process of setting and achieving goals. A certain portion of class time is therefore profitably spent in discussing reading tasks before they are begun. If the topic is a new one for the students, teachers are encouraged to provide and/or access background information for the students, adapting the activities under Before You Begin to specific teaching contexts. When confronted with a specific passage, students should become accustomed to the practice of skimming it quickly, taking note of titles and subheadings, pictures, graphs, etc., in an attempt to determine the most efficient approach to the task. In the process, they should develop expectations about the content of the passage and the amount of time and effort needed to accomplish their goals. In this type of setting students are encouraged to offer their opinions and ask for advice, to teach each other, and to learn from their errors.

*Reader's Choice* was written to encourage maximum flexibility in classroom use. Because of the large variety of exercises and reading selections, the teacher can plan several tasks for each class and hold in reserve a number of appropriate exercises to use as the situation demands. In addition, the exercises have been developed to make possible variety in classroom dynamics. The teacher should encourage the independence of students by providing opportunities for work in small groups, pairs, or individually. Small group work in which students self-correct homework assignments has also been successful.

Exercises do not have to be done in the order in which they are presented. In fact, we suggest interspersing skills work with reading selections. One way to vary reading tasks is to plan lessons around pairs of units, alternating skills exercises with the reading selections. In the process, the teacher can show students how focused skills work transfers to the reading of longer passages. For example, Sentence Study exercises provide intensive practice in analyzing grammatical structures to understand sentences; this same skill should be used by students in working through reading selections. When communication breaks down, the teacher can pull sentences from readings for intensive classroom analysis, thereby demonstrating the value of this skill.

It is important to *teach, then test.* Tasks should be thoroughly introduced, modeled, and practiced before students are expected to perform on their own. Although we advocate rapid-paced, demanding class sessions, we believe it is extremely important to provide students with a thorough introduction to each new exercise. At least for the first example of each type of exercise, some oral work is necessary. The teacher can demonstrate the skill using the example item, and work through the first few items with the class as a whole. Students can then work individually or in small groups.

## Specific Suggestions

*Reader's Choice* has been organized so that specific skills can be practiced before students use those skills to attack reading selections. Although exercises and readings are generally graded according to difficulty, it is necessary to use the material in the order in which it is presented.

Teachers are encouraged:
  *a*) to intersperse skills work with reading selections
  *b*) to skip exercises that are too easy or irrelevant to students' interests
  *c*) to do several exercises of a specific type at one time if students require intensive practice in that skill
  *d*) to jump from unit to unit, selecting reading passages that satisfy students' interests and needs
  *e*) to sequence longer readings as appropriate for their students either by interspersing them among other readings and skills work or by presenting them at the end of the course

## Language Skills Exercises

### Nonprose Reading

For students who believe they need to read only prose material, teachers can point out that nonprose reading provides more than an enjoyable change of pace. These exercises provide legitimate reading practice. The same problem-solving skills can be used for both prose and nonprose material. Just as one can skim a textbook for general ideas, it is possible to skim a menu for a general idea of the type of food offered, the price range of the restaurant, etc. Students may claim that they can't skim or scan; working with nonprose items shows them that they can.

Nonprose exercises are good for breaking the ice with new students, for beginning or ending class sessions, for role playing, or for those Monday blues and Friday blahs. Because they are short, rapid-paced exercises, they can be kept in reserve to provide variety, or to fill a time gap at the end of class.

The Bus Schedule and Road Map exercises present students with realistic language problems they might encounter in an English-speaking environment. The teacher can set up simulations to achieve a realistic atmosphere. The Questionnaire exercise is intended to provide practice in filling out forms. Since the focus is on following directions, students usually work individually.

With poetry, students' problem-solving skills are challenged by the economy of poetic writing. Poetry is especially good for reinforcing vocabulary from context skills, for comprehending through syntax clues, and for drawing inferences.

### Word Study

These exercises can be profitably done in class either in rapid-paced group work or by alternating individual work with class discussion. Like nonprose work, Word Study exercises can be used to fill unexpected time gaps.

Context Clues exercises appear frequently throughout the book, both in skills units and with reading selections. Students should learn to be content with a general meaning of a word and to recognize situations in which it is not necessary to know a word's meaning. In skills units, these exercises should be done in class to ensure that students do not look for exact definitions in the dictionary. When Vocabulary from Context exercises appear with reading selections, they are intended as tools for learning new vocabulary items and often for introducing ideas to be encountered in the reading. In this case they can be done at home as well as in class.

Stems and Affixes exercises must be done in the order in which they are presented. The exercises are cumulative: each exercise makes use of word parts presented in previous units and in Book 1. All stems and affixes taught in *Reader's Choice, International Edition: Books 1 and 2* are listed in Appendix C with their definitions. These exercises serve as an important foundation in vocabulary skills work for students whose native language does not contain a large number of words derived from Latin or Greek. Students should focus on improving their ability to analyze word parts as they work with the words presented in the exercises. During the introduction to each exercise students should be encouraged to volunteer other examples of words containing the stems and affixes presented. Exercises 1 and 2 can be done as homework; the matching exercise can be used as a quiz.

### Sentence Study

Students should not be concerned about unfamiliar vocabulary in these exercises; grammatical clues should provide enough information to allow them to complete the tasks. In addition, questions are syntax based; errors indicate structures that students have trouble reading, thus providing the teacher with a diagnostic tool for grammar instruction. An introduction to sentence study is provided in Appendix D.

### Paragraph Reading and Paragraph Analysis

If Main Idea paragraphs are read in class, they may be timed. If the exercises are done at home, students can be asked to come to class prepared to defend their answers in group discussion. One way to simulate discussion is to ask students to identify incorrect responses as too broad, too narrow, or false.

Restatement and Inference and Paragraph Analysis exercises are short enough to allow sentence-by-sentence analysis. These exercises provide intensive practice in syntax and vocabulary work. In the Paragraph Analysis exercises the lines are numbered to facilitate discussion. Introductions to paragraph exercises are provided in Appendix E (Main Idea), Appendix F (Restatement and Inference), and Appendix G (Reading for Full Understanding).

### Discourse Focus

Scanning and skimming activities should be done quickly in order to demonstrate to students the utility of these approaches for some tasks. The short mysteries can profit from group work, as students use specific elements of the text to defend their inferences. Prediction activities are designed to have students focus on the discourse signals that allow them to predict and sample texts. The diversity of student responses that emerges during group work can reinforce the notion that there is not a single correct answer, that all predictions are, by definition, only working hypotheses to be constantly revised. Introductions to scanning and skimming are provided in Appendixes H and I, respectively.

## Reading Selections

Teachers have found it valuable to introduce readings in terms of ideas, vocabulary, and syntax before students are asked to work on their own. The newly added section, Before You Begin, introduces the concepts and issues encountered in reading selections. Several types of classroom dynamics have been successful with reading selections after an introduction to the passage.

1. In class—the teacher reads entire selection orally; or the teacher reads part, students finish the selection individually; or students read the selection individually (perhaps under time constraint).
2. In class and at home—part of the selection is read in class, followed by discussion; students finish reading at home.
3. At home—students read the entire selection at home.

Comprehension questions are usually discussed in class with the class as a whole, in small groups, or in pairs. The paragraphs in the selections are numbered to facilitate discussion.

The teacher can pull out difficult vocabulary and/or sentences for intensive analysis and

Readings represent a variety of topics and styles. The exercises have been written to focus on the most obvious characteristics of each reading.

*a)* Fiction and personal experience narratives are to be read for enjoyment. Teachers often find it useful to read these to students, emphasizing humorous parts.

*b)* Well-organized readings with many facts and figures are appropriate for scanning and skimming. This type of reading can also be used in composition work as a model of organizational techniques.

*c)* If the reading is an editorial, essay, or other form of personal opinion, students should read critically to determine if they agree with the author. Students are encouraged to identify excerpts that reveal the author's bias or that can be used to challenge the validity of the author's argument.

*d)* Satire should be read both for enjoyment and for analysis of the author's comment on human affairs.

## Longer Readings

These readings can be presented in basically the same manner as other selections in the book. Longer readings can be read either at the end of the course or during the term. The schedule for working with longer readings is roughly as follows:

*a)* Readings are introduced by vocabulary exercises, discussion of the topic, reading and discussion of selected paragraphs.

*b)* Students read the selection at home and answer the comprehension questions. Students are allowed at least two days to complete the assignment.

*c)* In-class discussion of comprehension questions proceeds with students referring to the passage to support their answers.

*d)* The vocabulary review can be done either at home or in class.

*e)* Vocabulary questions raised on the off day between the assignment and the due day may be resolved with items from Vocabulary from Context exercises and Figurative Language and Idioms exercises.

"The Milgram Experiment" requires students to confront their own attitudes toward authority. The unit begins with a questionnaire that asks students to predict their behavior in particular situations and to compare their behavior with that of fellow natives of their culture and of Americans. Psychologist Stanley Milgram was concerned with the extent to which people would follow commands even when they thought they were hurting someone else. Because the results of the study are surprising and because most people have strong feelings about their own allegiance to authority and their commitment to independence, small group discussions and debriefing from the teacher will be important in this lesson.

"In the Shadow of Man" is well organized and may, therefore, be skimmed. Teachers can ask students to read the first and last sentences of the paragraphs, then paraphrase the general position of the author. Discussion of some Discussion/Composition items can serve as an effective introduction to the reading. In addition, some questions lead discussion away from the passage and might, therefore, lead to further reading on the topic. Some teachers may want to show the film *Miss Jane Goodall and the Wild Chimpanzees* (National Geographic Society; Encyclopedia Britannica Educational Films) in conjunction with this reading. Teachers should be aware that this selection raises the subject of evolution, a sensitive topic for students whose religious or personal beliefs deny evolutionary theory.

## Answer Key

Because the exercises in *Reader's Choice* are designed to provide students with the opportunity to practice and improve their reading skills, the processes involved in arriving at an answer are often more important than the answer itself. It is expected that students will not use the Answer Key until they have completed the exercises and are prepared to defend their answers. If a student's answer does not agree with the Key, it is important for the student to return to the exercise to discover the source of the error. In a classroom setting, students should view the Answer Key as a last resort, to be used only when they cannot agree on an answer. The Answer Key also makes it possible for students engaged in independent study to use *Reader's Choice*.

## Sample Lesson Plan

The following lesson plan is meant only as an example of how goals might be translated into practice. We do not imply that a particular presentation is the only one possible for a given reading activity, nor that the exercises presented here are the only activities possible to achieve our goals. The lesson plan demonstrates how skills work can be interspersed with reading selections.

It is assumed that the lessons described here would be presented after students have worked together for several weeks. This is important for two reasons. First, we hope that a nonthreatening atmosphere has been established in which people feel free to volunteer opinions and make guesses. Second, we assume that by now students recognize the importance of a problem-solving approach to reading and that they are working to improve skills and strategies using a variety of readings and exercises.

Although these lessons are planned for fifty-minute, daily classes, slight modification would make them appropriate for a number of other situations. Approximate time limits for each activity are indicated. The exercises and readings are taken from Units 1, 2, 5, and 6.

### Monday
Nonprose Reading: Poetry (20 minutes)
  *a*) The teacher points out that each poem is a puzzle; that students will have to use their reading skills to solve each one.
  *b*) The teacher reads the first poem aloud; students follow in their books.
  *c*) Discussion focuses on obtaining information from vocabulary and syntax clues and drawing inferences.
  *d*) If the students can't guess the subject of the poem, the class should do the Comprehension Clues exercise.
  *e*) The last two poems can be handled in the same manner or students can work individually with discussion following.
Reading Selection: Magazine Article ("Why We Laugh") (30 minutes)
  Introduction:
  *a*) Discussion: Why do we laugh? Is laughter culturally conditioned? Do students think English jokes are funny?
  *b*) Vocabulary: Vocabulary from Context exercises 1 and 2; students work as a class or individually, with discussion following.
  *c*) Skimming: the teacher skims the article aloud, reading first (and sometimes second and last) sentences of each paragraph.
  *d*) Discussion: What is the main idea? What type of article is it? Is the author an expert? Who are the experts she quotes?
  *e*) As a group, students review main ideas by answering questions in Comprehension exercise 1.
Homework: Read "Why We Laugh"; do Comprehension exercise 2.

### Tuesday

"Why We Laugh" (35 minutes)

  *a*) Work through Comprehension and Critical Reading exercises as a class, in small groups, or in pairs. Students should defend answers with portions of the text; emphasis is on convincing others or being convinced on the basis of the reading.

  *b*) Pull out, analyze, and discuss structure problems, difficult vocabulary.

  *c*) Wrap-up discussion proceeds from Critical Reading and Discussion questions.

Homework: Can include composition work based on Discussion/Composition topics.

Stems and Affixes (15 minutes)

  *a*) Introduction: students volunteer examples of words containing stems and affixes presented in the exercise.

  *b*) Class does exercise 1 orally as a group, if time permits.

Homework: Finish Stems and Affixes exercises.

### Wednesday

Stems and Affixes (15 minutes)

  *a*) Go over as a class; students volunteer and defend answers.

  *b*) The Appendix can be used if a dispute arises concerning one of the stems or affixes presented in *Reader's Choice, International Edition: Books 1 and 2.*

  *c*) Work is fast paced and skills focused. Students concentrate on learning word parts.

Sentence Study: Restatement and Inference (35 minutes)

  *a*) The first one or two items are done orally. The teacher reads the sentence and the choices aloud and students mark answers in the book.

  *b*) Discussion follows. Students must defend answers using grammatical analysis of sentences.

  *c*) Students complete the exercise individually after which answers are discussed.

Word Study: Context Clues (if time permits)

  *a*) Group or individual work.

  *b*) Students arrive at a definition, synonym, or description of each word, then defend their answers by referring to the syntax and other vocabulary items in the sentence.

### Thursday

Reading Selection: Narrative ("An Attack on the Family") (40 minutes)

  *a*) Discussion: What is it like to be the youngest child in the family?

  *b*) Vocabulary from Context: students work as a class or individually with discussion following.

  *c*) The teacher reads story aloud, students follow in their books.

  *d*) Students take ten minutes to answer Comprehension questions individually.

  *e*) Discussion follows. Students will have to examine the text carefully to answer the questions.

Paragraph Analysis: Reading for Full Understanding (10 minutes)

  *a*) The teacher reads the Example paragraph from Appendix G aloud. Students mark answers in their books.

  *b*) The class discusses the answers using the Explanation on pages 184–85.

Homework: Finish Paragraph Analysis exercise.

### Friday

Paragraph Analysis (25 minutes)

  *a*) Discussion of the homework: students must use excerpts from the paragraphs to defend their answers or to refute the choices of other students.

  *b*) Grammatical analysis can be used to develop convincing arguments supporting the correct answers. Context clues often furnish the definition of unfamiliar words.

Reading Selection: Narrative ("The Lottery") (25 minutes)

Introduction:

*a*) Discussion of lotteries in general, lotteries in the students' countries.

*b*) Vocabulary from Context exercise 1: students work as a class or individually with discussion following.

*c*) The teacher reads the first nine paragraphs, discusses content, vocabulary, syntax with students. Most of Vocabulary from Context exercises 2 and 3 can be covered during this discussion.

Homework: Read "The Lottery"; do Comprehension exercises for Monday.

This lesson plan represents an active, problem-solving approach to the teaching of ESL reading. Students are required to do more than merely read passages and answer questions. The type of reading that the students are asked to do varies from task to task. They skim "Why We Laugh" to determine the main idea, then scan to find the answers to some of the Comprehension questions. Sentence Study exercises require close grammatical analysis, just as Stems and Affixes exercises require analysis of word parts. "Why We Laugh" and "The Lottery" both require critical reading. The vocabulary and syntax work is presented as a tool for comprehension, appropriate for helping students solve persistent reading problems.

Within a single week, a great variety of activities is presented. In the course of any single lesson, the tempo and tasks change several times. In the course of the week, virtually all language and reading skills are reinforced in a variety of contexts and with a variety of materials. This variety has important implications for the nature of the class and for the role of the teacher.

The classroom dynamics change to fit the task. The poetry and the discussion sessions are class activities, the teacher encouraging students to volunteer answers and opinions. The vocabulary and structure exercises on Tuesday and Wednesday, as well as the paragraph work on Thursday and Friday, might be organized as workshop sessions, giving students the chance to work at their own pace and providing the teacher the opportunity to assist individuals.

The role of the teacher also changes from activity to activity. During vocabulary and structure work, the teacher teaches, providing help and encouragement as students work to solve language problems. The teacher is a facilitator during the poetry and short passage readings, intervening only in the event that linguistic expertise is needed to keep the discussion going. In discussions of how readings relate to the "real world," the teacher is primarily a participant on equal terms with the students in exploring mutually interesting topics. Of course, the role and behavior of the teacher can change a number of times in the course of a class session to suit the situation. It is hoped, however, that as the semester progresses, the teacher as teacher will gradually be replaced by the teacher as facilitator and participant.

Another important feature of this lesson plan is the opportunity provided to encourage students to choose their own reading strategies and to apply the skills dictated by the strategy chosen. It should be noted that "Why We Laugh" and "The Lottery" are introduced by the teacher through vocabulary work and discussion, followed by skimming and scanning. This type of introduction gives students the opportunity to develop expectations about the selection and, guided by their expectations, to read more effectively. It is hoped that this procedure will be repeated when students encounter similar readings in the future. Often the teacher will want to simulate a "real life" situation by giving the students a task and asking them how they would approach it. The approach to a newspaper editorial, for example, might be quite different depending on whether the selection is read for pleasure or for a university political science course.

Throughout the semester, students are taught to shift gears, to vary their reading strategies according to their goals for the selection at hand. As they become more proficient readers, we expect them to determine for themselves what they read, why they read it, and how they read it.

# Nonprose Reading

## Poetry

Because the goal of reading is to (re)create meaning, we can say that reading involves solving a puzzle for which the clues are the words we read. Reading poetry can be the most exciting kind of reading because more of the meaning seems hidden. The author provides the fewest but the richest clues. All of your reading skills will be needed if you are to "solve" the poems in this section.

Each of the following poems describes something.* Read each poem carefully to discover what is being described; do not be concerned if you do not know the meaning of some vocabulary items. If you are having trouble arriving at an answer, read the poem again. If the poem is still not clear, answering the questions on page 4 will give you more clues.

### Living Tenderly

My body a rounded stone
with a pattern of smooth seams.
My head a short snake,
retractive, projective,
My legs come out of their sleeves
or shrink within,
and so does my chin.
My eyelids are quick clamps.
My back is my roof.
I am always at home.
I travel where my house walks.
It is a smooth stone.
It floats within the lake,
or rests in the dust.
My flesh lives tenderly
inside its bone.

*May Swenson*

What is it? _____

---

*Poems from *Poems to Solve,* by May Swenson (New York: Charles Scribner's Sons, 1966).

### Southbound on the Freeway

A tourist came in from Orbitville,
parked in the air, and said:

The creatures of this star
are made of metal and glass.

Through the transparent parts
you can see their guts.

Their feet are round and roll
on diagrams—or long

measuring tapes—dark
with white lines.

They have four eyes.
The two in the back are red.

Sometimes you can see a 5-eyed
one, with a red eye turning

on the top of his head.
He must be special—

The others respect him,
and go slow,

when he passes, winding
among them from behind.

They all hiss as they glide,
like inches, down the marked

tapes. Those soft shapes,
shadowy inside

the hard bodies—are they
their guts or their brains?

*May Swenson*

What is it? _____

### By Morning

Some for everyone
    plenty

    and more coming

Fresh   dainty   airily arriving
    everywhere at once

Transparent at first
    each faint slice
    slow   soundlessly tumbling
    then quickly thickly a gracious fleece
    will spread like youth   like wheat
    over the city

Each building will be   a hill
    all sharps made round

        dark worn noisy arrows made still
        wide   flat   clean   spaces

Streets will be fields
    cars be   fumbling sheep

A deep bright harvest will be seeded
    in a night

By morning we'll be   children
    feeding on manna

    a new loaf on every doorsill

*May Swenson*

What is it? _____

## *Comprehension Clues*

"Living Tenderly": What is it?

1. What is the shape of its body?

2. What does its head look like?

3. T / F   Its legs don't move.

4. T / F   It carries its home wherever it goes.

5. T / F   It lives only in dry places.

"Southbound on the Freeway": What does the tourist see?

1. From where is the tourist observing the creatures?

2. What are the creatures made of?
   a. Describe their feet.
   b. Describe their eyes.

3. What is it that is described as "dark with white lines"?

4. What is different about the special ones:
   a. in appearance?
   b. in the way they affect the behavior of the other creatures?

5. What is a freeway?

"By Morning": What is it?

1. Which adjectives describe how it arrives?

2. How does it look at first?

3. What could make buildings suddenly look like hills?

4. What happens to the cars?

5. What could happen in the night to change a city like this?

# Word Study

## Context Clues

**Exercise 1**

*In the following exercise do NOT try to learn the italicized words. Concentrate on developing your ability to guess the meaning of unfamiliar words using context clues.\* Read each sentence carefully, and write a definition, synonym, or description of the italicized word on the line provided.*

1. _____   It is difficult to list all of my father's *attributes* because he has so many different talents and abilities.

2. _____   Mary, the president of the family council, *conferred* upon Robert the title of vice-president, because she thought he would do a good job.

3. _____   Mother was tall, fat, and middle-aged. The principal of the school was an older woman, almost as *plump* as Mother, and much shorter.

4. _____   When Mark was in one of his *pedantic* moods, he assumed the manner of a distinguished professor and lectured for hours, on minute, boring topics.

5. _____   Many members of the old wealthy families in society held themselves *aloof* from Gatsby, refusing even to acknowledge his existence.

6. _____   I became angrier and angrier as Don talked, but I *refrained* from saying anything.

7. _____   Mr. Doodle is always busy in an *ineffectual* way; he spends hours running around accomplishing nothing.

8. _____   Ian was proud of the neat rows of *marigolds* in his flower beds, which he tended with great care.

9. _____   Most dentists' offices are *drab* places, but Emilio's new office is a bright, cheerful place.

10. _____   The inner and outer events of a plant are interdependent; but this isn't saying that the *skin, cortex, membrane,* or whatever you want to call the boundary of the individual, is meaningless.

---

\*For an introduction to context clues, see Appendix A.

## Exercise 2

*This exercise is designed to give you practice using context clues from a passage. Use your general knowledge along with information from the entire text below to write a definition, synonym, or description of the italicized word on the line provided. Read through the entire passage before making a decision. Note that some of the words appear more than once; by the end of the passage you should have a good idea of their meaning. Do not worry if your definition is not exact; a general idea of the meaning will often allow you to understand the meaning of a written text.*

## *Babies Sound Off: The Power of Babble*

There is more to the *babbling* of a baby than meets the ear. A handful of scientists are picking apart infants' utterances and finding that not only is there an ordered *sequence* of vocal stages between birth and the first words, but in *hearing-impaired* babies a type of *babbling* thought to signal an emerging capacity for speech is delayed and distorted.

"The traditional wisdom [among developmental researchers] is that deaf babies *babble* like hearing babies," says linguist D. Kimbrough Oller of the University of Miami (Fla.). "This idea is a *myth*." Oller reported his latest findings on hearing and deaf infants last week at a National Institutes of Health seminar in Bethesda, Md. He and his colleagues demonstrated 8 years ago that hearing babies from a variety of language communities start out by cooing and gurgling; at about 7 months of age, they start to produce *sequences* of the same syllables (for instance, "da-da-da" or "dut-dut-dut") that are classified as *babbling* and can be recorded and acoustically measured in the laboratory, with words or wordlike sounds appearing soon after 1 year of age. *Babbling*—the emitting of identifiable consonant and vowel sounds—usually disappears by around 18 to 20 months of age.

In a just-completed study, Oller and his co-workers found that repeated *sequences* of syllables first appeared among 21 hearing infants between the ages of 6 and 10 months; in contrast, these vocalizations emerged among 9 severely to profoundly deaf babies between the ages of 11 and 25 months. In addition, deaf babies *babbled* less frequently than hearing babies, produced fewer syllables and were more likely to use single syllables than repeated *sequences*.*

babbling: _____

sequence: _____

hearing-impaired: _____

myth: _____

*From *Science News*, June 21, 1986, p. 390.

# Word Study

## Stems and Affixes

Below is a list of some commonly occurring stems and affixes.* Study their meanings; then do the exercises that follow. Your teacher may ask you to give examples of other words you know that are derived from these stems and affixes.

**Prefixes**

| | | |
|---|---|---|
| multi- | many | multiply, multiple |
| peri- | around | periscope, perimeter |
| semi- | half, partly | semisweet, semicircle |
| tri- | three | triangle |
| ultra- | beyond, excessive, extreme | ultramodern |
| uni- | one | unicycle, unify, universe |

**Stems**

| | | |
|---|---|---|
| -aster-, -astro-, -stellar- | star | astronomy, stellar |
| -auto- | self | automobile, automatic |
| -bio- | life | biology |
| -cycle- | circle | bicycle, cycle |
| -mega- | great, large | megaton, megalopolis |
| -mort- | death | mortal, immortality |
| -phil- | love | philosophy |
| -polis- | city | metropolis |
| -psych- | mind | psychology |
| -soph- | wise | philosophy, sophomore |

**Suffixes**

| | | |
|---|---|---|
| -ity | condition, quality, state of being | unity, ability |
| -ness | condition, quality, state of being | sadness, happiness |

### Exercise 1

*In each item, select the best definition of the italicized word or phrase or answer the question.*

1. To apply to some universities, you must fill out the application form and include a short *autobiography*.

    _____ a. sample of your writing  
    _____ b. account of your life written by you  
    _____ c. list of courses you have taken  
    _____ d. list of schools you have attended

*For a list of all stems and affixes taught in *Reader's Choice, International Edition: Books 1 and 2,* see Appendix C.

2. The police officer used a *megaphone*.

_____ a. a portable radio         _____ c. an instrument to make one's
_____ b. a long stick                          voice louder
                                  _____ d. a telephone in the car

3. Dr. Swanson has written articles about *interstellar* travel.

_____ a. underwater         _____ c. high-speed
_____ b. long-distance      _____ d. outer space

4. Janet is interested in *autographs* of famous people.

_____ a. pictures           _____ c. families
_____ b. personalities      _____ d. signatures

5. An *asterisk* is a written symbol that looks like _____

_____ a. /.                 _____ c. %.
_____ b. *.                 _____ d. @.

6. The government is financing a study of the effects on humans of living in a *megalopolis*.

_____ a. an apartment in a large building   _____ c. a dangerous part of a city
_____ b. an extremely large city            _____ d. a city with a large police force

7. Children learning to ride bicycles probably already know how to ride a _____

_____ a. unicycle.          _____ c. tricycle.
_____ b. megacycle.         _____ d. motorcycle.

8. What is the *perimeter* of this rectangle?

_____ a. 14                 _____ c. 2
_____ b. 4                  _____ d. 5

9. *Nautical* means *pertaining to sailors, ships, or navigation*. Explain how the word *astronaut* is formed.

_____

_____

10. Why are the clothes that nurses, police officers, and soldiers wear called *uniforms*?

_____

_____

11. People who study population often speak of the world mortality rate. What is the opposite of *mortality rate*?

_____

**Exercise 2**

*Word analysis can help you to guess the meaning of unfamiliar words. Using context clues and what you know about word parts, write a synonym, description, or definition of the italicized words.*

1. _____ I enjoy reading *biographies* of kings and queens.

2. _____ The Morrises hired a full-time nurse to help them care for their newborn *triplets*.

3. _____ The new art museum will be named for the *multimillionaire* who donated the money to build it.

4. _____ About 4 million people live in the Detroit *metropolitan* area.

5. _____ All the hospital's private rooms were occupied, so Michelle had to stay in a *semiprivate* one.

6. _____ Winston Churchill wrote a *multivolume* history of World War II.

7. _____ Race car drivers need to have good *peripheral* vision so they can see another car driving alongside them without turning their heads.

8. _____ That jeweler doesn't cut diamonds; he works mainly with *semiprecious* stones such as opals.

9. _____ He was shot during the robbery, but it is not a *mortal wound*.

10. _____ My teeth are falling out; my dentist wants me to make an appointment with a *periodontist*.

11. _____ The president's *popularity* with the voters has never been greater than it is today.

## Exercise 3

*Following is a list of words containing some of the stems and affixes introduced in this unit and the previous ones. Definitions of these words appear on the right. Put the letter of the appropriate definition next to each word.*

1. _____ psychologist

2. _____ philanthropist

3. _____ sophisticated

4. _____ biochemist

5. _____ biology

6. _____ antibiotic

a. worldly-wise; knowing; finely experienced

b. a substance capable of killing microorganisms

c. the science of life or living matter

d. one who studies the chemistry of living things

e. one who shows love for humanity by doing good works for society

f. one who studies mental processes and behavior

7. _____ multicolored

8. _____ asteroid

9. _____ periscope

10. _____ astronomer

11. _____ unilateral

12. _____ bilateral

a. starlike; shaped like a star

b. affecting two sides or parties

c. having many colors

d. pertaining to, involving, or affecting only one side

e. a scientific observer of the planets, stars, and outer space

f. an optical instrument that allows a submarine to observe the surface from below the water

13. _____ cycle

14. _____ semicircle

15. _____ trilogy

16. _____ astrology

17. _____ ultraviolet

18. _____ ultranationalism

a. a recurring period of time in which certain events repeat themselves in the same order and at the same intervals

b. the study of the influence of the stars on human affairs

c. excessive devotion to national interests as opposed to international considerations

d. a series or group of three related dramas, operas, novels, etc.

e. invisible rays of the spectrum lying beyond the violet end of the visible spectrum

f. a half circle

# Sentence Study

## Restatement and Inference

Each sentence below is followed by five statements.* The statements are of four types:
1. Some of the statements are restatements of the original sentence. They give the same information in a different way.
2. Some of the statements are inferences (conclusions) that can be drawn from the information given in the original sentence.
3. Some of the statements are false based on the information given.
4. Some of the statements cannot be judged true or false based on the information given in the original sentence.

Put a check (✓) next to all restatements and inferences (types 1 and 2). Note: do not check a statement that is true of itself but cannot be inferred from the sentence given.

---

**Example**

Heavy smokers and drinkers run a fifteen-times greater risk of developing cancer of the mouth and throat than nonsmokers and nondrinkers.

---

_____ a. Cancer of the mouth and throat is more likely to occur in heavy smokers and drinkers than in nonsmokers and nondrinkers.

_____ b. People who never drink and smoke will not get mouth or throat cancer.

_____ c. Heavy drinkers who run have a greater risk of developing cancer than nondrinkers.

_____ d. People who don't smoke and drink have less chance of getting cancer of the mouth and throat than those who smoke and drink heavily.

_____ e. People would probably be healthier if they did not drink and smoke too much.

*Explanation*

✓ a. This is a restatement of the original sentence. If heavy smokers and drinkers run a greater risk of developing cancer than those who do not drink or smoke, then cancer is more likely to occur in heavy smokers and drinkers.

_____ b. It is not true that people who never smoke and drink will never get mouth or throat cancer. We only know that they are *less likely* to get this kind of cancer.

_____ c. The word *run* in the original sentence is part of the phrase *to run a risk* which means *to be in danger*. The sentence does not tell us anything about heavy drinkers who enjoy the sport of running.

---

*For an introduction to sentence study, see Appendix D.

___✓___ d. This is a restatement of the original sentence. If people who drink and smoke heavily have a greater chance of getting mouth and throat cancer than those who don't, then it must be true that those who don't smoke and drink heavily have less chance of developing this kind of cancer.

___✓___ e. This is an inference that can be drawn from the information given. If people who smoke and drink heavily run a high risk of developing cancer, then we can infer that people probably would be healthier if they didn't smoke and drink too much (heavily).

1. Nine out of ten doctors responding to a survey said they recommend our product to their patients if they recommend anything.

_____ a. Nine out of ten doctors recommend the product.

_____ b. Of the doctors who responded to a survey, nine out of ten doctors recommend the product.

_____ c. If they recommend anything, nine out of ten doctors responding to a survey recommend the product.

_____ d. Most doctors recommend the product.

_____ e. We don't know how many doctors recommend the product.

2. This organization may succeed marvelously at what it wants to do, but what it wants to do may not be all that important.

_____ a. The organization is marvelous.

_____ b. The organization may succeed.

_____ c. Although the organization may reach its goals, the goals might not be important.

_____ d. What the organization wants is marvelous.

_____ e. The author questions the goals of the organization.

3. This book contains a totally new outlook that combines the wisdom of the past with scientific knowledge to solve the problems of the present.

_____ a. Problems of the past and present are solved in this book.

_____ b. In this book, current knowledge and past wisdom are combined to solve current problems.

_____ c. Only by using knowledge of the past and present can we solve problems.

_____ d. None of today's problems can be solved without scientific knowledge.

_____ e. This book is different because it combines the wisdom of the past with scientific knowledge.

4. Like other timeless symbols, flags have accompanied mankind for thousands of years, gaining ever wider meaning, yet losing none of their inherent and original force.

_____ a. In spite of losing some of their original force, flags are a timeless symbol that has accompanied mankind for thousands of years.

_____ b. Flags have existed for thousands of years.

_____ c. Timeless symbols typically gain wider meaning while not losing their inherent force.

_____ d. Thousands of years ago flags accompanied mankind but through time they have lost their force.

_____ e. Because flags are considered a timeless symbol, they have gained continually wider meaning without losing their inherent original force.

5. When there is an absence of reliable information about drugs, the risks involved in using them are greatly increased.

_____ a. There is no reliable information about drugs.

_____ b. Using drugs is more dangerous when we don't know what effects and dangers are involved.

_____ c. The risks involved in using drugs have increased.

_____ d. People should try to find out about drugs before using them.

_____ e. There are no risks involved in using drugs if we have reliable information about them.

6. The project of which this book is the result was first suggested in the summer of 1962, in the course of some leisurely conversations at the foot of and (occasionally) on top of the Alps of western Austria.

_____ a. This book was written in 1962.

_____ b. This book was written in Austria.

_____ c. This book is a collection of conversations held in 1962.

_____ d. This book is the end result of a project.

_____ e. This book is about western Austria.

7. Los Angeles' safety record with school buses is generally a good one, but of course this record is only as good as the school bus drivers themselves.

_____ a. In spite of a generally good safety record for their school buses, Los Angeles school bus drivers are not very good.

_____ b. If school bus drivers are not very good, the town's school bus safety record will not be very good either.

_____ c. If cities wish to maintain good safety records with school buses, they should hire good school bus drivers.

_____ d. With better school buses, drivers will be able to maintain better safety records.

_____ e. Los Angeles' safety record with school buses has improved because better bus drivers have been hired.

8. Taxes being so high, the descendents of the wealthy class of the nineteenth century are being forced to rent out their estates to paying guests.

_____ a. In the nineteenth century, the wealthy class rented out its estates.

_____ b. Because of high taxes, families that were rich one hundred years ago now rent out their estates.

_____ c. Guests pay high taxes when they rent old estates.

_____ d. Some families that were once wealthy are having trouble paying their taxes.

_____ e. High taxes have changed the lives of some of the old wealthy families.

9. According to the definition of Chinese traditional medicine, acupuncture is the treatment of disease—not just the alleviation of pain—by inserting very fine needles into the body at specific points called loci.

_____ a. The author believes some people do not know that acupuncture can be used to treat illness.

_____ b. Finely pointed needles called loci are used in acupuncture.

_____ c. In Chinese traditional medicine, acupuncture is known to treat disease and alleviate pain.

_____ d. Those using acupuncture treat disease by placing needles into the body at specific points.

_____ e. Only those who practice traditional Chinese medicine use acupuncture.

10. It would be difficult to overpraise this book.

_____ a. This is a difficult book.

_____ b. This book deserves much praise.

_____ c. It is difficult not to overpraise this book.

_____ d. It is difficult to praise this book.

_____ e. The author of this sentence thinks this is an excellent book.

# Paragraph Reading

## Main Idea

Read the following paragraphs and poem quickly. Concentrate on discovering the author's main idea.* Remember, don't worry about details in the selections. You only want to determine the author's general message.

After each of the first five paragraphs, select the statement that best expresses the writer's main idea. After paragraphs 6 and 7 and the poem, write a sentence that expresses the main idea in your own words. When you have finished, your teacher may want to divide the class into small groups for discussion.

**Paragraph 1**

John Cabot was the first Englishman to land in North America. However, this man who legitimized England's claim to everything from Labrador to Florida, left no sea journal, no diary or log, not even a portrait or a signature. Until 1956 most learned encyclopedias and histories indicated that Cabot's first landfall in America was Cape Breton, Nova Scotia. Then a letter was discovered in the Spanish archives, making it almost certain that he had touched first at the northernmost tip of Newfoundland, within five miles of the site of Leif Ericson's ill-fated settlement at L'Anse aux Meadows. Researchers studying the voyages of Columbus, Cartier, Frobisher, and other early explorers had a wealth of firsthand material with which to work. Those who seek to recreate the life and routes used by Cabot must make do with thirdhand accounts, the disloyal and untruthful boasts of his son, Sebastian, and a few hard dates in the maritime records of Bristol, England.†

*Select the statement that best expresses the main idea of the paragraph.*

_____ a. John Cabot claimed all the land from Labrador to Florida for England.

_____ b. Much of what is known about Cabot is based on the words of his son, Sebastian, and on records in Bristol, England.

_____ c. The lack of firsthand accounts of Cabot's voyage has left historians confused about his voyages to North America.

_____ d. Historians interested in the life and routes used by Cabot recently discovered an error they made in describing his discovery of North America.

---

*For an introduction to reading for the main idea, see Appendix E.

†From Allan Keller, "The Silent Explorer: John Cabot in North America," *American History Illustrated* 8, no. 9 (January 1974): 5.

**Paragraph 2**

The Bible, while mainly a theological document written with the purpose of explaining the nature and moral imperatives of the Christian and Jewish God, is secondarily a book of history and geography. Selected historical materials were included in the text for the purpose of illustrating and underlining the religious teaching of the Bible. Historians and archaeologists have learned to rely upon the amazing accuracy of historical memory in the Bible. The smallest references to persons and places and events contained in the accounts of the Exodus, for instance, or the biographies of such Biblical heroes as Abraham and Moses and David, can lead, if properly considered and pursued, to extremely important historical discoveries. The archaeologists' efforts are not directed at "proving" the correctness of the Bible, which is neither necessary nor possible, any more than belief in God can be scientifically demonstrated. It is quite the opposite, in fact. The historical clues in the Bible can lead the archaeologist to a knowledge of the civilizations of the ancient world in which the Bible developed and with whose religious concepts and practices the Bible so radically differed. It can be considered as an almost unfailing indicator, revealing to the experts the locations and characteristics of lost cities and civilizations.*

*Select the statement that best expresses the main idea of the paragraph.*

_____ a. The holy writings of the world's religions can provide valuable geographical information.

_____ b. The Bible is primarily a religious document.

_____ c. The Bible was intended by its authors to be a record of the history of the ancient world.

_____ d. The Bible, though primarily a religious text, is a valuable tool for people interested in history.

**Paragraph 3**

At one time it was the most important city in the region—a bustling commercial center known for its massive monuments, its crowded streets and commercial districts, and its cultural and religious institutions. Then, suddenly, it was abandoned. Within a generation most of its population departed and the once magnificent city became all but a ghost town. This is the history of a pre-Columbian city called Teotihuacán (the Aztec Indians' word for "the place the gods call home"), once a metropolis of as many as 200,000 inhabitants 33 miles northeast of present-day Mexico City and the focus of a far-flung empire that stretched from the arid plains of central Mexico to the mountains of Guatemala. Why did this city die? Researchers have

*From Nelson Glueck, "The Bible as Divining Rod," *Horizon* 2, no. 2 (November 1959): 6.

found no signs of epidemic disease or destructive invasions. But they have found signs that suggest the Teotihuacanos themselves burned their temples and some of their other buildings. Excavations revealed that piles of wood had been placed around these structures and set afire. Some speculate that Teotihuacán's inhabitants may have abandoned the city because it had become "a clumsy giant . . . too unwieldy to change with the times." But other archaeologists think that the ancient urbanites may have destroyed their temples and abandoned their city in rage against their gods for permitting a long famine.*

*Select the statement that best expresses the main idea of the paragraph.*

_____ a. Teotihuacán, once the home of 200,000 people, was the center of a large empire.

_____ b. Many archaeologists are fascinated by the ruins of a pre-Columbian city called Teotihuacán.

_____ c. Teotihuacán, once a major metropolitan area, was destroyed by an invasion.

_____ d. A still unsolved mystery is why the people of Teotihuacán suddenly abandoned their city.

**Paragraph 4**

In any archaeological study that includes a dig, the procedures are basically the same: 1) selecting a site 2) hiring local workers 3) surveying the site and dividing it into sections 4) digging trenches to locate levels and places to excavate 5) mapping architectural features 6) developing a coding system that shows the exact spot where an object is found 7) and recording, tagging, cleaning and storing excavated materials. Neilson C. Debevoise, writing on an expedition to Iraq in the early 1930's, described the typical "route" of excavated pottery. Workers reported an object to staff members before removing it from the ground. The date, level, location and other important information were written on a piece of paper and placed with the object. At noon the objects were brought in from the field to the registry room where they were given a preliminary cleaning. Registry numbers were written with waterproof India ink on a portion of the object previously painted with shellac. The shellac prevented the ink from soaking into the object, furnished a good writing surface, and made it possible to remove the number in a moment. From the registry room objects were sent to the drafting department. If a clay pot, for example, was of a new type, a scale drawing was made on graph paper. Measurements of the top, greatest diameter, base, height, color of the glaze, if any, the quality and texture of the body and the quality of the workmanship were recorded on paper with the drawing. When the drafting department had completed its work the materials were placed on the storage shelves, grouped according to type for division with the

*From "Twilight of the Gods," *Time,* November 24, 1975, p. 107.

Iraq government and eventually shipped to museums. Today, the steps of a dig remain basically the same, although specific techniques vary.*

*Select the statement that best expresses the main idea of the paragraph.*

_____ a. For a number of years, archaeologists have used basically the same procedure when conducting a dig.

_____ b. Neilson C. Debevoise developed the commonly accepted procedure for organizing a dig.

_____ c. Archaeologists take great care to assure that all excavated objects are properly identified.

_____ d. A great deal of important historical and archaeological information can be provided by a dig.

**Paragraph 5**            The unprecedented expansion of Modern architecture throughout the world must be considered one of the great events in the history of art. Within the space of the last generation, the contemporary movement has become the dominant style of serious building not only in the United States and Europe, where pioneers had been at work since the late nineteenth century, but also in nations such as Brazil and India, where almost no Modern architecture existed until much later. Only the Gothic perhaps, among all the styles of the past, gained popular acceptance with anything like the speed of the Modern. And like the Gothic—which required a full seventy-five years of experimentation before it produced the cathedral of Chartres—the Modern has continually improved its structural techniques, gained in scale, and revised its aesthetics as it has attempted to meet the full range of people's civilized needs.†

*Select the statement that best expresses the main idea of the paragraph.*

_____ a. Gothic architecture gained popular acceptance faster than Modern architecture did.

_____ b. Modern architecture has not changed fast enough to meet the needs of civilization.

_____ c. The rapid growth and development of Modern architecture (as an art form) is nearly unequaled in the history of art.

_____ d. If architectural styles are to endure, they must develop and improve in an attempt to meet society's needs.

---

*From "Unearthing the Past," *Research News* 23, no. 5 (November 1972): 6.
†Adapted from Allan Temko, "The Dawn of the 'High Modern'," *Horizon* 2, no. 1 (September 1959): 5.

**Paragraph 6**

A summit is not any old meeting between two heads of state. Potentates have been visiting each other since the beginning of time. The Queen of Sheba came to visit King Solomon and exchanged riddles with him. Mark Antony came to visit Cleopatra and stayed on. Royalty, presidents and prime ministers of allied nations have sometimes got together after a victorious war to divide the spoils, as they did at the Congress of Vienna in 1814 and then at Paris after World War I. But a summit, in the sense in which Winston Churchill introduced the word into the language when he called for one in 1950, is something quite different and quite specific: it is a meeting between the leaders of two or more rival or enemy Great Powers trying to satisfy their mutual demands and head off future conflict.*

*Write a sentence that expresses the main idea of the paragraph.* _____

_____

**Paragraph 7**

The ideals that children hold have important implications for their school experiences. Children who believe in the value of hard work and responsibility and who attach importance to education are likely to have higher academic achievement and fewer disciplinary problems than those who do not have these ideals. They are also less likely to drop out of school. Such children are more likely to use their out-of-school time in ways that reinforce learning. For example, high school students who believe in hard work, responsibility, and the value of education spend about 3 more hours a week on homework than do other students. This is a significant difference since the average student spends only about 5 hours a week doing homework.†

*Write a sentence that expresses the main idea of the paragraph.* _____

_____

---

*From Robert Wernick, "Summits of Yore: Promises, Promises and a Deal or Two," *Smithsonian* 17, no. 6 (September 1986): 58.
†From "Ideals," in *What Works: Research about Teaching and Learning* (U.S. Department of Education, 1986), p. 17.

**Poem**                        *Looking in the Album**

Here the formal times are surrendered
to the camera's indifferent gaze: weddings,
graduations, births and official portraits taken
every ten years to falsify appearances.
Even snapshots meant to gather afternoons
with casual ease are rigid. Smiles
are too buoyant. Tinny laughter echoes
from the staged scene on an artificial
beach. And yet we want to believe
this is how it was: That children's hair
always bore the recent marks of combs;
that trousers, even at picnics, were always
creased and we traveled years with the light
but earnest intimacy of linked hands or arms
arranged over shoulders. This is the record
of our desired life: Pleasant, leisurely on vacations,
wryly comic before local landmarks, competent
auditors of commencement speakers, showing
in our poses that we believed what we were told.
But this history contains no evidence
of aimless nights when the wilderness of ourselves
sprang up to swallow the outposts of what
we thought we were. Nowhere can we see
tears provoked by anything but joy. There
are no pictures of our brittle, lost intentions.
We burned the negatives that we felt did not give a true
account and with others made this abridgement of our lives.

*Vern Rutsala*

*Write a sentence that expresses the main idea of the poem.* _____

_____

*Vern Rutsala, "Looking in the Album," in *The Window* by Vern Rutsala (Middletown: Wesleyan University Press, 1964).

## Discourse Focus

### Prediction

Reading is an active process. Meaning does not exist only on the page or in the mind of the reader. It is created by an active *interaction* between reader and text. Based on their general knowledge and the information in a text, good readers develop predictions about what they will read next; then they read to see if their expectations will be confirmed. If they are not confirmed, readers reread, creating new predictions. Most often, however, readers are not greatly surprised; readers continue reading. This exercise is designed to give you practice in the process of consciously developing and confirming expectations. You will read an article, stopping at several points to consider what you expect to read about next. Readers cannot always predict precisely what an author will talk about next, but you can practice using clues from the text and your general knowledge to more efficiently predict content.

---

# The Troubled State of Calculus
## A Push to Revitalize College Calculus Teaching Has Begun

---

Calculus: a large lecture hall, 200 or so bored students, a lecturer talking to a blackboard filled with Greek symbols, a thick, heavy textbook with answers to even-numbered problems, a seemingly endless chain of formulas, theorems and proofs.

---

**Example**

1. Above are the title, subtitle, and an inset from an article on calculus.* On the basis of these, what aspect of calculus do you think the article might be about? List two possibilities:

   _____

   _____

2. Does the author seem to think that calculus instruction is successful

   or unsuccessful at the present time? _____ What words give

   you this impression? _____

   _____

---

*Adapted from *Science News,* April 5, 1986, pp. 220–21.

*Explanation*

1. The main title indicates that calculus instruction is *troubled*. The subtitle tells us that there is a movement to improve calculus teaching. The inset describes a "typical," boring calculus class, suggesting what is troubled, and what needs to be improved. Based on this information in the text you might have decided that the article would be about such things as current problems with calculus instruction, and proposals for improving instruction. If you have personal knowledge of calculus instruction, you may have some more specific ideas about the kinds of problems and solutions that might be mentioned.

2. Obviously the author has a negative opinion of calculus instruction. He refers to it as *troubled* in the main title, and indicates a need to *revitalize* (to give new life to) it in the subtitle. The inset describes a *large* lecture hall, with *bored* students and *heavy* books: the opposite of a lively situation.

---

3. Before you continue reading the article, decide how you expect it to begin. Remember, you cannot always predict precisely what an author will do, but you can use knowledge of the text and your general knowledge to make good guesses. Which of the following seems the most likely beginning?

   a. The author will describe traditional ways of teaching calculus.
   b. The author will describe math instruction in general.
   c. The author will describe new ways to teach calculus.
   d. The author will describe the general state of calculus instruction.

Now read to see if your expectations are confirmed.

> by Ivar Peterson
>
> More than half a million students take an introductory calculus course in any given year, and the number is growing. A large proportion have no choice. Calculus is a barrier that must be overcome on the way to a pro- fessional career in medicine or engineering. Even disciplines like history now sometimes require some college mathematics. But for many people who in the last few years have passed through such a course, the word "calculus" brings back painful memories.

4. The article appears to be critical of current teaching practices. Is this what you expected?

5. Did you expect the article to begin with a general description of calculus instruction?

6. What do you expect to read about next? What words or phrases point in this direction? What do you know about calculus and schools in general that would lead you to predict this?

_____

_____

_____

Now read to see if your expectations are confirmed.

In many universities about half of the students who take introductory calculus fail the course. A surprisingly large number must take the course several times to get through. At the same time, engineering and physical sciences professors complain that even the students who pass don't know very much about calculus and don't know how to use it.

"The teaching of calculus is a national disgrace," says Lynn A. Steen, president of the Mathematical Association of America, based in Washington, D.C., and a professor at St. Olaf College in Northfield, Minn. "Too often calculus is taught by inexperienced instructors to ill-prepared students in an environment with insufficient feedback," he says. "The result is a serious decline in the number of students pursuing advanced mathematics, and a majority of college graduates who have learned to hate mathematics."

7. Were your expectations confirmed? If not, why not? Did you misunderstand something in the previous section? Do you think your expectations were valid? Would they provide a better outline for the author than the one he used?

8. At this point, the author has summarized his criticisms of the teaching of calculus. What do you think he will say next?

_____

_____

Discuss your choices with your classmates. Then read to see if your expectations are confirmed.

Now a small group of educators has started a movement to change what is taught in an introductory calculus course, to improve the way it is taught and to bring the teaching of calculus into the computer age. Earlier this year, 25 faculty members, administrators, scientists and others representing diverse interests met at Tulane University in New Orleans to see what could be done.

One big surprise was a general agreement that there is room for change. When participants came to the meeting, says mathematician Peter L. Renz of Bard College in Annandale-on-Hudson, N.Y., although they recognized the problem, "we all believe that there was nothing we could do about calculus." Yet despite this pessimism, many of the participants brought worthwhile suggestions.

9. Were your expectations confirmed in these two paragraphs?

10. What do you think the author will do next? What aspects of the text and your general knowledge help you to create this prediction?

_____

_____

_____

Read to see if your expectations are confirmed.

A key question is the role of hand-held calculators and computers. For the price of a calculus textbook, students can buy a scientific calculator. "The first thing that one can do on that basis is to eliminate an awful lot of the routine problems," says mathematician Ronald G. Douglas, dean of the physical sciences school at the State University of New York at Stony Brook. The ideas are still important, and instructors may need some of these techniques to illustrate what is going on, he says, but drilling students in something that any calculator or computer can now do becomes much less important.

The conference participants agreed that the routine use of calculators would help shift the focus of calculus back to its fundamental ideas and away from students mechanically plugging numbers into formulas to get "nice" answers. Until now, says Douglas, "all we've been teaching people in some sense has been a kind of pattern recognition."

11. Were your predictions confirmed?

12. What other kinds of problems and solutions do you predict are discussed in the final sections of this article? Be prepared to defend your predictions.*

_____

_____

_____

*The rest of this article is not reprinted here; however, a summary of the ideas can be found in the Answer Key.

## Reading Selections 1A–1C

# Technical Prose

Following are three magazine articles that discuss issues and patterns of population growth. When writing about technical subjects, authors sometimes include graphs and tables because such visual aids present information clearly and concisely. You will need to use information from the graphs and chart as well as the prose sections of the following articles in order to complete the comprehension exercises.

**Before You Begin**   1. How many people live in your community?

2. Now imagine that twice as many people lived there. What effects would the increased population have on the way you live, travel, eat, work?

*Selection 1A*         **Magazine Article**

Read "Crowded Earth—Billions More Coming" quickly to get a general understanding of the article; do not be concerned if you do not know the meanings of some vocabulary items. Then scan* to answer the comprehension questions.

## *Comprehension*

Answer the following questions according to information given in the article and accompanying chart and graphs. Indicate if statements 1 through 18 are true (T) or false (F).

1. _F_ In the year 2000, the world population may be 12 billion people. (5)

2. _T_ The population estimate of 6.4 billion for the year 2000 is based on the present growth rate of 2 percent per year.

3. _F_ The population is increasing fastest in the more highly industrialized countries. (Poor)

4. _____ Generally speaking, the nations with the highest rates of population increase are the same countries that even today find it difficult to feed all their people.

---

*For an introduction to scanning, see Appendix H.

5. _____ By the year 2000, approximately four-fifths of the world's population will live in the "poorer" nations.

6. _F_ By the year 2000, 37 percent of the world population will be living in urban areas.

7. _F_ It took millions of years for the world population to reach 1 billion.

8. _T_ The world population doubled between 1830 and 1930.

9. _F_ The world population doubled between 1930 and 1960.

10. _T_ The world's birth rate is increasing while the death rate is decreasing.

11. _T_ Graph I shows that the world population is increasing faster now than it ever has before.

12. _F_ The percentage figures in Graph II indicate the expected percentage increase in population between 1972 and 2000.

13. _T_ The population of Russia is increasing about twice as fast as the population of Europe.

14. _T_ By the year 2000, it is estimated that Asia alone will have more people than are alive in the whole world today.

15. _T_ Chart III lists the 25 countries with the highest rate of population increase.

16. _T_ No figures are available on the rate of population increase in West Germany.

17. _F_ The population of Poland is increasing faster than the population of Italy.

18. _F_ According to Chart III, the United Kingdom has the lowest rate of population increase of any country in the world.

19. What two results of medical advances does the author say have caused the change in the

world death rate? _____

_____

_____

20. The author mentions that it will be difficult to feed 6 billion people. What other danger of

an overcrowded world is mentioned? _____

_____

21. In Chart III, the column titled "Years Until Population Will Double" is an estimation. What

is it based on? What factors affect population growth? _____

_____

_____

# CROWDED EARTH— BILLIONS MORE COMING

**M**ORE THAN 6 BILLION people in a world that already is having trouble supporting about 4 billion—

That is the prospect now being held out by population experts, and it frightens them.

A new projection by the United Nations shows that, if the present growth rate of 2 per cent per year continues, today's world population of 3.9 billion will hit 6.4 billion by the year 2000.

What's more, the great bulk of the growth—9 of every 10 people added to the earth's population—will be in the poorer, undeveloped countries. These are the nations where feeding billions of people already is proving a near-insurmountable challenge.

By the year 2000, today's "have not" nations will have a combined population of 5 billion people, comprising nearly four fifths of the world's population.

Food isn't the only problem that such a population explosion presents. The more people there are and the more crowded their living conditions, authorities warn, the greater grows the likelihood of violence and upheaval.

According to U. N. projections, half of all the earth's people will be living in urban areas by the year 2000, up from 37 per cent today.

**From time of Christ—.** To put this growth in perspective—

At the time of Christ, millions of years after man first appeared on the earth, demographers estimate there were 250 million people.

In 1830, world population reached 1 billion. It took only 100 more years to add another billion to world population; just 30 more to add a third billion. And it will have taken just 15 more years to reach the 4-billion mark in 1975.

Actually, the world's birth rate is on a decline. But so are death rates, as medical advances have increased life spans and reduced infant mortality.

Average world life expectancy, the U. N. says, has increased by 20 years over the past three decades.

It's mainly in advanced nations that population growth is being curbed.

The outlook beyond 2000 is even more threatening. Unless population growth is curtailed, a world population of 12 billion is foreseen in a century. One question raised by demographers:

Is the earth capable of providing a decent life for 12 billion people?

I.

**WORLD'S EXPLODING POPULATION**

| | | | | | | |
|---|---|---|---|---|---|---|
| 791 MIL. | 978 MIL. | 1.3 BIL. | 1.7 BIL. | 2.5 BIL. | 3.9 BIL. | 6.4 BIL. |
| 1750 | 1800 | 1850 | 1900 | 1950 | TODAY | 2000(est.) |

III.

## THE 25 MOST POPULATED COUNTRIES

| | Population 1973 | Years Until Population Will Double* |
|---|---|---|
| 1. China | 792,677,000 | 41 |
| 2. India | 596,000,000 | 32 |
| 3. U.S.S.R. | 248,626,000 | 77 |
| 4. United States | 209,123,000 | 116 |
| 5. Indonesia | 128,121,000 | 26 |
| 6. Japan | 106,663,000 | 53 |
| 7. Brazil | 101,582,000 | 25 |
| 8. Bangladesh | 75,382,000 | 26 |
| 9. Pakistan | 64,461,000 | 24 |
| 10. West Germany | 61,806,000 | † |
| 11. Nigeria | 58,148,000 | 29 |
| 12. United Kingdom | 55,956,000 | 231 |
| 13. Mexico | 54,963,000 | 20 |
| 14. Italy | 54,642,000 | 116 |
| 15. France | 51,921,000 | 116 |
| 16. Philippines | 41,288,000 | 22 |
| 17. Thailand | 39,075,000 | 25 |
| 18. Turkey | 37,737,000 | 27 |
| 19. Egypt | 34,705,000 | 32 |
| 20. Spain | 34,675,000 | 63 |
| 21. Korea | 33,435,000 | 35 |
| 22. Poland | 33,202,000 | 77 |
| 23. Iran | 32,778,000 | 22 |
| 24. Burma | 29,213,000 | 30 |
| 25. Ethiopia | 26,947,000 | 27 |

*Years to double assumes continuation of 1972 rate of increase.

†No increase in 1972

Source: U.S. Census Bureau

II.

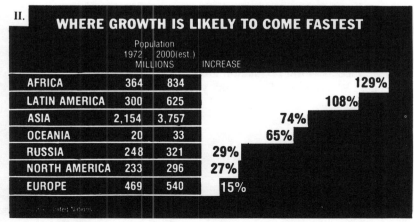

### WHERE GROWTH IS LIKELY TO COME FASTEST

| | Population 1972 MILLIONS | 2000(est.) MILLIONS | INCREASE |
|---|---|---|---|
| AFRICA | 364 | 834 | 129% |
| LATIN AMERICA | 300 | 625 | 108% |
| ASIA | 2,154 | 3,757 | 74% |
| OCEANIA | 20 | 33 | 65% |
| RUSSIA | 248 | 321 | 29% |
| NORTH AMERICA | 233 | 296 | 27% |
| EUROPE | 469 | 540 | 15% |

United Nations

Reprinted from *U.S. News and World Report,* October 21, 1974.

*Selection 1B*        **Magazine Article**

The article you just read was written in the 1970s. "The Global Community: On the Way to 9 Billion"* (opposite page) appeared in the 1980s in the same magazine. Read this article. As you read, ask yourself if the two articles make similar or different predictions.

## *Comprehension*

Indicate if statements 1 through 5 are true (T) or false (F) according to information given in this article and the accompanying charts.

1. _____ During the 50-year period between 1983 and 2033, the world population is likely to double.

2. _____ Generally speaking, the nations with the highest rates of population increase are the less-industrialized nations.

3. _____ China has the fastest-growing population.

4. _____ If current trends continue, the population of Nigeria will be relatively close to that of the Soviet Union in 2033.

5. _____ The population of Tokyo-Yokohama is not expected to change very much between 1983 and 2025.

## *Discussion/Composition*

1. Do the 1983 predictions about population seem consistent with the 1974 predictions? Cite evidence from the articles to support your answer.

2. The following is a quote from "The Global Community": "[humankind] will face a severe challenge to sustain itself in prosperity and peace." Would the author of "Crowded Earth" agree with this statement? Cite evidence from the article to support your answer.

3. What specific "challenges" will we face as world population grows? Consider economic, political, and/or personal challenges. Where possible, support your ideas with information from these two articles.

---

*From *U.S. News and World Report,* May 9, 1983.

# The Global Community: On the Way to 9 Billion

A child born today may share the earth with almost 9 billion other humans by age 50. About one third of these people will live in a broad swath stretching from the Philippines through the Indian subcontinent to the Middle East and Turkey. And all but 15 percent will reside in today's less developed nations. Should these projections by United Nations demographers come to pass, mankind will face a severe challenge to sustain itself in prosperity and peace.

**8.7** bil.

**4.4** bil.

## Estimated World Population

**1.8** bil.

**1.0** bil.

1850     1900     Today     2033

Though population is expected to almost double in the next 50 years, the actual pace of growth by 2033 will decline to roughly half of today's rate.

## Nations in Change

| | Population Now | 2033 | Change | |
|---|---|---|---|---|
| China | 1,000 mil. | 1,516 mil. | Up | 52% |
| India | 728 mil. | 1,311 mil. | Up | 80% |
| Soviet Union | 273 mil. | 366 mil. | Up | 34% |
| Nigeria | 85 mil. | 335 mil. | Up | 294% |
| Brazil | 131 mil. | 333 mil. | Up | 154% |
| U.S. | 232 mil. | 306 mil. | Up | 32% |
| Indonesia | 154 mil. | 261 mil. | Up | 69% |
| Japan | 120 mil. | 131 mil. | Up | 9% |
| Mexico | 73 mil. | 117 mil. | Up | 60% |
| Philippines | 53 mil. | 117 mil. | Up | 121% |
| France | 54 mil. | 57 mil. | Up | 6% |
| Italy | 58 mil. | 56 mil. | Down | 3% |
| West Germany | 62 mil. | 54 mil. | Down | 13% |
| Britain | 56 mil. | 53 mil. | Down | 5% |
| Canada | 25 mil. | 38 mil. | Up | 52% |

## Supercities Now and in 2025

| Now | Population | 2025 | Population |
|---|---|---|---|
| Tokyo–Yokohama | 20.0 mil. | Mexico City | 36.7 mil. |
| New York City area | 17.7 mil. | Shanghai | 36.1 mil. |
| Mexico City | 15.1 mil. | Peking | 31.9 mil. |
| Shanghai | 15.0 mil. | São Paulo | 29.6 mil. |
| São Paulo | 12.6 mil. | Bombay area | 27.0 mil. |
| Peking | 12.0 mil. | Calcutta | 26.4 mil. |
| Los Angeles– | | Jakarta | 23.6 mil. |
| Long Beach | 10.1 mil. | Dacca | 23.5 mil. |
| Buenos Aires area | 10.1 mil. | Tokyo– | |
| London | 10.0 mil. | Yokohama | 20.7 mil. |
| Paris | 9.7 mil. | Madras | 20.6 mil. |

USN&WR chart by Richard Gage—Basic data: United Nations, Population Reference Bureau, Inc., USN&WR Economic Unit

*Selection 1C* **Magazine Article**

***Before You Begin*** Consider the following:

1. Do you come from a small or large family? How many brothers and sisters do you have?

2. Do you think you will have more or fewer children than did your parents?

3. What factors influence family size?

The following article discusses changing patterns of childbearing and family size in the United States.

1. Consider the illustrations and the title of this article. What does a stork have to do with this article? If the article were written in your native language, could the illustrations remain the same?

2. People in the United States born between 1946 and 1964 are often called "baby boomers." What do you think this means?

3. Look at the subtitles and graphics. What do you expect this article to be about?

Read "The Stork Has a Busier Time, but—"* quickly to get a general understanding of the article. Then scan to answer the comprehension questions.

## *Comprehension*

Answer the following questions on the basis of information in the chart and graph from "The Stork Has a Busier Time, but—."

1. T / F   The size of the average U.S. family is increasing.

2. T / F   The number of births per year was higher in the early 1980s than in the 1970s.

3. T / F   Demographers are predicting a baby boom in the United States.

4. A baby boom is _____

_____ a. a time in which women have more babies.

_____ b. a time in which more women have babies.

---

*From *U.S. News and World Report,* November 29, 1982.

# The Stork Has a Busier Time, but--

**With more women of childbearing age, births are on the rise. Yet the trend toward smaller families continues unabated.**

Record numbers of women of childbearing age are producing a surge in the baby population but not in the birth rate.

With some 54 million women in that category, births in the U.S. are increasing. Last year there were 3.65 million babies born—almost half a million more than five years earlier.

Yet analysts see no baby boom in the cards. They say that, although more women are having babies, this is quite different from a boom—a period in which women have more babies.

Today, birth expectations among married women between 18 and 34 years of age are at an all-time low. "Over all, women are behaving as if they are going to have small families," says Peter Morrison, a demographer for the Rand Corporation.

**Later, fewer deliveries.** Many of those having babies today are older women. Between 1970 and 1979, the percentage of women age 30 and over having a first child doubled. Late motherhood is likely to mean smaller families since these women have fewer fertile years remaining.

Most women who have children are opting for only one or two youngsters, whereas two decades ago families of four or more were common. In 1965, nearly 1 mother in 4 bore at least four children, but by 1979 only 1 in 7 had such large families.

The move to smaller families, analysts say, represents the resumption of a trend going back decades, interrupted only by the tidal wave of births between 1946 and 1964.

One of the major reasons for smaller families these days: The changing role of women, who are continuing to enter the workplace in large numbers. The birth rate among working women is only one third that of those not in the labor force.

Another, and more troubling, finding is the continuing rise in the number of illegitimate births.

In 1979, the latest year for which figures are available, an unmarried mother accounted for 1 out of 6 births, while in 1950 only 1 out of 26 births came outside of marriage. Almost 1 in 10 of the white babies born in 1979 and close to half of the nonwhite babies had an unmarried mother.

Over the next few years, demographers expect no major change in current birth patterns. Any change at all is likely to be in the direction of even fewer births as Americans follow the example of many Western European nations and Japan, where small families are the rule.

Some analysts say the proportion of women who go through life childless could eventually reach 25 to 30 percent, about four times the current rate.

Observes Rand's Morrison: "Women are finding that they have roles to play other than reproduction." □

**More Babies...** Births in U.S.

3,646,000  122.9 Peak

3,137,000

Up 16% Since 1973

**...But No Baby Boom** Births Per 1,000 Women Age 15-44

67.7 Latest*

65.0 Low

*January-August at seasonally adjusted annual rate.

1973 '74 '75 '76 '77 '78 '79 '80 '81    1957                    1976   1982

## Anatomy of the Birth Rate

*Births in 1981 per 1,000 women age 18-44—*

**By Age**

| | |
|---|---|
| 18-24 | 92.1 |
| 25-29 | 112.8 |
| 30-34 | 67.3 |
| 35-39 | 28.6 |
| 40-44 | 7.1 |

**By Race**

| | |
|---|---|
| White | 68.5 |
| Black | 81.3 |
| Hispanic (all races) | 99.2 |

**By Marital Status**

| | |
|---|---|
| Married | 96.8 |
| Divorced, widowed | 27.8 |
| Never married | 27.0 |

**By Education**

| | |
|---|---|
| Not high-school graduates | 88.2 |
| High-school graduates | 70.3 |
| College graduates | 64.7 |

**By Status as Worker**

| | |
|---|---|
| Employed | 40.6 |
| Unemployed | 78.2 |
| Not in labor force | 126.1 |

**By Family Income**

| | |
|---|---|
| Less than $5,000 | 95.5 |
| $5,000-$14,999 | 80.4 |
| $15,000-$24,999 | 76.9 |
| More than $25,000 | 52.4 |

*USN&WR*—Basic data: U.S. Depts. of Commerce and Health and Human Services

5. T / F   Population experts think today's 18- to 34-year-old married women will end up having smaller families (that is, fewer children each) than women had 20 years ago.

6. T / F   The average age at which a woman in the U.S. has her first child is higher now than it was in 1970.

7. T / F   In 1965, most mothers in the U.S. had 4 children.

8. T / F   Before 1946, U.S. families tended to be larger than they were between 1946 and 1964.

9. T / F   The increasing number of women entering the work force affects family size.

10. T / F   Women with jobs outside the home have more children than women who are not in the work force.

11. T / F   In the U.S., more children are born to unmarried women now than at any time in the past.

12. T / F   Apparently, the term *illegitimate* refers to babies born to unmarried women.

13. T / F   Demographers predict that in the future, the size of the average U.S. family will either stay about the same or perhaps decrease.

14. T / F   Some demographers say that the number of women who never have children will increase greatly in the future.

15. T / F   In 1981, 96.8 percent of all children in the U.S. were born to married women.

16. T / F   Poor women were more likely to have a child in 1981 than were wealthy women.

17. T / F   In 1981, college graduates had a lower birth rate than women who had not graduated from college.

18. T / F   In 1981, no woman in the U.S. older than 44 had a child.

19. What reasons does the author cite to explain the trend toward smaller families? _____

_____

_____

## *Discussion/Composition*

Imagine you are the Minister of Health in your country. What actions, if any, would you take to respond to growing world population? Prepare a speech to present to government leaders supporting your position. You might want to comment on some of the following approaches to the problem.

1. It is not the role of government to attempt to control population.

2. The government should plan for population growth through economic development.

3. The government should take a role in controlling population growth through measures such as educational campaigns or financial incentives for small families.

4. The government should control population by prohibiting families from having more than one child.

# Reading Selection 2

# Magazine Article

*Before You Begin*   1. Why do people laugh? Do people laugh for different reasons?

2. Are there cultural differences that affect when and why people laugh?

3. Do you find jokes in English funny?

The following magazine article attempts to summarize scientific research for the general public. The author or the article on page 35 draws from the work of a number of experts in presenting an explanation for why we laugh.*

First skim† the article. In order to facilitate skimming, your teacher may want to read first (and sometimes second or last) lines of each paragraph aloud to you. Then complete exercise 1. Read the article a second time, more carefully, before completing the other exercises that follow. You may want to do the Vocabulary from Context exercise 1 on pages 38–39 before you begin reading.

## *Comprehension*

### Exercise 1

*Indicate if each statement is true (T) or false (F) according to your understanding of the article.*

1. _____ We laugh as a release for our normally repressed drives.

2. _____ Laughter strengthens social bonds.

3. _____ We laugh to express mastery over anxiety.

4. _____ We laugh to release energy after a crisis.

5. _____ We laugh at jokes of which we are the target.

6. _____ We never laugh when we are alone because we require company to laugh.

7. _____ We laugh immediately at birth.

8. _____ We sometimes laugh in times of sorrow.

9. _____ We sometimes laugh when nothing is funny.

10. _____ The ability to laugh takes a lifetime to perfect.

---

*"Why We Laugh" by Janet Spencer from *Ladies' Home Journal,* November 1974.
†For an introduction to skimming, see Appendix I.

**Are you a quiet giggler? Or can you let loose with hearty laughter? Your ability to laugh may mean more than you think. By Janet Spencer**

P icture this cartoon: A man is watering his lawn just as an attractive blonde walks by. As he ogles her, he accidentally turns the hose on his dowdy wife, who is sitting on the porch.

2) Men usually think the cartoon is funny. Women do not. And there's a good reason for the difference in opinion.

3) We start finding things laughable—or not laughable—early in life. An infant first smiles at approximately eight days of age. Many psychologists feel this is his first sign of simple pleasure —food, warmth and comfort. At six months or less, the infant laughs to express complex pleasures—such as the sight of Mother's smiling face.

4) In his book *Beyond Laughter*, psychiatrist Martin Grotjahn says that the earlier an infant begins to smile and laugh, the more advanced is his development. Studies revealed that children who did not develop these responses (because they lacked an intimate, loving relationship) "developed a schizophrenic psychosis in later life, or simply gave up and died."

5) Between the ages of six months and one year, the baby learns to laugh for essentially the same reasons he will laugh throughout his life, says Dr. Jacob Levine, associate professor of psychology at Yale University. Dr. Levine says that people laugh to express mastery over an anxiety. Picture what happens when a father tosses his child into the air. The child will probably laugh—but not the first time. In spite of his enjoyment of "flying," he is too anxious to laugh. How does he know Daddy will catch him? Once the child realizes he will be caught, he is free to enjoy the game. But more importantly, says Dr. Levine, the child laughs because he has mastered an anxiety.

6) Adult laughter is more subtle, but we also laugh at what we used to fear. The feeling of achievement, or lack of it, remains a crucial factor. Giving a

first dinner party is an anxious event for a new bride. Will the food be good? Will the guests get along? Will she be a good hostess? All goes well; the party is over. Now she laughs freely. Her pleasure from having proved her success is the foundation for her pleasure in recalling the evening's activities. She couldn't enjoy the second pleasure without the first, more important one—her mastery of anxiety.

7) Laughter is a social response triggered by cues. Scientists have not determined a brain center for laughter, and they are perplexed by patients with certain types of brain damage who go into laughing fits for no apparent reason. The rest of us require company, and a reason to laugh.

8) When we find ourselves alone in a humorous situation, our usual response is to smile. Isn't it true that our highest compliment to a humorous book is to say that "it made me laugh out loud"? Of course, we do occasionally laugh alone; but when we do, we are, in a sense, socializing with ourselves. We laugh at a memory, or at a part of ourselves.

9) Practically every philosopher since Plato has written on how humor and laughter are related, but Sigmund Freud was the first to evolve a conclusive theory. Freud recognized that we all repress certain basic but socially "unacceptable" drives, such as sex and aggression. Jokes, not accidentally, are often based on either sex or aggression, or both. We find these jokes funny because they provide a sudden release of our normally suppressed drives. We are free to enjoy the forbidden, and the energy we normally use to inhibit these drives is discharged in laughter.

10) Another reason laughter is pleasurable is because of the physical sensations involved. Laughter is a series of minor facial and respiratory convulsions that stimulates our respiratory and circulatory systems. It activates the secretion of adrenalin and increases the blood flow to the head and brain. The total effect is one of euphoria.

11) O f course, we don't always need a joke to make us laugh. People who survive frightening situations, such as a fire or an emergency plane landing, frequently intersperse their story of the crisis with laughter. Part of the laughter expresses relief that everything is now all right. During a crisis, everyone mobilizes energy to deal with the potential problem. If the danger is averted, we need to release that energy. Some people cry; others laugh.

12) Part of the integral pleasure of a joke *is* getting the point. But if the sexual or aggressive element of the joke is too thinly disguised, as in "sick" humor, the joke will leave us feeling guilty instead of amused. We may laugh—but in em-

barrassment. According to Dr. Grotjahn, "The disguise must go far enough to avoid guilt," but "not so far that the thrill of aggression is lost."

13) Which brings us to why women may not have found the joke about the man watering his wife very funny—because they get the point only too well. Many psychiatrists agree that the reason women aren't amused by this kind of joke is that most sex jokes (a hefty percentage of all jokes) employ women as their target. Women sometimes make poor joke tellers for the same reason; consciously or subconsciously, they express their resentment by "forgetting" the story.

14) W hen we are made the butt of a joke, either on a personal or impersonal level, we are emotionally involved in it. Consequently, we won't be able to laugh (except as a pretense). While we are feeling, we cannot laugh. The two do not mix. French essayist Henri Bergson called laughter a "momentary anesthesia of the heart." We call it comic relief.

15) Knowing that laughter blunts emotion, we can better understand why we sometimes laugh when nothing is funny. We laugh during moments of anxiety because we feel no mastery over the situation, claims Dr. Levine. He explains, "Very often compulsive laughter is a learned response. If we laugh, it expresses good feelings and the fact that we are able to cope. When we're in a situation in which we *can't* cope, we laugh to reassure ourselves that we *can!*"

16) How often have we laughed at a funeral or upon hearing bad news? We laugh to deny an unendurable reality until we are strong enough to accept it. Laughter also breaks our tension. However, we may also be laughing to express relief that the tragedy didn't happen to us. We laugh before giving a big party, before delivering a speech, or while getting a traffic ticket, to say, "This isn't bothering me. See? I'm laughing."

17) But if we sometimes laugh in sorrow, more often we laugh with joy. Laughter creates and strengthens our social bonds. And the ability to share a laugh has guided many marriages through hard periods of adjustment.

18) According to Dr. Levine, we can measure our adjustment to the world by our capacity to laugh. When we are secure about our abilities, we can poke fun at our foibles. If we can laugh through our anxieties, we will not be overpowered by them.

19) The ability to laugh starts early, but it takes a lifetime to perfect. Says Dr. Grotjahn, "When social relationships are mastered, when the individual has mastered . . . a peaceful relationship with himself, then he has . . . the sense of humor." And then he can throw back his head and laugh. **END**

11. _____ We laugh to break tension.

12. _____ Laughter is an unpleasant physical sensation.

13. _____ A sense of humor is a result of the mastery of human relationships.

14. _____ We always laugh when we understand a joke.

Now read the article again and complete the exercises that follow.

### Exercise 2

*The sentences in exercise 1 are general statements about laughter. Often authors will give specific examples to make an argument stronger or clearer. Following is a list of situations that the author of this article uses to illustrate some of the true statements in exercise 1. Match each of the examples below with the number of the appropriate general statement from the previous exercise. Some items have more than one possible answer. Choose what you feel to be the best answer. Be prepared to defend your choice.*

### Example

_3_ Infants laugh when their fathers throw them in the air.

1. _____ A new bride laughs after she gives her first successful dinner party.

2. _____ People who survive an emergency plane landing intersperse their story with laughter.

3. _____ We laugh before delivering a speech.

4. _____ We sometimes laugh at a funeral or when we hear bad news.

5. _____ We laugh at a sexual joke.

6. _____ Married couples laugh through hard periods of social adjustment.

## Critical Reading

### Exercise 1

*In order to evaluate an author's arguments, it is important to notice whom she quotes to support her statements. A number of experts are cited in this article. Next to each name below write the person's profession.*

**Example**

Sigmund Freud _psychiatrist_

1. Henri Bergson _____

2. Martin Grotjahn _____

3. Jacob Levine _____

4. Plato _____

## Exercise 2

*When an article combines information from many sources, it is sometimes difficult to determine the source of an individual piece of information. In this article it is especially difficult to determine if individual statements are those of the author or are based on the work of the experts cited.*

*Following is a list of statements made in the article. Indicate if each one has been made by the author or one of her sources.*

**Example**

_____Levine_____ We laugh to express mastery over anxiety.

1. _____ We laugh as a release for our normally repressed drives.

2. _____ Laughter strengthens social bonds.

3. _____ We laugh to release energy after a crisis.

4. _____ A sense of humor is a result of the mastery of human relationships.

5. _____ We sometimes laugh when nothing is funny.

6. _____ Laughter is a pleasurable physical sensation.

## Exercise 3

Now that you have examined the experts and information cited by the author, what is your opinion of the article? Why are the experts cited? How could this article be made more persuasive?

## Discussion/Composition

1. Tell a joke that you enjoy. How was your joke received? Are there ideas from the article that explain your classmates' reactions?

2. This article discusses situations that bring about laughter in the United States. Which situations given are similar to those in your country? Which are different? Which elements of laughter do you think are the same for all people?

## Vocabulary from Context

### Exercise 1

*Use the context provided to determine the meanings of the italicized words. Write a definition, synonym, or description of each of the italicized vocabulary items in the space provided.*

1. _____
2. _____
3. _____
4. _____
5. _____
6. _____
7. _____

Some people feel very nervous when they fly in airplanes. No matter how hard they try, they cannot lower their *anxiety*. Some of them enjoy talking about their fears while others *resent* being asked to discuss their personal feelings. Many are aware that they feel anxious but only a few are *conscious* of the way they express their *tension*. Some people try to hide their nervousness; they try to *disguise* their anxiety by telling jokes. Others become loud and *aggressive,* attacking people by making them the *butt* of cruel jokes.

8. _____
9. _____

Sometimes making someone else the *target* of jokes is an attempt to control one's own fears—to *master* anxiety.

10. _____

11. _____

A number of *factors* can be mentioned as important in explaining why some people have a fear of flying: early childhood experiences, general sense of security, fear of heights, trust in others, percentage of alcohol in blood, etc., but the *crucial* factor seems to be a feeling of no control.

12. _____

Usually, we are able to *suppress* our feelings so that they do not affect our behavior.

13. _____

By smiling foolishly and talking loudly, we are able to *repress* the rising feeling of fear so that it does not affect the way we behave.

14. _____

Most of us learn very young in life to control basic *drives* such as sex, hunger, and aggression.

15. _____     Sometimes the tension produced by our fears is so great that we cannot suppress it. At such times we need to *discharge* the tension by laughing or crying.

16. _____     The memory of a bad experience can sometimes *trigger* the same fear caused by that experience. Thus, a child might be frightened by the sight of a dog even though he is safe, merely because he once had a bad experience with a dog. A bad

17. _____     experience can be the *cue* that triggers our fears.

18. _____     Everyone experiences fear during major *crises*—such as fires, automobile accidents, etc.—but some people are even afraid of the dark.

19. _____     At the time of the crime, the man felt no emotion but later he began to feel *guilty,* so he went to the police and told them the whole story.

20. _____     Because it is necessary to recognize a problem before it can be solved, admitting that we are afraid is an *integral* part of the process of mastering our fears.

---

**Exercise 2**

*The following groups of sentences have been adapted from the article "Why We Laugh." Use context clues to determine the meanings of the italicized words. Write a definition, synonym, or description of each of the italicized vocabulary items in the space provided.*

1. People who survive frightening situations frequently *intersperse* their story of the crisis with laughter. Part of the laughter expressed is relief that everything is all right. During a crisis, everyone mobilizes energy to deal with the potential problem. If the danger is avoided we need to release that energy. For example, if a pilot *averts* a plane crash by making a safe emergency landing, he may laugh as he describes his experience.

   intersperse: _____

   averts: _____

2. We find these jokes funny because they provide a sudden release of our normally suppressed drives. We are free to enjoy the forbidden, and the energy we normally use to *inhibit* these drives is discharged as laughter.

   inhibit: _____

3. When we are secure about our abilities, we can joke about our *foibles*. If we can laugh at our small faults, we will not be overpowered by them.

   foibles: _____

4. A man is watering his lawn just as an attractive, well-dressed blond walks by. As he *ogles* her, he accidently turns the hose on his ugly, *dowdy* wife.

ogle: _____

dowdy: _____

## Vocabulary Review

Two of the words on each line in the following exercise are similar in meaning. Circle the word that does not belong.

1. cue            butt           target
2. inhibit        suppress       trigger
3. resent         release        discharge
4. crucial        conscious      integral
5. aggression     repression     suppression

# Reading Selection 3

## Short Story

***Before You Begin***      1. What is a lottery?

2. Why do you think lotteries have become popular throughout the world?

When "The Lottery" first appeared in the *New Yorker* in 1948, letters flooded the magazine expressing admiration, anger, and confusion at the story.* For a long time, Shirley Jackson refused to discuss the story, apparently believing that people had to make their own evaluation of it and come to a personal understanding of its meaning. Whatever people may think of it, they all agree that it is unusual.

Read "The Lottery" carefully and make your own judgment. You may want to do Vocabulary from Context exercise 1 on page 46 before you begin reading.

# The Lottery

**Shirley Jackson**

1    The morning of June 27th was clear and sunny, with the fresh warmth of a full-summer day; the flowers were blossoming profusely, and the grass was richly green. The people of the village began to gather in the square, between the post office and the bank, around ten o'clock; in some towns there were so many people that the lottery took two days and had to be started on June 26th, but in this village, where there were only about three hundred people, the whole lottery took only about two hours, so it could begin at ten o'clock in the morning and still be through in time to allow the villagers to get home for noon dinner.

2    The children assembled first, of course. School was recently over for the summer, and the feeling of liberty sat uneasily on most of them; they tended to gather together quietly for a while before they broke into boisterous play, and their talk was still of the classroom and the teacher, of books and reprimands. Bobby Martin had already stuffed his pockets full of stones, and the other boys soon followed his example, selecting the smoothest and roundest stones; Bobby and Harry Jones and Dickie Delacroix—the villagers pronounced the name "Dellacroy"—eventually made a great pile of stones in one corner of the square and guarded it against the raids of the other boys. The girls stood aside, talking among themselves, looking over their shoulders at the boys, and the very small children rolled in the dust or clung to the hands of their older brothers or sisters.

3    Soon the men began to gather, surveying their own children, speaking of planting and rain, tractors and taxes. They stood together, away from the pile of stones in the corner, and their jokes were quiet, and they smiled rather than laughed. The women, wearing faded house dresses and sweaters, came shortly after their menfolk. They greeted one another and exchanged bits of gossip as they went to join their husbands. Soon the women, standing by their husbands, began to call to their children, and the children came reluctantly, having to be called four or five times. Bobby Martin ducked under his mother's grasping hand and ran, laughing, back to the pile of stones. His father spoke up sharply, and Bobby came quickly and took his place between his father and his oldest brother.

4    The lottery was conducted—as were the square dances, the teen-age club, the Halloween program—by Mr. Summers, who had time and energy to devote to civic activities. He was a round-faced, jovial man, and he ran the coal business; and people were sorry for him, because he had no children and his wife was a scold. When he arrived in the square, carrying the black wooden box, there was a murmur of conversation among the villagers, and he waved and called, "Little late today, folks." The postmaster, Mr. Graves, followed him, carrying a three-legged stool; and the stool was put in the center of the square, and Mr. Summers set the black box down on it. The villagers kept their distance, leaving a space between themselves and the stool, and when Mr. Summers said, "Some of you fellows want to give me hand?" there was a hesitation before two men, Mr. Martin and his oldest son, Baxter, came forward to

---

*Reprinted from *The Lottery* by Shirley Jackson (New York: Farrar, Straus and Giroux, 1949).

hold the box steady on the stool while Mr. Summers stirred up the papers inside it.

5   The original paraphernalia for the lottery had been lost long ago, and the black box now resting on the stool had been put into use even before Old Man Warner, the oldest man in town, was born. Mr. Summers spoke frequently to the villagers about making a new box, but no one liked to upset even as much tradition as was represented by the black box. There was a story that the present box had been made with some pieces of the box that had preceded it, the one that had been constructed when the first people settled down to make a village here. Every year, after the lottery, Mr. Summers began talking again about a new box, but every year the subject was allowed to fade off without anything's being done. The black box grew shabbier each year; by now it was no longer completely black but splintered badly along one side to show the original wood color, and in some places faded or stained.

6   Mr. Martin and his oldest son, Baxter, held the black box securely on the stool until Mr. Summers had stirred the papers thoroughly with his hand. Because so much of the ritual had been forgotten or discarded, Mr. Summers had been successful in having slips of paper substituted for the chips of wood that had been used for generations. Chips of wood, Mr. Summers had argued, had been all very well when the village was tiny, but now that the population was more than three hundred and likely to keep on growing, it was necessary to use something that would fit more easily into the black box. The night before the lottery, Mr. Summers and Mr. Graves made up the slips of paper and put them into the box, and it was then taken to the safe of Mr. Summers' coal company and locked up until Mr. Summers was ready to take it to the square next morning. The rest of the year, the box was put away, sometimes one place, sometimes another; it had spent one year in Mr. Graves's barn and another year underfoot in the post office, and sometimes it was set on a shelf in the Martin grocery and left there.

7   There was a great deal of fussing to be done before Mr. Summers declared the lottery open. There were the lists to make up—of heads of families, heads of households in each family, members of each household in each family. There was the proper swearing-in of Mr. Summers by the postmaster, as the official of the lottery; at one time, some people remembered, there had been a recital of some sort, performed by the official of the lottery, a perfunctory, tuneless chant that had been rattled off duly each year; some people believed that the official of the lottery used to stand just so when he said or sang it; others believed that he was supposed to walk among the people; but years and years ago this part of the ritual had been allowed to lapse. There had been also a ritual salute, which the official of the lottery had had to use in addressing each person who came up to draw from the box, but this also had changed with time, until now it was felt necessary only for the official to speak to each person approaching. Mr. Summers was very good at all this; in his clean white shirt and blue jeans, with one hand resting carelessly on the black box, he seemed very proper and important as he talked interminably to Mr. Graves and the Martins.

8   Just as Mr. Summers finally left off talking and turned to the assembled villagers, Mrs. Hutchinson came hurriedly along the path to the square, her sweater thrown over her shoulders, and slid into place in the back of the crowd. "Clean forgot what day it was," she said to Mrs. Delacroix, who stood next to her, and they both laughed softly. "Thought my old man was out back stacking wood," Mrs. Hutchinson went on, "and then I looked out the window and the kids was gone, and then I remembered it was the twenty-seventh and came a-running." She dried her hands on her apron, and Mrs. Delacroix said, "You're in time, though. They're still talking away up there."

9   Mrs. Hutchinson craned her neck to see through the crowd and found her husband and children standing near the front. She tapped Mrs. Delacroix on the arm as a farewell and began to make her way through the crowd. The people separated good-humoredly to let her through; two or three people said, in voices just loud enough to be heard across the crowd, "Here comes your Mrs., Hutchinson," and "Bill, she made it after all." Mrs. Hutchinson reached her husband, and Mr. Summers, who had been waiting, said cheerfully, "Thought we were going to have to get on without you, Tessie." Mrs. Hutchinson said, grinning, "Wouldn't have me leave m'dishes in the sink, now, would you Joe?" and soft laughter ran through the crowd as the people stirred back into position after Mrs. Hutchinson's arrival.

10   "Well, now," Mr. Summers said soberly, "guess we better get started, get this over with, so's we can go back to work. Anybody ain't here?"

"Dunbar," several people said. "Dunbar, Dunbar."

Mr. Summers consulted his list. "Clyde Dunbar," he said. "That's right. He's broke his leg, hasn't he? Who's drawing for him?"

11   "Me, I guess," a woman said, and Mr. Summers turned to look at her. "Wife draws for her husband," Mr. Summers said. "Don't you have a grown boy to do it for you, Janey?" Although Mr. Summers and everyone else in the village knew the answer perfectly well, it was the business of the official of the lottery to ask such questions formally. Mr. Summers waited with an expression of polite interest while Mrs. Dunbar answered.

"Horace's not but sixteen yet," Mrs. Dunbar said regretfully. "Guess I gotta fill in for the old man this year."

"Right," Mr. Summers said. He made a note on the list he was holding. Then he asked, "Watson boy drawing this year?"

12   A tall boy in the crowd raised his hand. "Here," he said. "I'm drawing for m'mother and me." He blinked his eyes nervously and ducked his head as several voices in the crowd said things like "Good fellow, Jack," and "Glad to see your mother's got a man to do it."

"Well," Mr. Summers said, "guess that's everyone. Old Man Warner make it?"

"Here," a voice said, and Mr. Summers nodded.

13   A sudden hush fell on the crowd as Mr. Summers cleared his throat and looked at the list. "All ready?" he called. "Now, I'll read the names—heads of families first—and the men come up and take a paper out of the box. Keep the paper folded in your hand without looking at it until everyone has had a turn. Everything clear?"

14   The people had done it so many times that they only half listened to the directions; most of them were

quiet, wetting their lips, not looking around. Then Mr. Summers raised one hand high and said, "Adams." A man disengaged himself from the crowd and came forward. "Hi, Steve," Mr. Summers said, and Mr. Adams said, "Hi, Joe." They grinned at one another humorlessly and nervously. Then Mr. Adams reached into the black box and took out a folded paper. He held it firmly by one corner as he turned and went hastily back to his place in the crowd, where he stood a little apart from his family, not looking down at his hand.

"Allen," Mr. Summers said. "Anderson . . . Bentham."

15  "Seems like there's no time at all between lotteries any more," Mrs. Delacroix said to Mrs. Graves in the back row. "Seems like we got through with the last one only last week."

"Time sure goes fast," Mrs. Graves said.

"Clark . . . Delacroix."

"There goes my old man," Mrs. Delacroix said. She held her breath while her husband went forward.

"Dunbar," Mr. Summers said, and Mrs. Dunbar went steadily to the box while one of the women said, "Go on, Janey," and another said, "There she goes."

16  "We're next," Mrs. Graves said. She watched while Mr. Graves came around from the side of the box, greeted Mr. Summers gravely, and selected a slip of paper from the box. By now, all through the crowd there were men holding the small folded papers in their large hands, turning them over and over nervously. Mrs. Dunbar and her two sons stood together, Mrs. Dunbar holding the slip of paper.

"Harburt . . . Hutchinson."

"Get up there, Bill," Mrs. Hutchinson said, and the people near her laughed.

"Jones."

17  "They do say," Mr. Adams said to Old Man Warner, who stood next to him, "that over in the north village they're talking of giving up the lottery."

Old Man Warner snorted. "Pack of crazy fools," he said. "Listening to the young folks, nothing's good enough for them. Next thing you know, they'll be wanting to go back to living in caves, nobody work any more, live *that* way for a while. Used to be a saying about 'Lottery in June,

corn be heavy soon.' First thing you know, we'd all be eating stewed chickweed and acorns. There's always been a lottery," he added petulantly. "Bad enough to see young Joe Summers up there joking with everybody."

18  "Some places have already quit lotteries," Mrs. Adams said.

"Nothing but trouble in that," Old Man Warner said stoutly. "Pack of young fools."

"Martin." And Bobby Martin watched his father go forward. "Overdyke . . . Percy."

"I wish they'd hurry," Mrs. Dunbar said to her older son. "I wish they'd hurry."

"They're almost through," her son said.

"You get ready to run tell Dad," Mrs. Dunbar said.

19  Mr. Summers called his own name and then stepped forward precisely and selected a slip from the box. Then he called, "Warner."

"Seventy-seventh year I been in the lottery," Old Man Warner said as he went through the crowd. "Seventy-seventh time."

"Watson." The tall boy came awkwardly through the crowd. Someone said, "Don't be nervous, Jack," and Mr. Summers said, "Take your time, son."

"Zanini."

20  After that, there was a long pause, a breathless pause, until Mr. Summers, holding his slip of paper in the air, said, "All right, fellows." For a minute, no one moved, and then all the slips of paper were opened. Suddenly, all the women began to speak at once, saying, "Who is it?" "Who's got it?" "Is it the Dunbars?" "Is it the Watsons?" Then the voices began to say, "It's Hutchinson. It's Bill." Bill Hutchinson's got it."

"Go tell your father," Mrs. Dunbar said to her older son.

21  People began to look around to see the Hutchinsons. Bill Hutchinson was standing quiet, staring down at the paper in his hand. Suddenly, Tessie Hutchinson shouted to Mr. Summers, "You didn't give him time enough to take any paper he wanted. I saw you. It wasn't fair!"

"Be a good sport, Tessie," Mrs. Delacroix called, and Mrs. Graves said, "All of us took the same chance."

"Shut up, Tessie," Bill Hutchinson said.

22  "Well, everyone," Mr. Summers

said, "that was done pretty fast, and now we've got to be hurrying a little more to get done in time." He consulted his next list. "Bill," he said, "you draw for the Hutchinson family. You got any other households in the Hutchinsons?"

"There's Don and Eva," Mrs. Hutchinson yelled. "Make *them* take their chance!"

"Daughters draw with their husbands' families, Tessie," Mr. Summers said gently. "You know that as well as anyone else."

"It wasn't *fair*!" Tessie said.

23  "I guess not, Joe," Bill Hutchinson said regretfully. "My daughter draws with her husband's family. That's only fair. And I've got no other family except the kids."

"Then, as far as drawing for families is concerned, it's you," Mr. Summers said in explanation, "and as far as drawing for households is concerned, that's you, too. Right?"

"Right," Bill Hutchinson said.

"How many kids, Bill?" Mr. Summers asked formally.

"Three," Bill Hutchinson said. "There's Bill, Jr., and Nancy, and little Dave. And Tessie and me."

"All right, then," Mr. Summers said. "Harry, you got their tickets back?"

24  Mr. Graves nodded and held up the slips of paper. "Put them in the box, then," Mr. Summers directed. "Take Bill's and put it in."

"I think we ought to start over," Mrs. Hutchinson said, as quietly as she could. "I tell you it wasn't *fair*. You didn't give him time enough to choose. *Everybody* saw that."

Mr. Graves had selected the five slips and put them in the box, and he dropped all the papers but those onto the ground, where the breeze caught them and lifted them off.

"Listen, everybody," Mrs. Hutchinson was saying to the people around her.

"Ready, Bill?" Mr. Summers asked, and Bill Hutchinson, with one quick glance around at his wife and children, nodded.

25  "Remember," Mr. Summers said, "take the slips and keep them folded until each person has taken one. Harry, you help little Dave." Mr. Graves took the hand of the little boy, who came willingly with him up to the box. "Take a paper out of the box, Davy," Mr. Summers said. Davy put his hand into the box and laughed. "Take just one paper," Mr.

Summers said. "Harry, you hold it for him." Mr. Graves took the child's hand and removed the folded paper **28** from the right fist and held it while little Dave stood next to him and looked up at him wonderingly.

**26**   "Nancy next," Mr. Summers said. Nancy was twelve, and her school friends breathed heavily as she went forward, switching her skirt, and took a slip daintily from the box. "Bill, Jr.," Mr. Summers said, and Billy, his face red and his feet over-large, nearly knocked the box over as he got a paper out. "Tessie," Mr. Summers said. She hesitated for a minute, looking around defiantly, and then set her lips and went up to the box. She snatched a paper out and held it behind her.              **29**

**27**   "Bill," Mr. Summers said, and Bill Hutchinson reached into the box and felt around, bringing his hand out at last with the slip of paper in it.

The crowd was quiet. A girl whispered, "I hope it's not Nancy," and the sound of the whisper reached the edges of the crowd.

"It's not the way it used to be," Old Man Warner said clearly. "Peo- **30** ple ain't the way they used to be."

"All right," Mr. Summers said.

"Open the papers. Harry, you open little Dave's."

Mr. Graves opened the slip of paper, and there was a general sigh through the crowd as he held it up and everyone could see that it was blank. Nancy and Bill, Jr., opened theirs at the same time, and both beamed and laughed, turning around to the crowd and holding their slips above their heads.

"Tessie," Mr. Summers said. There was a pause, and then Mr. Summers looked at Bill Hutchinson, and Bill unfolded his paper **31** and showed it. It was blank.

"It's Tessie," Mr. Summers said, and his voice was hushed. "Show us her paper, Bill."

Bill Hutchinson went over to his wife and forced the slip of paper out of her hand. It had a black spot on it, the black spot Mr. Summers had made the night before with the heavy pencil in the coal-company office. Bill Hutchinson held it up, and there was a stir in the crowd.

"All right, folks," Mr. Summers said, "Let's finish quickly."

Although the villagers had forgotten the ritual and lost the original black box, they still remembered to use stones. The pile of stones the boys had made earlier was ready; there were stones on the ground with the blowing scraps of paper that had come out of the box. Mrs. Delacroix selected a stone so large she had to pick it up with both hands and turned to Mrs. Dunbar. "Come on," she said. "Hurry up."

Mrs. Dunbar had small stones in both hands, and she said, gasping for breath, "I can't run at all. You'll have to go ahead and I'll catch up with you."

The children had stones already, and someone gave little Davy Hutchinson a few pebbles.

Tessie Hutchinson was in the center of a cleared space by now, and she held her hands out desperately as the villagers moved in on her. "It isn't fair," she said. A stone hit her on the side of the head.

Old Man Warner was saying, "Come on, come on, everyone." Steve Adams was in the front of the crowd of villagers, with Mrs. Graves beside him.

"It isn't fair, it isn't right," Mrs. Hutchinson screamed, and then they were upon her.

---

# Comprehension

## Exercise 1

*Without referring to the story, indicate if each statement below is true (T) or false (F).*

1. _____ The lottery was always held in summer.

2. _____ The lottery had not changed for many generations.

3. _____ The villagers were angry at Mrs. Hutchinson for being late.

4. _____ In the first drawing, only one person from each family drew a paper from the black box.

5. _____ The lottery was a custom only in this small village.

6. _____ Bill Hutchinson thought the first drawing was unfair.

7. _____ Tessie Hutchinson drew the paper with the black dot in the final drawing.

8. _____ The people wanted to finish in a hurry because they didn't like Tessie.

9. _____ The lottery was a form of human sacrifice.

---

**Exercise 2**

*The following exercise requires a careful reading of "The Lottery." Indicate if each statement below is true (T) or false (F) according to your understanding of the story. Use information in the passage and inferences that can be drawn from the passage to make your decisions. You may refer to the story if necessary.*

1. _____ Old Man Warner believed that the lottery assured the prosperity of the village.

2. _____ The date of the lottery was not rigidly fixed but occurred any time in summer when all of the villagers could be present.

3. _____ Mr. Summers never managed to make a new box for the lottery because people were unwilling to change the traditions that remained from the past.

4. _____ A family might contain several households.

5. _____ Mr. Warner felt that stopping the lottery would be equal to returning to prehistoric times.

6. _____ Only Mr. Warner remembered when the lottery was started.

7. _____ The villagers were hesitant to take part in the final step in the lottery.

---

## Drawing Inferences

1. When did you first realize that this was a strange lottery? That winning the lottery was not desirable?

2. What details did the author add to make the lottery seem like a "normal" lottery? What details indicated that the lottery was strange? What details had double meanings?

3. Why do you think everyone had to take part in the final step of the lottery?

4. What was Mr. Warner's attitude toward the lottery? In what way and why did his attitude differ from other members of the community? What group in every society does Mr. Warner represent?

5. Why did Tessie want to include Tom and Eva in the final drawing?

6. Which aspects of the lottery have changed? Which have not changed?

## Discussion

1. How do you think the lottery began? Why was it started? Why does it take place at that time of year?

2. Why do you think the community continues the lottery?

3. Would you take part in the lottery if you were a member of the community?

4. This story is about a physical sacrifice in which a person is killed. Sacrifice is characterized by the suffering of one member of a group for the benefit of the group as a whole, and by a sense of relief when one realizes that he or she has not been selected. This relief is so great that it leads to unconcern toward the fate of the person(s) to be sacrificed. Using this definition, can you think of specific institutions in modern societies in which sacrifices take place? Aside from physical sacrifice, what other types of sacrifice are possible?

## Discussion/Composition

Was the lottery fair?

## Vocabulary from Context

### Exercise 1

*Use the context provided to determine the meanings of the italicized words. Write a definition, synonym, or description of each of the italicized vocabulary items in the space provided.*

1. _____

2. _____

3. _____
4. _____
5. _____
6. _____

7. _____

8. _____

I like any game of chance, but I most enjoy taking part in a lottery. The lottery is like an unchanging religious ceremony, and it is perhaps this *ritual* quality of the lottery that people enjoy. Unlike other games of chance, a lottery does not require a great deal of *paraphernalia*. The only equipment needed is a bowl filled with slips of paper. I enjoy the excitement of watching the official pick the winning number. The moment before the *drawing* is very serious. The judge *gravely* approaches the bowl and looks at the crowd *soberly*. The crowd is quiet except for the low *murmur* of excitement. Suddenly the winner is selected. After the lottery is over, everyone but the winner throws away his or her piece of paper, and the *discarded* slips are soon blown away by the wind. People begin to *disengage* themselves from the crowd and the lottery is over.

## Exercise 2

*This exercise is designed to give you additional clues to determine the meanings of unfamiliar vocabulary items in context. In the paragraph of "The Lottery" indicated by the number in parentheses, find the word that best fits the meaning given. Your teacher may want to read these aloud as you quickly scan the paragraph to find the answer.*

1. (2) Which word means *noisy and excited?*

2. (2) Which word means *criticisms; severe or formal scoldings?*

3. (3) Which word means *information, usually about other people, not always factual?*

4. (7) Which word at the beginning of the paragraph means *taking care of details?*

5. (7) Which word at the bottom of the paragraph means *endlessly?*

## Exercise 3

*This exercise should be done after you have finished reading "The Lottery." The exercise is designed to determine how well you have been able to use context clues to guess the meaning of unfamiliar vocabulary in "The Lottery." Give a definition, synonym, or description of each of the words and phrases below. The number in parentheses indicates the paragraph in which the word can be found. This exercise can be done orally or in writing.*

1. devote (first sentence, paragraph 4) _____

2. stirred up (last sentence, paragraph 4) _____

3. fade off (bottom, paragraph 5) _____

4. shabbier (last sentence, paragraph 5) _____

5. lapse (middle, paragraph 7) _____

6. craned (first sentence, paragraph 9) _____

7. tapped (second sentence, paragraph 9) _____

8. consulted (paragraph 10) _____

# 3

---

## Nonprose Reading

## Bus Schedule

Nonprose writing consists of disconnected words and numbers instead of the sentences and paragraphs you usually learn to read. Each time you need information from a train schedule, a graph, a menu, or the like, you must read nonprose material. This activity will help you practice the problem-solving skills you will need in order to read nonprose material.

The United States is a country that has depended heavily on the automobile. In recent years, because of concern about oil resources and the pollution caused by auto emissions, large cities have tried to change commuter habits by encouraging people to ride buses rather than drive their cars. Bus schedules such as the one that follows are a part of this effort.

**Before You Begin**   Reflect on bus travel in your country:

1. How convenient is the bus service in your country? How often do the buses run? Are there many buses to choose from?

2. Do buses serve small towns as well as cities? Rural areas as well as urban areas? Do many people ride buses?

3. Do drivers adhere to a strict schedule? Do drivers wait for passengers who are running to catch the bus?

4. How do you find out about the buses? Do you use printed schedules to find the appropriate bus routes and times?

Consider bus travel as a visitor to the U.S.:

1. In the U.S., bus travelers rely on printed bus schedules. Why do you think this might be?

2. Imagine you are visiting a large city in the United States for the first time. You plan to take city buses to see some of the city's parks, museums, and important landmarks. What would you need to know about the city's bus system in order to plan your tour?

Bus schedules are often difficult to read. Following are pages of a Denver, Colorado, bus schedule. The accompanying exercises are designed to help you solve typical problems encountered by bus travelers.

---
**Exercise 1**

*At the top of page 51 are the cover pages of a Denver bus schedule. Skim them to get a general idea of the kinds of information they provide. Then use questions 1 through 8 to guide you in finding specific information.*

1. Within the Denver bus system there are many different bus routes. Each route, or line, has a different name and a separate printed schedule. What bus route is this schedule for?

_____

2. Do you know if this bus goes to the campus of the University of Colorado at Denver? To the Denver Museum of Natural History?

_____

3. What are "peak hours"? Why is it important to know if your bus is traveling during peak hours?

_____

_____

4. How much would it cost two adults and a 5-year-old child to take a local bus ride on a Saturday?

_____

5. Suppose that all you have is a five-dollar bill. Will you need to get change before you board the bus?

_____

6. If you left your umbrella on a Denver bus, what number would you call to see if it had been found?

_____

7. If you have questions about bus routes, what number should you call? _____

8. How much would it cost a handicapped passenger (with proper RTD identification) to ride a bus at noon on a Monday?

_____

## Exercise 2

*The map on the bottom of page 51 shows the routes followed by eastbound and westbound 20th Avenue buses. Use the map to answer the following questions.*

1. Can you connect to a route 76 bus from a route 20 bus? _____

2. T / F   The westbound bus passes Mercy Hospital.

3. T / F   The eastbound bus stops in front of Children's Hospital.

4. When do 20th Avenue buses pass the corner of West 26th and Lowell? _____

5. You want to visit a friend at Fitzsimons Hospital. Does the 20th Avenue bus go directly there?

   _____

## Exercise 3

*Within the 20th Avenue bus schedule, there are separate time tables for buses that travel east and buses that travel west. On page 52 are the time tables for the eastbound 20th Avenue buses. Suppose that you are staying near the Denver West Marriott Hotel. Use the time tables to answer the following questions. For some questions you may want to use the map in exercise 2 as well as the time tables.*

1. T / F   It costs more to take the 8:55 A.M. weekday bus from the Marriott than to take the 9:57 A.M. bus.

2. If you use a wheelchair, which 20th Avenue bus would you take? _____

3. If you wanted to meet a friend at Mile High Stadium at 10:00 A.M. on a Wednesday, what

   bus would you need to catch from the hotel? _____

4. It's Friday. You want to meet a friend for an 8:00 P.M. dinner at a restaurant on the corner

   of E. 17th and York. What is the latest bus you could catch from your hotel? _____

5. How many buses go from the Marriott Hotel to Union Station? _____

6. T / F   The Marriott is a convenient place to stay if you want to visit downtown Denver on the weekend.

7. T / F   20th Avenue buses do not run on Christmas Day.

8. T / F   The bus schedule is bilingual.

# RTD The Ride

# 20

**Stops**

## 20th Avenue

Service to:
**Auraria**
**Beth Israel Hospital**
**Children's Hospital**
**City Park**
**Colorado Women's College**
**Denver Museum of**
**Natural History**
**Denver West Marriott**
**Downtown Denver**
**Fitzsimons Hospital**
**Kaiser Permanente**
**McNichols Arena**
**Mercy Hospital**
**Mile High Stadium**
**Sloans Lake**
**St. Anthony Hospital Central**
**St. Joseph's Hospital**
**St. Luke's Hospital**
**Union Station**

This route makes "X" stops
on 15th/17th Streets

**For information call: 778-6000**

**11 January, 1987**

## Fares/Tarifas

| Type of Service | Peak | Off-Peak | Monthly Passes | |
| --- | --- | --- | --- | --- |
| | | | Regular | Elderly-Handicapped Youth (6-19 yrs.) |
| Mall Shuttle | **free** | free | — | — |
| Circulator | **35¢** | 35¢ | $12.00 | $ 8.00 |
| Boulder City | **50¢** | 35¢ | 17.00 | 11.00 |
| Local/Ltd | **70¢** | 35¢ | 24.00 | 16.00 |
| Express | **$1.05** | $1.05 | 36.00 | 24.00 |
| Regional long-distance | 1.75 | 1.75 | 60.00 | 40.00 |
| Transfers | **free** | free | | |

**Peak Hours** are 6:00-9:00 AM and 4:00-6:00 PM weekdays only.

**Off-Peak Hours** are all other times including holidays.

**Exact Fare, Token or Monthly Pass Only!** Drivers carry no change.

**Transfers** are intended for one continuous trip in the same direction. Request transfers at the time a fare is paid by cash or token.

**Passes and Tokens** are available at selected RTD offices and all King Soopers and Safeway stores. Tokens are sold at all Albertsons stores. Charge your pass or tokens by the roll to your MasterCard, Visa or Choice Card at selected RTD locations, by mail or by phone. To charge by phone, call 777-8893, seven days a week, 24 hours a day.

**Elderly (65+), Handicapped and Youth** pass discounts are available at selected RTD locations. Youth show proof of age. Elderly show a Medicare card, driver's license or Colorado ID. Handicapped show an authorized RTD identification card available through RTD, call 777-8600. To receive discounted passes by mail, initial eligibility must be established at an RTD location.

**Elderly and Handicapped** passengers ride for just 5¢ during off-peak hours by showing identification noted above for pass discounts.

**Children** 5 and under ride free if accompanied by adult passenger (limit 3).

**RTD's Downtown Information Center** is located at Civic Center Station, Broadway and Colfax. Passes, tokens and customer schedules are available here. Hours are from 8:00 AM-6:00 PM Monday-Friday.

**RTD's Customer Service** is located at Civic Center Station, Broadway and Colfax. For compliments or concerns call 573-2343. Hours are from 8:00 AM-5:00 PM Monday-Friday.

**Lost and Found** articles can be reclaimed at the following locations:

**Denver:** Civic Center Station, Broadway and Colfax
Hours: 8:00 AM-5:00 PM Monday-Friday. Call 573-2288

**Boulder:** Boulder Transit Center, 14th and Walnut
Hours: 7:00 AM-7:00 PM Monday-Friday. Call 442-7332

**Longmont:** Longmont Terminal, 815 South Main
Hours: 8:00 AM-5:00 PM Monday-Friday. Call 776-4141

**TTY** information service for patrons with hearing and speech impairments ONLY: call 753-9405.

**Notice:** Although RTD makes every effort to operate its service as scheduled, bus schedules may vary because of road, traffic, equipment, and other conditions. RTD makes no warranty or guarantee, express or implied, that bus service will be provided as scheduled. The RTD's liability is limited to the value of the fare for a one-way ride.

**For information call: 778-6000,** 5:00 AM to 10:00 PM Mon-Fri and 7:00 AM to 10:00 PM Sat/Sun/Holiday.

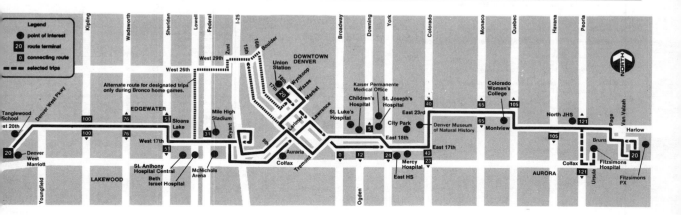

## Denver West to Fitzsimons—Eastbound

### Monday-Friday   Lunes-Viernes

Times listed are approximate

| H | Denver West Marriott | West 20th-Youngfield (Lakewood) | West 20th-Wadsworth | West 17th-Sheridan | West 17th-Bryant (Mile High Stadium) | Lawrence-9th (Auraria) | Wynkoop-17th (Union Station) | 17th-Champa** | East 17th-York | Colorado-East 17th | East 23rd-Monaco | Montview-Havana | Fitzsimons PX | Fitzsimons Hospital (Aurora) |
|---|---|---|---|---|---|---|---|---|---|---|---|---|---|---|
| H | 524 | 528 | 538 | 544 | 549 | 555 | -- | 601 | 608 | 611 | 618 | 627 | 634 | -- |
| H | -- | -- | -- | -- | -- | -- | 620 | 623 | 630 | 633 | 640 | 649 | 656 | -- |
| H | 601 | 605 | 616 | 622 | 627 | 634 | -- | 641 | 651 | 654 | 701 | 710 | 717 | -- |
| H | 621 | 625 | 636 | 642 | 647 | 654 | -- | 701 | 711 | 714 | 721 | 730 | 737 | -- |
| H | -- | -- | -- | -- | -- | -- | 717 | 721 | 731 | 734 | 741 | 750 | 757 | -- |
| H | 652 | 656 | 708 | 714 | 719 | 726 | -- | 735 | 745 | 748 | 755 | 804 | 811 | -- |
| H | -- | -- | -- | -- | -- | -- | 745 | 750 | 800 | 803 | 810 | 819 | 826 | -- |
| H | 722 | 726 | 738 | 744 | 749 | 756 | -- | 805 | 815 | 818 | 825 | 834 | 841 | -- |
| H | -- | -- | -- | -- | -- | -- | 818 | 820 | 830 | 833 | 840 | 849 | 856 | -- |
| H | 755 | 759 | 809 | 815 | 820 | 826 | -- | 835 | 845 | 848 | 855 | 904 | 911 | -- |
| H | -- | -- | -- | -- | -- | -- | 845 | 850 | 900 | 903 | 910 | 919 | 926 | -- |
| H | 825 | 829 | 839 | 845 | 850 | 856 | -- | 905 | 915 | 918 | 925 | 934 | 941 | -- |
| H | -- | -- | -- | -- | -- | -- | 915 | 920 | 930 | 933 | 940 | 949 | 956 | -- |
| H | 855 | 859 | 909 | 915 | 920 | 926 | -- | 935 | 945 | 948 | 955 | 1004 | 1011 | -- |
| H | -- | -- | -- | -- | -- | -- | 945 | 950 | 1000 | 1003 | 1010 | 1019 | 1026 | -- |
| H | -- | -- | -- | -- | -- | -- | 1000 | 1005 | 1015 | 1018 | 1025 | 1034 | 1041 | -- |
| H | -- | -- | -- | -- | -- | -- | 1015 | 1020 | 1030 | 1034 | 1041 | 1050 | 1057 | -- |
| H | 957 | 1001 | 1011 | 1017 | 1022 | 1028 | -- | 1035 | 1045 | 1049 | 1056 | 1105 | 1112 | -- |
| H | -- | -- | -- | -- | -- | -- | 1045 | 1050 | 1100 | 1104 | 1111 | 1120 | 1127 | -- |
| H | -- | -- | -- | -- | -- | -- | 1100 | 1105 | 1115 | 1119 | 1126 | 1135 | 1142 | -- |
| H | -- | -- | -- | -- | -- | -- | 1115 | 1120 | 1130 | 1134 | 1141 | 1150 | 1157 | -- |
| H | 1057 | 1101 | 1111 | 1117 | 1122 | 1128 | -- | 1135 | 1145 | 1149 | 1156 | 1205 | 1212 | -- |
| H | -- | -- | -- | -- | -- | -- | 1145 | 1150 | 1200 | 1204 | 1211 | 1220 | 1227 | -- |
| H | -- | -- | -- | -- | -- | -- | 1200 | 1205 | 1215 | 1219 | 1226 | 1235 | 1242 | -- |
| H | -- | -- | -- | -- | -- | -- | 1215 | 1220 | 1230 | 1234 | 1241 | 1250 | 1257 | -- |
| H | 1157 | 1201 | 1211 | 1217 | 1222 | 1228 | -- | 1235 | 1245 | 1249 | 1256 | 105 | 112 | -- |
| H | -- | -- | -- | -- | -- | -- | 1245 | 1250 | 100 | 104 | 111 | 120 | 127 | -- |
| H | -- | -- | -- | -- | -- | -- | 100 | 105 | 115 | 119 | 126 | 135 | 142 | -- |
| H | -- | -- | -- | -- | -- | -- | 115 | 120 | 130 | 134 | 141 | 150 | 157 | -- |
| H | 1257 | 101 | 111 | 117 | 122 | 128 | -- | 135 | 145 | 149 | 156 | 205 | 212 | -- |
| H | -- | -- | -- | -- | -- | -- | 145 | 150 | 200 | 204 | 211 | 220 | 227 | -- |
| H | -- | -- | -- | -- | -- | -- | 200 | 205 | 215 | 219 | 226 | 235 | 242 | -- |
| H | -- | -- | -- | -- | -- | -- | 215 | 220 | 231 | 235 | 243 | 253 | 300 | -- |
| H | -- | -- | -- | -- | -- | -- | -- | -- | 244 | 247 | 255 | -- | -- | -- |
| H | 157 | 201 | 211 | 217 | 222 | 228 | -- | 235 | 246 | 250 | 258 | 308 | 315 | -- |
| H | -- | -- | -- | -- | -- | -- | 245 | 250 | 301 | 305 | 313 | 323 | 330 | -- |
| H | -- | -- | -- | -- | -- | -- | 300 | 305 | 316 | 320 | 328 | 338 | 345 | -- |
| H | -- | -- | -- | -- | -- | -- | 310 | 315 | 327 | 331 | 339 | 349 | 357 | -- |
| H | -- | -- | -- | -- | -- | -- | 320 | 325 | 337 | 341 | 349 | 359 | 407 | -- |
| H | 254 | 258 | 310 | 316 | 321 | 327 | -- | 335 | 347 | 351 | 359 | 407 | 417 | -- |
| H | -- | -- | -- | -- | -- | -- | 340 | 345 | 357 | 401 | 409 | 419 | 427 | -- |
| H | -- | -- | -- | -- | -- | -- | 350 | 355 | 407 | 411 | 419 | 429 | 437 | -- |
| H | 324 | 328 | 340 | 346 | 351 | 357 | -- | 405 | 417 | 421 | 429 | 439 | 447 | -- |
| H | -- | -- | -- | -- | -- | -- | 410 | 415 | 427 | 431 | 439 | 449 | 457 | -- |
| H | -- | -- | -- | -- | -- | -- | 420 | 425 | 437 | 441 | 449 | 459 | 507 | -- |
| H | 354 | 358 | 410 | 416 | 421 | 426 | -- | 435 | 447 | 451 | 459 | 509 | 517 | -- |
| H | -- | -- | -- | -- | -- | -- | 440 | 445 | 457 | 501 | 509 | 519 | 527 | -- |
| H | -- | -- | -- | -- | -- | -- | 450 | 455 | 506 | 510 | 518 | 528 | 536 | -- |
| H | 424 | 428 | 440 | 446 | 451 | 456 | -- | 505 | 516 | 520 | 528 | 538 | 546 | -- |
| H | -- | -- | -- | -- | -- | -- | 510 | 515 | 526 | 530 | 538 | 548 | 555 | -- |
| H | -- | -- | -- | -- | -- | -- | 525 | 530 | 540 | 544 | 552 | 602 | 609 | -- |
| H | -- | -- | -- | -- | -- | -- | 555 | 600 | 610 | 614 | 622 | 632 | -- | 639 |
| H | 507 | 511 | 520 | 526 | 531 | 536 | -- | 545 | 555 | 559 | 607 | 617 | 624 | -- |
| H | -- | -- | -- | -- | -- | -- | 615 | 625 | 629 | 637 | 647 | -- | -- | 654 |
| H | 537 | 541 | 550 | 556 | 601 | 606 | -- | 625 | 630 | 640 | 644 | 652 | 702 | 709 |
| H | 607 | 611 | 620 | 626 | 631 | 636 | -- | 645 | 655 | 659 | 707 | 717 | -- | 724 |
| H | -- | -- | -- | -- | -- | -- | 710 | 715 | 722 | 725 | 731 | 739 | -- | 748 |
| H | -- | -- | -- | -- | -- | -- | 740 | 745 | 752 | 755 | 801 | 810 | -- | 817 |
| H | -- | -- | -- | -- | -- | -- | 810 | 815 | 822 | 825 | 831 | 840 | -- | 847 |
| H | -- | -- | -- | -- | -- | -- | 840 | 845 | 852 | 855 | 901 | 910 | -- | 917 |
| H | -- | -- | -- | -- | -- | -- | 910 | 915 | 922 | 925 | 931 | 940 | -- | 947 |
| H | -- | -- | -- | -- | -- | -- | 940 | 945 | 952 | 955 | 1001 | 1010 | -- | 1017 |
| H | -- | -- | -- | -- | -- | -- | 1010 | 1015 | 1022 | 1025 | 1031 | 1040 | -- | 1047 |
| H | -- | -- | -- | -- | -- | -- | 1040 | 1045 | 1052 | 1055 | 1101 | 1110 | -- | 1117 |
| H | -- | -- | -- | -- | -- | -- | 1110 | 1115 | 1122 | 1125 | 1131 | 1140 | -- | 1147 |
| H | -- | -- | -- | -- | -- | -- | 1140 | 1145 | 1152 | 1155 | 1201 | 1210 | -- | 1217 |

## Denver West to Fitzsimons—Eastbound

### Saturday   Sabado

| H | Wynkoop-17th (Union Station) | 17th-Champa** | East 17th-York | Colorado-East 17th | East 23rd-Monaco | Montview-Havana | Fitzsimons PX | Fitzsimons Hospital (Aurora) |
|---|---|---|---|---|---|---|---|---|
| H | 508A | 511 | 520 | 523 | 530 | 539 | -- | 546 |
| H | 538 | 541 | 550 | 553 | 600 | 609 | 616 | -- |
| H | 608 | 611 | 620 | 623 | 630 | 639 | 646 | -- |
| H | 645 | 648 | 657 | 700 | 707 | 716 | 723 | -- |
| H | 715 | 718 | 727 | 730 | 737 | 746 | 753 | -- |
| H | 745 | 748 | 757 | 800 | 807 | 816 | 823 | -- |
| H | 815 | 818 | 827 | 830 | 837 | 846 | 853 | -- |
| H | 841 | 846 | 858 | 902 | 909 | 919 | 926 | -- |
| H | 911 | 916 | 928 | 932 | 939 | 949 | 956 | -- |
| H | 941 | 946 | 958 | 1002 | 1009 | 1019 | 1026 | -- |
| H | 1011 | 1016 | 1028 | 1032 | 1039 | 1049 | 1056 | -- |
| H | 1041 | 1046 | 1058 | 1102 | 1109 | 1119 | 1126 | -- |
| H | 1111 | 1116 | 1128 | 1132 | 1139 | 1149 | 1156 | -- |
| H | 1141 | 1146 | 1158 | 1202P | 1209 | 1219 | 1226 | -- |
| H | 1211P | 1216 | 1228 | 1232 | 1239 | 1249 | 1256 | -- |
| H | 1241 | 1246 | 1258 | 102 | 109 | 119 | 126 | -- |
| H | 111 | 116 | 128 | 132 | 139 | 149 | 156 | -- |
| H | 141 | 146 | 158 | 202 | 209 | 219 | 226 | -- |
| H | 211 | 216 | 228 | 232 | 239 | 249 | 256 | -- |
| H | 241 | 246 | 258 | 302 | 309 | 319 | 326 | -- |
| H | 311 | 316 | 328 | 332 | 339 | 349 | 356 | -- |
| H | 341 | 346 | 358 | 402 | 409 | 419 | 426 | -- |
| H | 411 | 416 | 428 | 432 | 439 | 449 | 456 | -- |
| H | 441 | 446 | 458 | 502 | 509 | 519 | 526 | -- |
| H | 511 | 516 | 528 | 532 | 539 | 549 | 556 | -- |
| H | 541 | 546 | 558 | 602 | 609 | 619 | 626 | -- |
| H | 605 | 610 | 622 | 626 | 633 | 643 | -- | 650 |
| H | 635 | 640 | 652 | 656 | 703 | 712 | -- | 719 |
| H | 715 | 718 | 725 | 728 | 734 | 743 | -- | 750 |
| H | 745 | 748 | 755 | 758 | 804 | 813 | -- | 820 |
| H | 815 | 818 | 825 | 828 | 834 | 843 | -- | 850 |
| H | 845 | 848 | 855 | 858 | 904 | 913 | -- | 920 |
| H | 915 | 918 | 925 | 928 | 934 | 943 | -- | 950 |
| H | 945 | 948 | 955 | 958 | 1004 | 1013 | -- | 1020 |
| H | 1015 | 1018 | 1025 | 1028 | 1034 | 1043 | -- | 1050 |
| H | 1045 | 1048 | 1055 | 1058 | 1104 | 1113 | -- | 1120 |
| H | 1115 | 1118 | 1125 | 1128 | 1134 | 1143 | -- | 1150 |

## Downtown to Fitzsimons—Eastbound

### Sunday/Holiday   Domingo/Dia de Fiesta

| H | Wynkoop-17th (Union Station) | 17th-Champa** | East 17th-York | Colorado-East 17th | East 23rd-Monaco | Montview-Havana | Fitzsimons PX | Fitzsimons Hospital (Aurora) |
|---|---|---|---|---|---|---|---|---|
| H | 528A | 531 | 539 | 542 | 548 | 557 | 604 | -- |
| H | 558 | 601 | 609 | 612 | 618 | 627 | 634 | -- |
| H | 628 | 631 | 639 | 642 | 648 | 657 | 704 | -- |
| H | 658 | 701 | 709 | 712 | 718 | 727 | 734 | -- |
| H | 738 | 741 | 749 | 752 | 758 | 807 | 814 | -- |
| H | 814 | 817 | 825 | 828 | 834 | 843 | 850 | -- |
| H | 844 | 847 | 855 | 858 | 904 | 913 | 920 | -- |
| H | 914 | 917 | 925 | 928 | 934 | 943 | 950 | -- |
| H | 944 | 947 | 955 | 958 | 1004 | 1013 | 1020 | -- |
| H | 1014 | 1017 | 1025 | 1028 | 1034 | 1043 | 1050 | -- |
| H | 1044 | 1047 | 1055 | 1058 | 1104 | 1113 | 1120 | -- |
| H | 1114 | 1117 | 1125 | 1128 | 1134 | 1143 | 1150 | -- |
| H | 1144 | 1147 | 1155 | 1158 | 1204P | 1213 | 1220 | -- |
| H | 1214P | 1217 | 1225 | 1228 | 1234 | 1243 | 1250 | -- |
| H | 114 | 117 | 125 | 128 | 134 | 143 | 150 | -- |
| H | 144 | 147 | 155 | 158 | 204 | 213 | 220 | -- |
| H | 214 | 217 | 225 | 228 | 234 | 243 | 250 | -- |
| H | 244 | 247 | 255 | 258 | 304 | 313 | 320 | -- |
| H | 314 | 317 | 325 | 328 | 334 | 343 | 350 | -- |
| H | 344 | 347 | 355 | 358 | 404 | 413 | 420 | -- |
| H | 414 | 417 | 425 | 428 | 434 | 443 | 450 | -- |
| H | 444 | 447 | 455 | 458 | 504 | 513 | 520 | -- |
| H | 514 | 517 | 525 | 528 | 534 | 543 | 550 | -- |
| H | 544 | 547 | 555 | 558 | 604 | 613 | 620 | -- |
| H | 615 | 618 | 626 | 629 | 635 | 644 | -- | 651 |
| H | 645 | 648 | 656 | 659 | 705 | 714 | -- | 721 |
| H | 715 | 718 | 725 | 728 | 734 | 743 | -- | 750 |
| H | 745 | 748 | 755 | 758 | 804 | 813 | -- | 820 |
| H | 815 | 818 | 825 | 828 | 834 | 843 | -- | 850 |
| H | 845 | 848 | 855 | 858 | 904 | 913 | -- | 920 |
| H | 915 | 918 | 925 | 928 | 934 | 943 | -- | 950 |
| H | 945 | 948 | 955 | 958 | 1004 | 1013 | -- | 1020 |
| H | 1015 | 1018 | 1025 | 1028 | 1034 | 1043 | -- | 1050 |
| H | 1045 | 1048 | 1055 | 1058 | 1104 | 1113 | -- | 1120 |
| H | 1115 | 1118 | 1125 | 1128 | 1134 | 1143 | -- | 1150 |

**This route makes the following "X" stops on 17th Street
  17th - Lawrence
  17th - Champa
  17th - Welton

H - accessible service - wheelchair lift equipped buses serving local routes

Shaded area indicates peak hours.

El area sombreada indica horas de trafico de gran volumen.

Holidays: New Year's Day, Memorial Day, Independence Day, Labor Day, Thanksgiving Day, and Christmas Day.

# Word Study

## Stems and Affixes

Below is a list of some commonly occurring stems and affixes.* Study their meanings; then do the exercises that follow. Your teacher may ask you to give examples of other words you know that are derived from these stems and affixes.

**Prefixes**

| | | |
|---|---|---|
| by- | aside or apart from the common, secondary | bypass, byproduct |
| de- | down from, away | descend, depart |
| dia- | through, across | diameter, diagonal |
| epi- | upon, over, outer | epidermis |
| hyper- | above, beyond, excessive | hypersensitive |
| hypo- | under, beneath, down | hypothesis, hypothermia |

**Stems**

| | | |
|---|---|---|
| -capit- | head, chief | captain, cap, decapitate |
| -corp- | body | corporation, incorporate |
| -derm- | skin | epidermis, dermatology |
| -geo- | earth | geology, geography |
| -hydr-, -hydro- | water | hydrogen, hydrology |
| -ortho- | straight, correct | orthodox, orthography |
| -pod-, -ped- | foot | podiatrist, pedestrian |
| -son- | sound | sound, sonic |
| -therm-, -thermo- | heat | thermal, hypothermia |
| -ver- | true | verity, veritable |

**Suffixes**

| | | |
|---|---|---|
| -ate | to make | activate |
| -fy | to make | liquify |
| -ize | to make | crystallize |

---

**Exercise 1**

*Word analysis can help you to guess the meaning of unfamiliar words. Using context clues and what you know about word parts, write a synonym, description, or definition of the italicized words.*

1. _____  Mr. Adams is employed at a *hydroelectric* power plant.

2. _____  Before Cindy gets dressed in the morning, she looks at the *thermometer* hanging outside her kitchen window.

3. _____  Some doctors prescribe medication to slow down *hyperactive* children.

---

*For a list of all stems and affixes taught in *Reader's Choice, International Edition: Books 1 and 2,* see Appendix C.

4. _____    I'm not sure if that information is correct, but I'll look in our records to *verify* it.

5. _____    Susan wants to replace the *pedals* on her bicycle with a special kind that racers use.

6. _____    After spending so many days lost in the desert, he was suffering from severe *dehydration*.

7. _____    June's father's hobby is photography, so she bought him a top-quality *tripod* for his birthday.

8. _____    He will never learn how to improve his writing unless he stops being so *hypersensitive* to criticism.

9. _____    Dr. Robinson said that just the sight of a *hypodermic* needle is enough to frighten many of his patients.

10. _____    Although she finished her degree in dentistry in 1960, she wants to go back to school next year to specialize in *orthodontics*.

11. _____    The immigration authorities *deported* Mr. Jensen because he did not have a legal passport.

12. _____    The average *per capita* annual income in this country for people between the ages of sixteen and sixty-five has risen dramatically in the last ten years.

13. _____    Mr. Thompson made an appointment with a *dermatologist* because he noticed small red spots on his hands.

14. _____    Scientists have developed a sensitive instrument to measure *geothermal* variation.

15. _____    Anthropologists say that bipedalism played an important role in the cultural evolution of the human species. Because early humans were *bipedal,* their hands were free to make and use tools.

16. _____    They doubted the *veracity* of his story.

17. _____    The Concorde, which flies at *supersonic* speed, can cross the Atlantic in about three hours.

---

**Exercise 2**

*Following is a list of words containing some of the stems and affixes introduced in this unit and the previous ones. Definitions of these words appear on the right. Put the letter of the appropriate definition next to each word.*

1. ＿＿＿ hyperbole

a. the tissue immediately beneath the outer layer of the tissue of plants

2. ＿＿＿ hypodermis

b. a quotation printed at the beginning of a book or chapter to suggest its theme

3. ＿＿＿ epicenter

4. ＿＿＿ epidermis

c. the outer layer of skin of some animals

5. ＿＿＿ epigraph

d. an exaggeration; a description that is far beyond the truth

e. the part of the earth's surface directly above the place of origin of an earthquake

6. ＿＿＿ orthography

a. fear of water

7. ＿＿＿ hydrate

b. agreeing with established beliefs

8. ＿＿＿ decapitate

c. fat; large of body

9. ＿＿＿ orthodox

d. to cut off the head of

10. ＿＿＿ hydrophobia

e. correct spelling; writing words with the proper, accepted letters

11. ＿＿＿ corpulent

f. to cause to combine with water

12. ＿＿＿ bypass

a. of or related to walking; a person who walks

13. ＿＿＿ pedestrian

b. a dead body

14. ＿＿＿ byproduct

c. a passage to one side; a route that goes around a town

15. ＿＿＿ corporeal

d. a secondary and sometimes unexpected result; something produced (as in manufacturing) in addition to the principal product

16. ＿＿＿ corpse

17. ＿＿＿ podiatry

e. the care and treatment of the human foot in health and disease

f. bodily; of the nature of the physical body; not spiritual

18. ＿＿＿ deflect

a. to turn aside from a fixed course

19. ＿＿＿ decentralize

b. of or relating to the form of the earth or its surface features

20. ＿＿＿ diaphanous

c. to divide and distribute what has been concentrated or united

21. ＿＿＿ verisimilitude

d. the quality of appearing to be true

22. ＿＿＿ geomorphic

e. characterized by such fineness of texture as to permit seeing through

## Sentence Study
## Comprehension

Read these sentences carefully.* The questions that follow are designed to test your comprehension of complex grammatical structures. Select the *best* answer.

1. Like physical anthropology, orthodontics (dentistry dealing with the irregularities of teeth) tries to explain how and why men are different; unlike anthropology, it also tries to correct those differences for functional or aesthetic reasons.
   How does orthodontics differ from physical anthropology?
   _____ a. Physical anthropology is concerned with aesthetics; orthodontics is not.
   _____ b. Physical anthropology deals with the irregularities of teeth.
   _____ c. Orthodontics tries to explain why men are different, anthropology does not.
   _____ d. Anthropology does not try to correct differences among men; orthodontics does.

2. What is most obvious in this book are all those details of daily living that make Mrs. Richards anything but common.
   According to this statement, what kind of person is Mrs. Richards?
   _____ a. She is very obvious.
   _____ b. She is an unusual person.
   _____ c. She is anything she wants to be.
   _____ d. She is quite ordinary.

3. A third island appeared gradually during a period of volcanic activity that lasted over four years. Later, the 1866 eruptions, which brought to Santorin those volcanologists who first began archeological work there, enlarged the new island through two new crater vents.
   What enlarged the third island?
   _____ a. the eruptions of 1866
   _____ b. a four-year period of volcanic activity
   _____ c. the activities of the men who came to study volcanoes
   _____ d. archeological work, which created two new crater vents

4. Just before his tenth birthday John received a horse from his father; this was the first of a series of expensive gifts intended to create the impression of a loving parent.
   Why did John receive the horse?
   _____ a. because he was ten
   _____ b. because his father loved him
   _____ c. because his father wanted to seem loving
   _____ d. because his father wouldn't be able to give him expensive gifts in the future

5. Since industry and commerce are the largest users of electrical energy, using less electricity would mean a reduced industrial capacity and fewer jobs in the affected industries and therefore an unfavorable change in our economic structure.
   According to this sentence, decreasing the use of electricity _____
   _____ a. must begin immediately.     _____ c. will cause difficulties.
   _____ b. isn't important.            _____ d. won't affect industry.

___

*For an introduction to sentence study, see Appendix D.

6. The medical journal reported that heart attack victims who recover are approximately five times as likely to die within the next five years as those people without a history of heart disease.

What did this article say about people who have had a heart attack?

_____ a. They are more likely to die in the near future than others.

_____ b. They will die in five years.

_____ c. They are less likely to die than people without a history of heart disease.

_____ d. They are likely to recover.

7. Few phenomena in history are more puzzling than this one: that men and women with goals so vague, with knowledge so uncertain, with hopes so foggy, still would have risked dangers so certain and tasks so great.

What historical fact is puzzling?

_____ a. that people had such vague goals

_____ b. that people took such great risks

_____ c. that people had foggy hopes and uncertain knowledge

_____ d. that people completed such great tasks

8. Next he had to uncover the ancient secret—so jealously guarded by the ancients that no text of any kind, no descriptive wall painting, and no tomb inscriptions about making papyrus are known to exist.

What secret did this man want to discover?

_____ a. how to understand wall paintings

_____ b. how to read tomb inscriptions

_____ c. how to read the ancient texts

_____ d. how to produce papyrus

9. Alexis, ruler of a city where politics was a fine art, concealed his fears, received the noblemen with extravagant ceremonies, impressed them with his riches, praised them, entertained them, bribed them, made promises he had no intention of keeping—and thus succeeded in keeping their troops outside his city walls.

Why did Alexis give money and attention to the noblemen?

_____ a. because they praised him

_____ b. in order to prevent their armies from entering the city

_____ c. in order to impress them with his riches

_____ d. because they were his friends

# Paragraph Reading

## Restatement and Inference

Each paragraph below is followed by five statements.* The statements are of four types:
1. Some of the statements are restatements of ideas in the original paragraph. They give the same information in a different way.
2. Some of the statements are inferences (conclusions) that can be drawn from the information given in the paragraph.
3. Some of the statements are false based on the information given.
4. Some of the statements cannot be judged true or false based on information given in the original paragraph.

Put a check (✓) next to all restatements and inferences (types 1 and 2). Note: do not check a statement that is true of itself but cannot be inferred from the paragraph.

**Paragraph 1**

It was the weekend before the exam. We were at the Walkers' house and it was pouring rain. Jack came in late, drenched to the skin. He explained that a car had broken down on the road and he had stopped to help push it onto the shoulder and out of the traffic. I remember thinking then how typical that was of Jack. So helpful, so accommodating.

\_\_\_\_\_ a. Jack came in late because it was raining.

\_\_\_\_\_ b. Jack came in late because his car had broken down.

\_\_\_\_\_ c. The narrator thinks Jack is typical.

\_\_\_\_\_ d. The narrator bases his opinion of Jack on this one experience.

\_\_\_\_\_ e. Jack often helps other people.

**Paragraph 2**

The illustrations in books make it easier for us to believe in the people and events described. The more senses satisfied, the easier is belief. Visual observation tends to be the most convincing evidence. Children, being less capable of translating abstractions into actualities, need illustration more than adults. Most of us, when we read, tend to create only vague and ghostlike forms in response to the words. The illustrator, when he reads, must see. The great illustrator sees accurately.

\_\_\_\_\_ a. Illustrations help us to believe events described in words.

\_\_\_\_\_ b. When most people read, they do not picture events as accurately as can a great illustrator.

---

*For an introduction to restatement and inference, see Appendix F.

_____ c. Children are less able than adults to visualize events described in books.

_____ d. The author believes illustrators are especially able to imagine visual details described with words.

_____ e. The author believes all illustrators see accurately.

---

**Paragraph 3**
        Surveys reveal that most adults consider themselves "well informed about the affairs of the nation and the world." Yet a regularly taken Roper poll that asks, "From where do you obtain most of your information about the world?" has found the percentage of people who reply, "Television" has been increasing steadily over the past decade. The latest questionnaire found that well over 60 percent of the respondents chose television over other media as their major source of information. These two facts are difficult to reconcile since even a casual study of television news reveals it is only a headline service and not a source of information enabling one to shape a world view.

_____ a. Most adults obtain most of their information about world affairs from the newspaper.

_____ b. The author of this passage does not believe that television provides enough information to make people well informed.

_____ c. The number of people answering the questionnaire has increased.

_____ d. Sixty percent of the people questioned get all their news from television.

_____ e. Most adults are well informed about the affairs of the nation and the world.

---

**Paragraph 4**
        The dusty book room whose windows never opened, through whose panes the summer sun sent a dim light where gold specks danced and shimmered, opened magic windows for me through which I looked out on other worlds and times than those in which I lived. The narrow shelves rose halfway up the walls, their tops piled with untidy layers that almost touched the ceiling. The piles on the floor had to be climbed over, columns of books flanked the window, falling at a touch.

_____ a. The room is dusty and shadowy, filled with books from floor to ceiling.

_____ b. The sun never enters the room.

_____ c. The author spent time in this room as a child.

_____ d. The author did not like the room.

_____ e. Through the windows in the room, the author saw worlds other than those in which he lived.

**Paragraph 5**

By voting against mass transportation, voters have chosen to continue on a road to ruin. Our interstate highways, those much praised golden avenues built to whisk suburban travelers in and out of downtown, have turned into the world's most expensive parking lots. That expense is not only economic—it is social. These highways have created great walls separating neighborhood from neighborhood, disrupting the complex social connections that help make a city livable.

_____ a. Interstate highways have created social problems.

_____ b. Highways create complex social connections.

_____ c. By separating neighborhoods, highways have made cities more livable.

_____ d. The author supports the idea of mass transportation.

_____ e. The author agrees with a recent vote by the citizens.

# Discourse Focus

## Careful Reading/Drawing Inferences

Mystery stories, like most other texts, require readers to note important facts and draw inferences based on these. To solve the following mysteries, you must become a detective, drawing inferences from the clues provided. Each mystery below has been solved by the fictional Professor Fordney, a master detective—the expert the police call for their most puzzling cases. Your job is to match wits with the great professor.* Your teacher may want you to work with your classmates to answer the question following each mystery. Be prepared to defend your solution with details from the passage.

**Mystery 1:**
**Murder on Board**

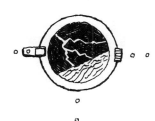

During a lull in the storm which tossed and rocked the sturdy little steamer *Dauntless,* a shot rang out on A deck.

Professor Fordney threw down the detective story he was somewhat unsuccessfully trying to read and hastened into the companionway. Where it turned at the far corner, he found Steward Mierson bending over the body of a man who had been instantly killed. Just then the heavens opened; lightning flashed and thunder boomed as if in ghoulish mockery.

The dead man's head bore powder burns. Captain Larson and the criminologist started checking the whereabouts of everyone aboard, beginning with those passengers nearest where the body was discovered.

The first questioned was Nathan Cohen, who said he was just completing a letter in his cabin when he heard the shot.

"May I see it?" Larson asked.

Looking over the captain's shoulder, Fordney saw the small, precise handwriting, on the ship's stationery. The letter was apparently written to a woman.

The next cabin was occupied by Miss Margaret Millsworth. On being questioned regarding what she was doing at the time, Miss Millsworth became excited and nervous. She stated that she had become so frightened by the storm, that about fifteen minutes before the shot was fired she had gone to the cabin of her fiancé, James Montgomery, directly opposite. The latter corroborated her statement, saying they hadn't rushed into the passageway because it would have looked compromising were they seen emerging together at that hour. Fordney noticed a dark red stain on Montgomery's dressing gown.

The whereabouts of the rest of the passengers and crew were satisfactorily checked.

Whom did the captain hold on suspicion? Why? _____

_____

*From *Minute Mysteries* by Austin Ripley (New York: Pocket Books, 1949).

**Mystery 2:**
**Death in the Mountains**

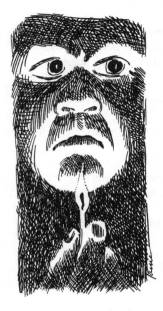

While hunting in the Adirondacks, Fordney was informed of a tragedy at one of the camps. Thinking he might be of some help, he went over and introduced himself and was told of the accident by Wylie, the victim's companion.

"When Moore hadn't returned to camp at nine o'clock last night, I was a bit worried, because he didn't know these mountains. There wasn't a star out and it was dark and moonless, so I decided to look around for him. We're five miles from anyone, you know.

"Putting more wood on the fire, I set out. After searching for an hour I was coming up the slope of a ravine when I saw a pair of eyes shining at me.

"Calling twice, and getting no answer, I fired, thinking it was a mountain lion. Imagine my horror when I reached the spot, struck a match, and saw I had nearly blown off Moore's head. A terrible experience!

"I carried him back to camp and then walked to the nearest house to report the accident."

"How far from camp did you find him?"

"About a quarter of a mile."

"How did you manage to shoot with your right hand bandaged?"

"Oh—I use either hand."

"Mind if I look at the gun?"

"Not at all." Wylie handed it over.

"H'mmmm. European make. Had it long?"

"No. It's rather new."

"Why did you deliberately murder Moore?" Fordney abruptly demanded. "For that's what you did!"

How did he know? _____

_____

**Mystery 3:**
**Case #194**

Rudolph Mayer stumbled into the police station of the little village of Monroe, shook water from his clothes, and collapsed. A local physician was summoned and brought Mayer around. He told the following story.

"My wife and I, fond of winter sports, registered at the Fox Head Resort this afternoon—I've spent several vacations here. Shortly before dusk we decided to go skating on Lake Howard. We'd been out probably twenty minutes, as nearly as I can figure it, when my wife, who was about ten yards in front of me, suddenly dropped into the water through a large hole. Someone must have been cutting ice. I swerved, took off my skates, and jumped in after her. Despite my efforts, however, I couldn't locate her. I was barely able to pull myself out, and as I called and there was no help at hand, made my way here, somehow. It's about half a mile, I guess, and I didn't think I'd be able to do it. For God's sake send someone out there!"

Again the man fainted but was revived in a few minutes, mumbling incoherently about skates.

Two constables were dispatched through the ten below zero weather to the scene and returned with Mayer's skates found on the edge of a large hole where a local concern had been cutting ice. At the sight of them Mayer again collapsed.

Professor Fordney read no further in the above newspaper account.

"Mayer is certainly lying," he said to himself.

How did he know? _____

_____

**Mystery 4:**
**The Break**

Four tough prisoners in the county jail tore plumbing from the wall, beat two guards with iron pipes, brutally killing one, and escaped through a hole in the wall, after arming themselves with guns and ammunition. They were Dan Morgan, Sam Chapin, Louis Segal and Anton Kroll, all being held for armed robbery.

A posse was quickly organized and the gang surrounded in a small valley fifteen miles from the jail. Two of the mob were wounded and all captured, but not before one of the gang killed State Trooper Don Burton with a bullet through his head.

Professor Fordney interrogated the sullen four separately but each refused any information concerning himself or the others. From outside sources, however, the criminologist learned the following facts.

1. A dancer, one of the four, acted as leader of the gang. He spoke several languages fluently.
2. For some time the ugly Segal and the handsome leader had been suspicious of each other.
3. A week before their arrest, Sam Chapin and the leader won $4,000 each in a crap game at Anton Kroll's lake cabin. Kroll does not gamble.
4. The leader and the prisoner who killed Trooper Don Burton are good friends. They once ran a gambling house in Cuba.
5. Anton Kroll and the killer have been going with twin sisters who knew nothing of their criminal backgrounds.

Fordney sat in his study evaluating the above data. After a few moments he reached for the phone, called the prosecuting attorney and advised him to issue a murder warrant for . . . .

Who killed Trooper Don Burton? _____

_____

# 4

## Reading Selections 1A–1B

## Feature Articles

**Before You Begin**    In his book *With Respect to the Japanese,** John Condon, a specialist in intercultural relations, describes American interest in Japan:

> A New York bookdealer said he had never seen anything like the surge of interest American readers have recently shown for books on Japanese management. . . . Many have argued that Americans have much to learn from the Japanese, while others have raised doubts about transferring methods from one culture to another. In this writer's opinion, the most remarkable fact about the Japan boom in the U.S. is that for the first time Americans have considered the possibility of learning from another culture in areas where Americans had thought they excelled. In that regard Japan deserves special credit, for this might lead to a greater openness and curiosity and learning across other cultural boundaries that rarely occur in the U.S.

1. Why do you think Americans have recently become fascinated by Japan?

2. Why does the author feel that this interest is positive? Do you agree?

---

*Selection 1A*    **Feature Article**

This first feature article is an example of U.S. interest in Japan.† It is reprinted from the *New York Times.* Unlike news articles that seek to inform the public about important events, feature articles are essays that describe persons and topics of general interest. Read this article quickly to discover the major ways in which the author contrasts the Japanese and United States styles of decision-making, and to see whether or not you agree. You will need to do Vocabulary from Context exercise 1 on pages 67–68 before you begin reading.

---

*John C. Condon, *With Respect to the Japanese: A Guide for Americans*. (Yarmouth, Maine: Intercultural Press, 1984), p. 61.
†Adapted from "Japanese Style in Decision-Making" by Yoshio Terasawa, *New York Times,* May 12, 1974.

# Japanese Style in Decision-Making

By YOSHIO TERASAWA

1 To talk about problem-solving or decision-making within a national environment means examining many complex cultural forces. It means trying to measure the impact of these forces on contemporary life, and also coming to grips with changes now taking place.

2 It also means using dangerous comparisons — and the need to translate certain fundamental concepts which resist translation and comparisons.

3 For example, the concept of vocational or professional identity differs markedly between the United States and Japan.

4 In the West, the emphasis is on what a man, or woman does for a living. Here in the U.S., if you ask children what their fathers do, they will say "My daddy drives a truck" or "My daddy is a stock broker" or "My daddy is an engineer."

5 But in Japan, the child will tell you "My daddy works for Mitsubishi" or "My daddy works for Nomura Securities" or for "Hitachi." But you will have no idea whether the father is president of Hitachi or a chauffeur at Hitachi.

6 In Japan, the most important thing is what organization you work for. This becomes very significant when you try to analyze the direction-taking or decision-making process. At the least, it explains the greater job stability in Japan, in contrast to the great job mobility in America.

7 While we differ in many ways, such differences are neither superior nor inferior to each other. A particular pattern of management behavior develops from a complexity of unique cultural factors — and will only work within a given culture.

8 Let me try to describe three or four characteristics of the Japanese environment that in some way affect decision-making or direction-taking and problem-solving. These characteristics are interrelated.

9 First, in any approach to a problem and in any negotiations in Japan, there is the "you to you" approach, as distinguished from the Western "I to you" approach.

10 The difference is this: in "I to you," both sides present their arguments forthrightly from their own point of view — they state what they want and what they expect to get. Thus, a confrontation situation is set up, and Westerners are very adroit in dealing with this.

11 The "you to you" approach practiced in Japan is based on each side — automatically and often unconsciously — trying to understand the other person's point of view, and for the purpose of the discussion actually declaring this understanding. Thus, the direction of the meeting is a mutual attempt at minimizing confrontation and achieving harmony.

12 A second characteristic is based on "consensus opinion" and "bottom-up direction." In Japan great consideration is given to and reliance placed on the thoughts and opinions of everyone at all levels. This is true of corporate enterprises and Government agencies.

Japan, direction can be formulated at the lowest levels, travel upward through an organization and have an impact on the eventual decision. This is "bottom up."

17 There is also a characteristic style of communications in Japan that is different from the Western way.

18 The Japanese business person works to achieve harmony, even if the deal falls through, and will spend whatever time is necessary to determine a "you to you" approach, communicating personal views only indirectly and with great sensitivity.

19 This places time in a different perspective. In Japan the Western

*In Japan, negotiations seek a basis of harmony rather than confrontation, as in West.*

13 To understand this, it is important to realize that Japan is a very densely populated homogeneous country. Moreover, the people are aware and are articulate. Literacy is almost 100 per cent. Problems are shared. In Japan there is a drive for the group — whether it is family, company, or Government — to act as a unit.

14 Tremendous weight is given to the achievement of solidarity and unanimity. Unilateral decision-making or direction-taking is generally avoided, or where it does occur for very practical urgent reasons, it usually happens along with a sounding out of all concerned.

15 This brings us to the second part of this characteristic. When I use the term "bottom-up," I am referring to a style of management — perhaps what you would call keeping your finger on the pulse of the public, or the labor force, or other audiences.

16 The difference is that in Japan we record the pulse and it has real meaning, and it influences the direction finally taken at the top regarding a specific important issue. In other words, Western style decision-making proceeds predominantly from top management and often does not consult middle management or the worker while in

deadline approach is secondary to a thorough job. Japanese are thorough in their meetings as well as in their production. Thus Americans are often exasperated by the seemingly endless sequences of meetings in many Japanese businesses.

20 But where the American is pressing for a specific decision, the Japanese is trying to formulate a rather broad direction.

21 On the other hand, once agreement is established, it is the Japanese who sometimes wonder at the leisurely pace of execution of Westerners. The Japanese are eager for execution and Westerners, perhaps, like to take the time for in-depth planning.

22 Now, while Japan's industry and technology are highly developed, they have not replaced the fundamental force of human energy and motivation. By that I mean that the Japanese take great pride in doing a job well and getting it done no matter how much time is required.

23 There is a dedication and sense of responsibility which have not been replaced by the machine age. Perhaps we are not so sophisticated yet.

24 In my field — finance and securities — I am often asked by West-

erners how Nomura Securities has managed to escape the paper log-jam that American brokerage firms have faced. We, too have had that problem.

25 The Tokyo Stock Exchange often has a turnover of between 200 and 300 million shares a day. This volume is many times more than that of the New York Stock Exchange. How can we possibly handle this load?

26 First, we have very advanced computerization. Second, and most important, the personnel responsible for processing all these transactions stay and stay till all hours until the job is done. And their families understand that this is something that they must do, for the survival and progress of the company and for their own mutual security as well.

27 Perhaps in 20 years — or sooner — they will be more Westernized and insist on going home at five o'clock. But today, still, most insist on staying until the job is done. There is concern for quality.

28 This willingness to pitch in is an important aspect of Japanese problem-solving, and you find it at every level.

29 Some years ago, the Matsushita company was having a very bad time. Among the many measures taken, Mr. Matsushita, the founder and then chairman, became the manager of the sales department.

30 Also, when we at Nomura converted to computers about five years ago, the new system eliminated the jobs of 700 bookkeepers and accountants who were using abacuses. We got rid of the abacuses but we did not get rid of the people. We converted our bookkeepers and accountants to securities sales people and some of these today are our leading sales people.

31 Where there is willingness and intelligence, there is a place within the company to try and to succeed. In Japan, a person's capabilities are not forced into an inflexible specialty. And we feel the company owes a worker something for loyalty and commitment.

\* \* \*

This article is adapted from a speech by Mr. Terasawa, president of Nomura Securities International, Inc., before the Commonwealth Club of San Francisco.

## *Comprehension*

### Exercise 1

*Each of the statements below would be true of the business world in either the United States or Japan according to the information in the article or inferences that can be drawn from the article. Indicate whether each statement below is characteristic of Japan (J) or the United States (US) according to this article. Be prepared to use parts of the article to support your decisions.*

1. _____ In business meetings, confrontations are avoided by communicating one's personal views indirectly.

2. _____ An important decision is made by the president of a company and a memo is sent to all employees informing them of the decision.

3. _____ Several weeks of meetings pass before a policy decision is made.

4. _____ Several weeks pass after agreement is reached before action is taken.

5. _____ A new machine is installed to increase production and as a result 100 workers lose their jobs.

6. _____ When asked what his father does, a child answers, "My daddy is an engineer."

7. _____ Young employees move from one company to another in order to improve their position.

8. _____ Employees often stay at work after hours, until a job is finished.

9. _____ Most companies employ workers of several different cultural and national backgrounds.

### Exercise 2

*The following questions will help you summarize "Japanese Style in Decision-Making."*

1. According to the article, how does the concept of professional identity differ between the United States and Japan?

2. According to the article, what is the difference between the Western "I to you" approach and the Japanese "you to you" approach? What is the difference between Western-style unilateral decision-making and Japanese "consensus opinion" and "bottom-up direction"?

3. Compare the American and Japanese sense of time in business transactions.
   a. Why do Japanese seem to take longer to reach an agreement?
   b. Why do Americans seem to take longer to act after an agreement has been reached?

4. According to the author, how have the Japanese managed to "escape the paper logjam that American . . . firms have faced"?

5. Who is the author of this article? From what source has the article been adapted?

## Discussion/Composition

1. The author admits that "to talk about problem-solving or decision-making within a national environment . . . means using dangerous comparisons." Are there generalizations in the article that you find unconvincing either for lack of information or because of your personal experience?

2. Do you think it's possible to transfer management methods from one culture to another? Support your position.

3. Write an article or prepare a speech similar to the one above, explaining to American business people how to do business in your community.

## Vocabulary from Context

### Exercise 1

*Both the ideas and the vocabulary in the exercise below are taken from "Japanese Style in Decision-Making." Use the context provided to determine the meanings of the italicized words. Write a definition, synonym, or description of each of the italicized vocabulary items in the space provided.*

1. _____
2. _____

When *formulating* business decisions, Japanese businesses do not depend only on the opinions of a few at the top of the company; rather, *reliance* is placed on the opinions of everyone, at all levels.

3. _____
4. _____

In the United States business people are skilled at handling strong disagreements in meetings. The Japanese, on the other hand, are *adroit* at avoiding such *confrontations*.

5. _____
6. _____

The Japanese business person tries to create a situation in which all people present feel comfortable. Only in such an atmosphere of *harmony* are decisions made. *Consensus* decision-making, a process by which action is taken only after everyone is in agreement, is an important part of Japanese business practices.

7. _____

It is important that people from different cultures come to understand each other and develop *mutual* trust. Only when people trust each other is international cooperation possible.

8. _____
9. _____

The majority of people in Japan are *literate*. Because most people are able to read newspapers and magazines, they generally have opinions on most important matters. In addition, they are quite *articulate* and therefore able to state their ideas clearly to their superiors.

10. _____   People are more likely to change jobs in the United States
                          than they are in Japan. There are several possible explanations
                          for the greater job *stability* in Japan in contrast to the great job
11. _____   *mobility* in the United States.

12. _____   The Japanese are often *exasperated* by the seriousness with
                          which Americans approach time limits. Similarly, Americans
                          are often impatient with the Japanese seeming lack of concern
13. _____   for *deadlines*.

14. _____   Because Japanese workers willingly stay after hours to finish
                          work, they are well known for their *dedication* to their
                          company.

15. _____   We thought we were in complete agreement and we expected a
                          *unanimous* vote. However, one person voted against the plan.

16. _____   Unlike the United States, where many different nationalities
                          make up the population, Japan's population is quite
                          *homogeneous*.

17. _____   A company's structure should not be so *inflexible* that it does
                          not allow people to change jobs as their abilities and the needs
                          of the company change.

18. _____   Unlike decisions that are made on the basis of mutual
                          concerns, *unilateral* decisions can be unpopular because they
                          are made by only one of the parties concerned.

19. _____   Some *firms* offer their employees company-paid health
                          insurance.

---

### Exercise 2

*This exercise should be done after you have finished reading "Japanese Style in Decision-Making." The exercise is designed to determine how well you have been able to use context clues to guess the meaning of unfamiliar vocabulary in the article. Give a definition, synonym, or description of each of the words below. The number in parentheses indicates the paragraph in which the word can be found. Your teacher may want you to do these orally or in writing.*

1. (3) vocational (Find a synonym in the same paragraph.) _____

2. (10) forthrightly _____

3. (13) densely _____

4. (16) consult _____

5. (16) impact _____

6. (30) converted _____

## Figurative Language and Idioms

In the paragraph indicated by the number in parentheses, find the phrase that best fits the definition given. Your teacher may want to read these aloud as you quickly scan the paragraph to find the answer.

1. (1) What phrase means *understanding and taking appropriate action?*

2. (4) What phrase means *as a profession; to support oneself?*

3. (14) What phrase means *trying to find out someone's opinion?*

4. (15) What phrase means *knowing the feelings of a group of people?*

5. (18) What phrase means *fails; comes to nothing?*

6. (24) What phrase means *a situation in which progress is stopped because there is too much paper work?*

7. (28) What phrase means *begin to work energetically; help do a job?*

## Vocabulary Review

### Exercise 1

*Place the appropriate word from this list in each of the blanks below. Do not use any word more than once.*

| | | | |
|---|---|---|---|
| formulate | articulate | exasperated | adroit |
| dedicated | deadlines | transactions | reliance |

There are two reasons why Lynn was made president of her company last week. First,

Lynn is very _____ at handling people. She is a(n) _____ woman who is

able to express her thoughts and desires very precisely. Her ability helps her in

business _____. When other people become _____ because they cannot find

the right words to express their thoughts, Lynn can make everyone feel comfortable by helping

them to find the right words.

*(Continued on page 70)*

Lynn's second characteristic is her ability to get work done on time, to

meet _____. She has always been a(n) _____ employee

whose _____ on hard work has earned her the respect of her superiors. In fact,

Lynn's success is due to her hard work and her ability to _____ plans that will get

work done efficiently.

## Exercise 2

*The words in this list are opposite in meaning to the italicized words in the following passage.*
*Change the story below by substituting an* antonym *for each of the italicized words or phrases.*
*Each word should be used at least once.*

| | | |
|---|---|---|
| unilaterally | mobility | unilateral |
| confrontation | inflexible | heterogeneous |

1. _____    In my company all decisions are made *by consensus* in an

2. _____    atmosphere of *harmony*. The employees are educationally

3. _____    *homogeneous*. Like most workers in this country, employees

4. _____    here experience great job *stability*. However, the policy for

5. _____    changing jobs within the company is quite *flexible*. Requests to

6. _____    change jobs are approved on the basis of *mutual* concerns.

*Selection 1B*          **Feature Article**

*Before You Begin*   1. Have you ever felt that salespeople in another community or country were rude?

2. In what ways was their behavior different from what you expected? What did you do?

3. Is it possible for salespeople to be too polite?

Here is another feature article on Japan that appeared in a newspaper in the United States.* The article contrasts customer service in the U.S. and Japan. Read the article quickly to get a general idea of the areas of contrast. Your teacher may want you to do the Vocabulary from Context exercise on page 73 before you begin.

**FOCUS/A YEN TO PLEASE**

# Happy Customers Matter of Honor among Japanese

By John Burgess
The Washington Post   TOKYO

1   In an age when personal service as a significant aspect of merchandising is dying out in the United States, Japan clings tenaciously to it.

2   Service is viewed by people in Japan not as a luxury, but as an essential ingredient for the success of individual companies and the Japanese economy as a whole.

3   Americans who move to Japan never get used to the range of services and courtesies taken for granted here. To those old enough to remember how things used to be at home, life can bring on twinges of nostalgia.

4   Supermarket check-out counters have two or three people ringing up and bagging groceries. Some stores deliver, with each bag arriving neatly stapled closed. Dry ice is inserted alongside the frozen foods to ensure that they don't spoil on the way.

5   Television shops normally send a technician to install and fine-tune a newly purchased set. The technician will rush back if anything goes wrong. Car salespeople are known to bring new models around to customers' homes for test drives and loaners are available for people whose cars are in for repairs.

6   There are no limits to what is home-delivered — video movies, dry cleaning, health foods, rented tailcoats (this last one requires two visits from the sales staff, first for a fitting, second for delivery of the altered and freshly pressed garment). Office deliveries are common, too, especially of lunch.

7   Japanese barbers often give back massages as part of an ordinary haircut. If they remove a customer's eyeglasses, they may polish the lenses before returning them.

Self-service gasoline has yet to make its appearance here in any significant way. At the minimum, attendants fill the tank and wipe the windshield. They often empty ashtrays and stop traffic to let the motorist back on the road.

8   Department stores seem to have twice, if not three times the floor staff of American ones. Many stores wrap everything they sell. Upscale customers don't have to come in at all — the goods are taken to their homes for display and selection.

9   Feudal Japan evolved tight rituals of personal service. Many survive in the traditional inns called *ryokan*. Proprietors bow when guests arrive and straighten the shoes they step out of. Welcoming tea and elaborate meals are brought to the rooms. Bedding is laid out and cleared away in the morning. On departure, the bows may be held until a guest's car is out of sight.

10   But even in modern businesses, the culture's attention to detail and doing things the "correct" way fit well into the service mentality. While Americans may find it demeaning to fuss over a customer, Japanese worry — with reason — that their shop will be laughed at if they don't.

11   Perhaps the darkest spot on personal service in Japan is how remarkably impersonal it can be. Everyone is treated exactly

*From the *Washington Post*.

alike. Employee's cheery greetings and directions, in fact, are often memorized from a company manual. After a month's stay in a hotel, guests may find the staff still has no idea who they are.

12   Still, the Japanese view service as the glue that holds commercial relationships together. If the correct personal contact and follow-up come with the first sale, a second is sure to come. Market share and loyal customers are the first goal, not short-term profit. Service may cost but it helps ensure these more important objectives.

13   While Americans in need of something think of stores, Japanese often think of dealers, individuals who supply and advise over the years on product lines like sake, clothing and electronic equipment.

14   Memories of service may help a company weather hard times. If a computer firm drops behind in product quality or price, its customers will not abandon it en masse. They would feel treacherous doing so. After all, didn't the company send a technician to the office a dozen times to answer questions on that little desk-top model? Expand that to national scale and you have a more stable, predictable economy and job market in the Japanese view.

15   Japanese officials often say one reason why many American companies do poorly in Japan is because people can't believe they will give good service. Even if an American machine tops a Japanese one in price and quality, the buyer will be suspicious. Will I have to phone Houston every time

something goes wrong? he may wonder.

16   Service is plugged as being "free," but of course, is not. Each woman who wraps and each man who lugs groceries is part of why prices are so high in Japan. They are also part of why unemployment is so low. Some economists, in fact, view some of these jobs as disguised welfare programs, financed through high prices rather than taxes.

17   Invariably, as Japan internationalizes, some firms are opting to follow the foreign pattern and cut service to lower prices. Supermarkets and chain stores have gained ground. Department stores have done away with the women who once bowed to every customer who stepped onto an escalator. Some shops now have a tape machine, not a person, saying

"*irashaimase,*" or welcome, at the door.

18   Proliferation of American fast-food is another sign of these times. McDonald's now has 573 outlets in Japan. But characteristically, cleanliness and employee courtesy seem to be generally higher than in the United States.

19   The Japanese over the years have borrowed heavily in commercial ideas from the United States but generally look elsewhere concerning service. There are exceptions, however, such as American-style home-delivery pizza. In the last two years, motorbikes darting around with pizza have been growing in numbers on Tokyo streets. Delivery in 30 minutes is guaranteed, or the customer gets about $5 back.

## *Critical Reading*

### Exercise 1

*Indicate if each of the statements below is true (T) or false (F) according to your understanding of the article.*

1. _____ In a Japanese supermarket, you will find several employees at a single check-out counter.

2. _____ Japanese customers are suspicious of the quality of products manufactured in the United States.

3. _____ The author prefers the courtesy of Japanese hotels to the impersonal practices in U.S. hotels.

4. _____ Japanese customers don't pay for these personal services.

5. _____ The author believes that as Japan internationalizes, it will do away with some services that are not economical.

### Exercise 2

*Although this article is about Japan, it provides a good deal of information about the United States. For the reader, the contrasts mentioned can only be significant in contrast to what is considered "normal" in the U.S.*

*For each of the activities listed below infer how the author assumes service people behave in the United States. What is your experience of this activity in the U.S. or elsewhere? Your teacher may want you to do this in small groups or pairs.*

1. shopping for food

2. purchasing a T.V.

3. getting a haircut

4. buying gas for a car

5. shopping in a department store

6. staying at a hotel

## Discussion/Composition

What do you think mainstream U.S. culture could learn from your culture? Compare the two, pointing out the advantages of your native culture.

## Vocabulary from Context

Both the ideas and the vocabulary in the following exercise are taken from "Happy Customers Matter of Honor among Japanese." Use the context provided to determine the meanings of the italicized words. Write a definition, synonym, or description of each of the italicized vocabulary items in the space provided.

1. _____

2. _____
3. _____

4. _____

5. _____

6. _____

7. _____

8. _____

9. _____
10. _____
11. _____

In Japan, good service is not considered a *luxury,* but a necessity. In most stores you will find more salespeople than you would in a comparable store in the United States. This larger sales *staff* allows the *proprietor* of the store to spend time greeting customers.

What is considered an unnecessary bother in the U.S., too much of a *fuss,* is considered fundamental in Japan. Owners of American shops might find giving personal attention to customers to be beneath them. But this is not considered *demeaning* in Japan. On the contrary, personal attention is considered one of the necessary *ingredients* for business success. If a company provides good service, it hopes for customer loyalty during bad times. The hope is that customers would feel *treacherous* if they left a company with which they had a personal relationship.

Thus, for the business person, being polite is as necessary for poor customers as it is for more *upscale* customers. And the *courtesies* shown customers exist throughout Japan *on a national scale.* One hopes that this will not change with the introduction and *proliferation* of American-style stores.

# Reading Selection 2

## Satire

***Before You Begin***   1. T / F   Men have more power in society.

2. T / F   A briefcase is the same as a purse.

3. T / F   Clothing is an important aspect of men's position in society.

Satire is a style of writing that pretends to be serious in order to demonstrate the humor of a particular situation. Read the following article to determine what the author is satirizing.*

You may want to do the Vocabulary from Context exercise on page 77 and the Dictionary Study exercise on page 78 before you begin reading.

### Pockety Women Unite?

*Jane Myers*

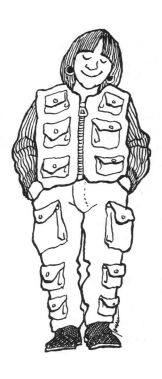

1    Pockets are what women need more of. The women's movement in the past decade has made giant strides in achieving greater social justice for females, but there's a great deal of work yet to be done. And it can't be done without pockets.

2    It has been commonly thought that men get the best jobs and make the most money and don't have to wash the dinner dishes simply because they're men, that cultural traditions and social conditioning have worked together to give them a special place in the world order.

3    While there is undoubtedly some truth to this, the fact remains that no one has investigated the role that pockets have played in preventing women from attaining the social status and rights that could and should be theirs.

4    Consider your average successful executive. How many pockets does he wear to work? Two in the sides of his trousers, two in the back, one on the front of his shirt, three on his suit coat, and one on the inside of the suit coat. Total: nine.

5    Consider your average woman dressed for office work. If she is wearing a dress or skirt and blouse, she is probably wearing zero pockets, or one or two at the most. The pantsuit, that supposedly liberating outfit, is usually equally pocketless.

6    Now, while it is always dangerous to generalize, it seems quite safe to say that, on the whole, the men of the world, at any given time, are carrying about a much greater number of pockets than are the women of the world. And it is also quite clear that, on the whole, the men enjoy more power, prestige, and wealth than women do.

7    Everything seems to point to a positive correlation between pockets, power, prestige, and wealth. Can this be?

*Adapted from "Pockety Women Unite?" by Jane Myers, Staff Reporter, *Ann Arbor News,* September 22, 1975.

8      An examination of the function of the pocket seems necessary. Pockets are for carrying money, credit cards, identification (including access to those prestigious clubs where people presumably sit around sharing powerful secrets about how to run the world), important messages, pens, keys, combs, and impressive-looking handkerchiefs.

9      All the equipment essential to running the world. And held close to the body. Easily availablle. Neatly classified. Pen in the inside coat pocket. Keys in the back left trouser pocket. Efficiency. Order. Confidence.

10     What does a woman have to match this organization? A purse.

The most hurried examination will show that a purse, however large or important-looking, is no match for a suitful of pockets. If the woman carrying a purse is so lucky as to get an important phone number or market tip from the executive with whom she is lunching, can she write it down? Can she find her pen? Perhaps she can, but it will probably be buried under three old grocery lists, two combs, a checkbook, and a wad of Kleenex. All of which she will have to pile on top of the lunch table before she can find the pen.

11     Will she ever get another tip from this person of power? Not likely. Now she has lost any psychological advantage she may have had. He may have been impressed with her intelligent discussion of the current economic scene before she opened her handbag, but four minutes later, when she is still digging, like a busy little prairie dog, for that pen, he is no longer impressed.

12     He knows he could have whipped his pen in and out of his pocket and written fourteen important messages on the table napkin in the time she is still searching.

What can a pocketless woman do?

Two solutions seem apparent. The women can form a pocket lobby (Pocket Power?) and march on the New York garment district.*

13     Or, in the event that effort fails (and well it might, since it would, by necessity, have to be run by a bunch of pocketless women) an alternate approach remains.

14     Every man in the country for his next birthday finds himself the lucky recipient of one of those very stylish men's handbags, and to go with it, one of those no-pocket body shirts.

---

*A major center of fashion design in the United States

## *Comprehension*

### Exercise 1

*Answer the following questions. Your teacher may want you to do this exercise orally, in writing, or by underlining appropriate parts of the text.*

1. What are reasons commonly given to explain why men hold better positions in society than women? _____

   _____

2. How many pockets does the average successful male executive wear to work? _____

3. How many pockets does the average woman wear for office work? _____

4. According to the author, what is the correlation between power and pockets?

   _____

5. According to the author, why do people need pockets? _____

   _____

6. According to the author, what are the disadvantages of women's purses? _____

   _____

7. What two solutions does the author propose for women's pocket problems? _____

   _____

### Exercise 2

*In your opinion which of the following groups of people does the author find humorous (make fun of)? Be prepared to defend your choices with portions of the text.*

1. _____ people who are well organized

2. _____ people who judge the efficiency of others on the basis of the way they dress

3. _____ people who feel that women can improve their situation in life by being more like men

4. _____ women

5. _____ businessmen

6. _____ people who make correlations between unrelated events

7. _____ people who describe human behavior by counting things

## Discussion/Composition

1. Give examples of the ways in which clothing contributes to people's success.

2. Approaching the issue of the unequal position of women and men satirically, why do you think men have more power? For example, how do men's shoes contribute to their position in society?

## Vocabulary from Context

Both the ideas and the vocabulary in this exercise are taken from "Pockety Women Unite?" Use the context provided to determine the meanings of the italicized words. Write a definition, synonym, or description of each of the italicized vocabulary items in the space provided.

1. _____   It is always dangerous to generalize; however, it seems obvious that, on the whole, men hold a higher position in society than women. Because of this *status,* men enjoy more power than women.

2. _____   People's *prestige* often depends on their title or profession. For example, in many countries, doctors and lawyers are greatly admired.

3. _____   There seems to be a *correlation* between one's sex and one's status in society. On the whole, men enjoy higher status than women.

4. _____   Most women's clothing is made without pockets. As a result, women are forced to carry their belongings in a *purse.*

5. _____   Despite the fact that women often make valuable contributions, they have not been able to *attain* the same social and economic status as men.

## Dictionary Study

Many words have more than one meaning. When you use the dictionary* to discover the meaning of an unfamiliar word, you need to use the context to determine which definition is appropriate. Use the portions of the dictionary provided to select the best definition for each of the italicized words below.†

1. As long as women insist on using purses, they will never be as organized as men. A purse, however large or important-looking, is no *match* for a suitful of pockets.

2. If a woman with a purse is lucky enough to get a business *tip* from the executive with whom she is lunching, she will not be able to find a pen with which to write it down.

3. Women should become *lobbyists* and try to influence the garment industry.

**lob·by** (lob'i), *n*. [*pl.* LOBBIES (-iz)], [ML. *lobium, lobia;* see LODGE], 1. a hall or large anteroom; waiting room or vestibule, as of an apartment house, hotel, theater, etc. 2. a large hall adjacent to the assembly hall of a legislature and open to the public. 3. a group of lobbyists representing the same special interest: as, a cotton *lobby*. *v.i.* [LOBBIED (-id), LOBBYING], to act as a lobbyist. *v.t.* to get or try to get legislators to vote for (a measure) by acting as a lobbyist (often with *through*).
**lob·by·ism** (lob'i-iz'm), *n*. the practice of lobbying.
**lob·by·ist** (lob'i-ist), *n*. [*lobby* + *-ist*], a person who tries to get legislators to introduce or vote for measures favorable to a special interest that he represents.

**match** (mach), *n*. [ME. *macche*; OFr. *mesche* (Fr. *mèche*), wick of a candle, match; prob. < L. *myxa*, wick of a candle; Gr. *myxa*, nozzle of a lamp], 1. originally, a wick or cord prepared to burn at a uniform rate, used for firing guns or explosives. 2. a slender piece of wood, cardboard, waxed cord, etc. tipped with a composition that catches fire by friction, sometimes only on a specially prepared surface. 3. [Obs.], a slip of paper, splinter of wood, etc. dipped in sulfur so that it can be ignited with a spark, for lighting candles, lamps, etc.
**match** (mach), *n*. [ME. *macche*; AS. *gemæcca*, one suited to another, mate < base of *macian*, to make, form (see MAKE, *v. & n.*); sense development: what is put together—what is suitable (for putting together), etc.], 1. any person or thing equal or similar to another in some way; specifically, *a*) a person, group, or thing able to cope with or oppose another as an equal in power, size, etc.; peer. *b*) a counterpart or facsimile. *c*) either of two corresponding things or persons; one of a pair. 2. two or more persons or things that go together in appearance, size, or other quality; pair: as, her purse and shoes were a good *match*. 3. a contest or game involving two or more contestants. 4. *a*) an agreement to marry or mate. *b*) a marriage or mating: as, she made a good *match*. 5. a person regarded as a suitable or possible mate. *v.t.* 1. to join in marriage; get a (suitable) match for; mate. 2. *a*) formerly, to meet as an antagonist; hence, *b*) to compete with successfully. 3. to put in opposition (*with*); pit (*against*). 4. to be equal, similar, suitable, or corresponding to in some way: as, his looks *match* his character. 5. to make, show, produce, or get a competitor, counterpart, or equivalent to: as, I want to *match* this cloth. 6. to suit or fit (one thing) to another. 7. to fit (things) together; make similar or corresponding. 8. to compare. 9. *a*) to flip or reveal (coins) as a form of gambling or to decide something contested, the winner being determined by the combination of faces thus exposed. *b*) to match coins with (another person), usually betting that the same faces will be exposed. *v.i.* 1. to get married; mate. 2. to be equal, similar, suitable, or corresponding in some way.

**tip** (tip), *n*. [ME. *tippe*; prob. < MD. or MLG. *tip*, point, top; akin to G. *zipf-* in *zipfel*, an end, tip; prob. IE. base *dā(i)-*, to part, divide up (cf. TIDE, TIME)], 1. the pointed, tapering, or rounded end or top of something long and slim. 2. something attached to the end, as a cap, ferrule, etc. 3. a top or apex, as of a mountain. *v.t.* [TIPPED (tipt), TIPPING], 1. to make a tip on. 2. to cover the tip or tips of (*with* something). 3. to serve as the tip of.
**tip** (tip), *v.t.* [TIPPED (tipt), TIPPING], [prob. < ME. *tippe*, a tip, or its base], 1. to strike lightly and sharply; tap. 2. to give a small present of money to (a waiter, porter, etc.) for some service. 3. [Colloq.], to give secret information to in an attempt to be helpful: often with *off*. 4. in *baseball*, etc., to hit (the ball) a glancing blow. *v.i.* to give a tip or tips. *n*. 1. a light, sharp blow; tap. 2. a piece of information given secretly or confidentially in an attempt to be helpful: as, he gave me a *tip* on the race. 3. a suggestion, hint, warning, etc. 4. a small present of money given to a waiter, porter, etc. for services; gratuity.
**tip** (tip), *v.t.* [TIPPED (tipt), TIPPING], [ME. *tipen* (short vowel prob. < p.t. *tipte*); Northern word, prob. < ON.], 1. to overturn or upset: often with *over*. 2. to cause to tilt or slant. 3. to raise slightly or touch the brim of (one's hat) in salutation. *v.i.* 1. to tilt or slant. 2. to overturn or topple: often with *over*. *n*. a tipping or being tipped; tilt; slant.

---

*For an introduction to dictionary use, see Appendix B.
†From *Webster's New World Dictionary*, College Edition (World Publishing Company, 1966).

# Reading Selection 3
# Poetry

In Unit 1 you read poems to determine the main ideas, to discover what the poems were about. But poetry can be enjoyed on many levels, and read in many ways. You can read a poem once, simply to enjoy the language or the main message of the poem. Or you can decide to experience a poem more fully, by reading it several times for different purposes or meanings. The two poems that follow describe this process of intense discovery.*

### How to Eat a Poem

1　Don't be polite.
　 Bite in.
　 Pick it up with your fingers and lick the juice that
　　　may run down your chin.
5　It is ready and ripe now, whenever you are.

6　You do not need a knife or fork or spoon
　 or plate or napkin or tablecloth.

8　For there is no core
　 or stem
　 or rind
　 or pit
12　or seed
　 or skin
　 to throw away.

*Eve Merriam*

### Unfolding Bud

1　One is amazed
　 By a water-lily bud
　 Unfolding
　 With each passing day,
　 Taking on a richer color
6　And new dimensions.

*(Continued on page 80)*

*"How to Eat a Poem" by Eve Merriam, from *Jamboree: Rhymes for All Times* (New York: Dell, 1984); "Unfolding Bud" by Naoshi Koriyama, *Christian Science Monitor,* July 13, 1957.

7   One is not amazed,
    At a first glance,
    By a poem,
    Which is as tight-closed
11  As a tiny bud.

12  Yet one is surprised
    To see the poem
    Gradually unfolding,
15  Revealing its rich inner self,
    As one reads it
    Again
18  And over again.

*Naoshi Koriyama*

## Comprehension

Answer the following questions. Your teacher may want you to discuss these questions as a class, in small groups, or in pairs.

1. Eve Merriam, the author of "How to Eat a Poem," compares the process of reading a poem to eating a fruit. What does she mean?

   a. In what ways is reading a poem like eating?

   b. What does the author mean when she advises us, "Don't be polite"?

   c. Why don't you need a plate or a napkin in order to eat a poem?

   d. Why do you think the author chose eating a fruit instead of a piece of bread for her analogy?

   e. The author gives us a model for reading poetry. Are there other things that you read in this way?

2. Naoshi Koriyama compares poetry to an unfolding bud. What does she mean?

   a. In what ways is a poem like a water-lily bud?

   b. According to Koriyama, what is a difference between our reaction to a water-lily and to a poem?

   c. What are the similarities and differences in these two poets' views of reading poetry?

The three selections that follow* will give you an opportunity to eat poems, to watch them unfold. Read each poem once. Then work with your classmates to answer the questions that follow. Because so much of poetry depends upon individual response, there is no single correct answer to many of these questions. Your teacher may want you to discuss these questions as a class, in small groups, or in pairs.

### This is Just to Say

1   I have eaten
     the plums
     that were in
     the icebox

5   and which
     you were probably
     saving
     for breakfast

9   Forgive me
     they were delicious
     so sweet
     and so cold.

*William Carlos Williams*

## Comprehension

1. Some people think this is a wonderful poem, others don't think it is a poem at all. What do you think accounts for these different reactions?

2. The poem seems to be in the form of a note. Why do you think it was written? Did this note need to be written? Do you think the writer believes that the reader will be angry with him? Is this really an apology?

3. What do you think is the relationship between the writer and the addressee of the note? Do they live together? Are they close? What is their relationship?

4. Why do you think this poem/note was written?

5. Do you think this is a poem? If you had found it in your kitchen, would you experience it as a poem?

---

*"This is Just to Say" by William Carlos Williams, from *Collected Poems, Volume I: 1909–1939* (New York: New Directions, 1938); "in Just-" by e.e. cummings, from *Tulips & Chimneys* (New York: Liveright, 1976); "Spring and Fall: To a Young Child" by Gerald Manley Hopkins, from *Poetry: From Statement to Meaning* (New York: Oxford University Press, 1965).

The poet e. e. cummings is noted for the unusual placement of words on the page and his lack of capital letters. Your teacher will read the following poem aloud to show the effects achieved by this unusual spacing.

*in Just-*

*1*   in Just-
    spring      when the world is mud-
    luscious the little
    lame balloonman

*5*   whistles   far   and wee

    and eddieandbill come
    running from marbles and
    piracies and it's
    spring

*10*   when the world is puddle-wonderful

    the queer
    old balloonman whistles
    far   and   wee
    and bettyandisbel come dancing

*15*   from hop-scotch and jump-rope and

    it's
    spring
    and
      the

*20*         goat-footed

    balloonMan   whistles
    far
    and
    wee

*e. e. cummings*

## Comprehension

1. This poem describes spring. What aspects of springtime does it mention?

2. What are the names of the children?

3. Cummings is also noted for inventing words. In this poem, the words *mud-luscious* and *puddle-wonderful* have been created by combining common English words. What do you think each of these means? Do you find cummings's unusual spacing and invented words effective?

4. What is e. e. cummings's attitude toward spring? Toward the balloonman? What is the spirit or mood of the poem? Is it happy? sad? threatening? Use evidence from the poem to support your position.

5. Both Williams and cummings use the word *just*. Is this *just* spring; was Williams's poem *just* an apology?

### Spring and Fall:
### To a Young Child

1   Margaret, are you grieving
Over Goldengrove unleaving?
Leaves, like the things of man, you
With your fresh thoughts care for, can you?
5   Ah! as the heart grows older
It will come to such sights colder
By and by, nor spare a sigh
Though worlds of wanwood leafmeal lie;
And yet you will weep and know why.
10   Now no matter child, the name:
Sorrow's springs are the same.
Nor mouth had, no nor mind, expressed
What heart heard of, ghost guessed:
It is the blight man was born for,
15   It is Margaret you mourn for.

*Gerard Manley Hopkins*

## *Comprehension*

1. This poem begins with a question: Why is Margaret grieving? The poem unfolds in a way that answers this question. To discover the answer, first we must untangle some unusual syntax.

   a. Rearrange the words in lines 3 and 4 so that the word order is closer to standard English.

   _____

   _____

   b. Change lines 12 and 13 so that they too are closer to standard English. In this case you may want to change or add words, for example *neither* usually precedes *nor*.

   _____

   _____

2. In this poem, Hopkins has invented a number of new words. These have been created by combining words or word forms. What do you think is the meaning of each of the following? Feel free to use your dictionary to look up the meanings of parts of these compound words.

   Goldengrove (line 2) _____

   unleaving (line 2) _____

   wanwood (line 8) _____

   leafmeal (line 8) _____

3. Now that you have looked more closely at the language of the poem, read it through once again. Why is Margaret grieving?

# Reading Selection 4

## Short Story

*Before You Begin*   There is a saying in English, "Be careful, or your wishes will come true."

1. What does this mean?

2. Do you believe there is wisdom in this saying?

Alan Austen is a troubled young man. Luckily, he finds a strange old man who can help him. There's just one problem. . . .

Read the selection,* then do the exercises that follow. Your teacher may want you to do Vocabulary from Context exercise 1 on page 89 before you begin reading.

### The Chaser

*John Collier*

1       Alan Austen, as nervous as a kitten, went up certain dark and creaky stairs in the neighborhood of Pell Street, and peered about for a long time on the dim hallway before he found the name he wanted written obscurely on one of the doors.

2       He pushed open this door, as he had been told to do, and found himself in a tiny room, which contained no furniture but a plain kitchen table, a rocking-chair, and an ordinary chair. On one of the dirty buff-coloured walls were a couple of shelves, containing in all perhaps a dozen bottles and jars.

3       An old man sat in the rocking-chair, reading a newspaper. Alan, without a word, handed him the card he had been given. "Sit down, Mr. Austen," said the old man very politely. "I am glad to make your acquaintance."

4       "Is it true," asked Alan, "that you have a certain mixture that has-er-quite extraordinary effects?"

        "My dear sir," replied the old man, "my stock in trade is not very large—I don't deal in laxatives and teething mixtures—but such as it is, it is varied. I think nothing I sell has effects which could be precisely described as ordinary."

        "Well, the fact is . . ." began Alan.

5       "Here, for example," interrupted the old man, reaching for a bottle from the shelf. "Here is a liquid as colourless as water, almost tasteless, quite imperceptible in coffee, wine, or any other beverage. It is also quite imperceptible to any known method of autopsy."†

---

*"The Chaser" by John Collier. Originally published in the *New Yorker*.
†autopsy: the examination of a dead body, to determine the cause of death

6       "Do you mean it is a poison?" cried Alan, very much horrified.

"Call it a glove-cleaner if you like," said the old man indifferently. "Maybe it will clean gloves. I have never tried. One might call it a life-cleaner. Lives need cleaning sometimes."

7       "I want nothing of that sort," said Alan.

"Probably it is just as well," said the old man. "Do you know the price of this? For one teaspoonful, which is sufficient, I ask five thousand dollars. Never less. Not a penny less."

"I hope all your mixtures are not as expensive," said Alan apprehensively.

8       "Oh dear, no," said the old man. "It would be no good charging that sort of price for a love potion, for example. Young people who need a love potion very seldom have five thousand dollars. Otherwise they would not need a love potion."

"I am glad to hear that," said Alan.

9       "I look at it like this," said the old man. "Please a customer with one article, and he will come back when he needs another. Even if it is more costly. He will save up for it, if necessary."

"So," said Alan, "you really do sell love potions?"

10      "If I did not sell love potions," said the old man, reaching for another bottle, "I should not have mentioned the other matter to you. It is only when one is in a position to oblige that one can afford to be so confidential."

"And these potions," said Alan. "They are not just-just-er-"

11      "Oh, no," said the old man. "Their effects are permanent, and extend far beyond the mere casual impulse. But they include it. Oh, yes, they include it. Bountifully, insistently. Everlastingly."

"Dear me!" said Alan, attempting a look of scientific detachment. "How *very* interesting!"

12      "But consider the spiritual side," said the old man.

"I do, indeed," said Alan.

"For indifference," said the old man, "they substitute devotion. For scorn, adoration. Give one tiny measure of this to the young lady—its flavour is imperceptible in orange juice, soup, or cocktails—and however gay and giddy she is, she will change altogether. She will want nothing but solitude and you."

13      "I can hardly believe it," said Alan. "She is so fond of parties."

"She will not like them *any* more," said the old man. "She will be afraid of the pretty girls you may meet."

"She will actually be jealous?" cried Alan in a rapture. "Of me?"

"Yes, she will want to be everything to you."

"She is, already. Only she doesn't care about it."

14      "She will, when she has taken this. She will care intensely. You will be her sole interest in life."

"Wonderful!" cried Alan.

"She will want to know *all* you do," said the old man. "*All* that has happened to you during the day. *Every* word of it. She will want to know what you are thinking about, why you smile suddenly, why you are looking sad."

"That is love!" cried Alan.

15   "Yes," said the old man. "How carefully she will look after you! She will never allow you to be tired, to sit in a draught, to neglect your food. If you are an hour late, she will be terrified. She will think you are killed, or that some siren has caught you."

"I can hardly imagine Diana like that!" cried Alan, overwhelmed with joy.

16   "You will not have to use your imagination," said the old man. "And, by the way, since there are always sirens, if by any chance you *should,* later on, slip a little, you need not worry. She will forgive you, in the end. She will be terribly hurt, of course, but she will forgive you—in the end."

"That will not happen," said Alan fervently.

17   "Of course not," said the old man. "But, if it did, you need not worry. She would never divorce you. Oh, no! And, of course, she will never give you the least, the very least, grounds for—uneasiness."

"And how much," said Alan, "is this wonderful mixture?"

"It is not as dear," said the old man, "as the glove-cleaner, or life-cleaner, as I sometimes call it. No. That is five thousand dollars, never a penny less. One has to be older than you are, to indulge in that sort of thing. One has to save up for it."

18   "But the love potion?" said Alan.

"Oh, that," said the old man, opening the drawer in the kitchen table, and taking out a tiny, rather dirty-looking phial. "That is just a dollar."

"I can't tell you how grateful I am," said Alan, watching him fill it.

19   "I like to oblige," said the old man. "Then customers come back, later in life, when they are better off, and want more expensive things. Here you are. You will find it very effective."

"Thank you again," said Alan. "Good-bye."

"*Au revoir,*"* said the old man.

## Comprehension

Answer the following questions. Your teacher may want you to do this exercise orally, in writing, or by underlining appropriate parts of the text. True/False items are indicated by a T / F preceding a statement.

1. T / F   Alan Austen accidentally discovered the old man's room.

2. T / F   The old man sold a large number of mixtures commonly found in pharmacies.

3. What did the old man call the $5,000 mixture? _____

4. What was the $5,000 mixture? _____

5. T / F   Alan Austen loved Diana more than she loved him.

---

*\*au revoir*: (French) goodbye; until we meet again

6. How would you describe Diana? _____

_____

7. According to the old man, what effect would the love potion have on Diana? _____

_____

8. T / F   Alan felt that he could never love anyone but Diana.

9. A chaser is a drink taken to cover the unpleasant taste of a preceding drink. What is the first drink in this story? What is its unpleasant "taste"? What is the chaser?

_____

10. How could the old man make enough money to live if he sold his love potion for only one dollar?

_____

_____

## Drawing Inferences

In part, what makes "The Chaser" an interesting story is the fact that the author and the reader share a secret: they know something that Alan Austen doesn't know. Each reader will discover the meaning of the title, "The Chaser," at a different moment in the story. However, even if you finished the story before you realized the real meaning of the old man's words, you were probably able to go back and find double meanings in many of the passages in the story.

The following quotations are taken from "The Chaser." Read each one, then give two possible meanings: (1) the meaning Alan Austen understands, and (2) what you consider to be the real meaning. The number in parentheses indicates the paragraph where the quotation can be found. Your teacher may want you to do this exercise orally or in writing.

1. (14) "She will want to know *all* you do," said the old man. "*All* that has happened to you during the day. *Every* word of it. She will want to know what you are thinking about, why you smile suddenly, why you are looking sad."

2. (17) ". . . you need not worry. She would never divorce you."

3. (19) "I like to oblige," said the old man. "Then customers come back, later in life, when they are better off, and want more expensive things."

4. (19) "Thank you again," said Alan. "Goodbye."
   "*Au revoir,*" said the old man.

## Discussion/Composition

1. This short story suggests that love potions require an antidote. By this logic, are there other desires that, if fulfilled, require an antidote? What are some of these?

2. Write a scene between Alan and the old man or Alan and Diana that takes place in the future.

## Vocabulary from Context

**Exercise 1**

*Use the context provided to determine the meanings of the italicized words. Write a definition, synonym, or description of each of the italicized vocabulary items in the space provided.*

1. _____   The doctor said that if a person ate even one leaf of the hemlock plant, he would die, because the plant is a deadly *poison*.

2. _____   The murderer had developed a poison which could not be tasted or smelled when mixed with food. Because it was *imperceptible,* he was able to murder a number of people without being caught.

3. _____   "When making this mixture," the man said, "you don't need two teaspoons of salt, because one teaspoon is *sufficient.*"

4. _____   "Since you are my best friend, and because I can trust you, I know I can be *confidential* with you. Listen carefully, because what I am going to tell you is a secret," said Henry.

5. _____   "I am able to *oblige* you sir; I can give you the item you wanted so badly."

6. _____   There are times when one wants to be surrounded by people, and there are times when one needs *solitude.*

7. _____   The man was so *jealous* of his wife that he would not allow her to talk to other men.

---

### Exercise 2

*This exercise is designed to give you additional clues to determine the meanings of unfamiliar vocabulary items in context. In the paragraph indicated by the number in parentheses, find the word that best fits the meaning given. Your teacher may want to read these aloud as you quickly scan the paragraph to find the answer.*

1. (1)   Which word means *poorly lighted; dark?*

2. (4)   Which word means *objects for sale; items kept for sale?*

3. (7)   Which word means *worriedly; with alarm or concern?*

4. (10)  Which word means *to perform a service; to please or help someone?*

5. (16)  Which word means *women who attract, seduce, lure men?*

6. (17)  Which word means *reason; basis; foundation?*

---

### Exercise 3

*This exercise should be done after you have finished reading "The Chaser." The exercise is designed to determine how well you have been able to use context clues to guess the meaning of unfamiliar vocabulary. Give a definition, synonym, or description of each of the words or phrases below. The number in parentheses indicates the paragraph in which the word can be found. Your teacher may want you to do these orally or in writing.*

1. (1)   peered ———————————————————————————————

2. (8)   potion ———————————————————————————————

3. (16)  slip a little ———————————————————————————————

4. (17)  dear ———————————————————————————————

5. (19)  better off ———————————————————————————————

# 5

## Nonprose Reading

## Road Map

Nonprose writing consists of disconnected words and numbers instead of the sentences and paragraphs you usually learn to read. Each time you need information from a train schedule, a graph, a menu, or the like, you must read nonprose material. This activity will help you practice the problem-solving skills you will need in order to read nonprose material.

If you travel by car in an English-speaking country, you will need to read road maps in English. This exercise is designed to give you practice in many aspects of map reading.

*Before You Begin*  Reflect on road travel in your country:

1. If you are traveling to an unfamiliar area, how do you find out about the route? Do you ever rely on road maps?

2. Why do you think road maps are important to travel in the United States?

## *Introduction*

### Exercise 1

*Examine the parts of the map you will need to use in order to answer the questions below.*

1. On page 221 is a section of a *map* of Tennessee (Tenn.) and Kentucky (Ky.), two states of the United States.

   Find the Kentucky-Tennessee border.

2. On page 220 is a section of the *Tennessee City and Town Index*. This lists the larger cities and towns in Tennessee with coordinates to help you find the names of these cities and towns on the map.

   a. What are the coordinates of Clarksville, Tenn.? _____

   b. Locate Clarksville on the map on page 95.

3. On page 96 is an *inset* (a larger, more detailed reproduction) of Nashville, Tenn. You will need to use the inset of Nashville to find information about major roads and landmarks within Nashville.

Riverside Hospital (on the north side of the city) is located near the intersection of which two streets?

_____

4. On page 97 is a *legend,* that is, a list of symbols to help you interpret the map on page 95. On the legend is the *distance scale,* which tells you the relationship of both miles and kilometers to inches on the map. Examine the legend carefully to see if you have any questions.

   a. Using the distance scale, estimate the distance in both miles and kilometers from Bowling Green, Ky. (coordinates: J-13), to the Ky.-Tenn. border.

   _____

   b. What is the difference between the two roads, route 31W and route 65, that connect Bowling Green and Nashville?

   _____

   _____

5. Finally, on page 97 you will find a *driving distance map.* This map will tell you the exact distance in miles between many of the large cities in Kentucky, Tennessee, and surrounding states. It also estimates the driving time from city to city.

What is the distance between Bowling Green, Ky., and Nashville, Tenn.? _____

**Exercise 2**

*This exercise is designed to give you practice in deciding where to look for specific pieces of information. Below are questions you might ask if you needed to find information from a map. Read each question, then decide if you would look for the answer on the map itself, in the Tennessee City and Town Index, on the inset of Nashville, on the legend, or on the driving distance map. Put the appropriate letter in the blank provided.*

   a. map
   b. city and town index
   c. inset
   d. legend
   e. driving distance map

Where should you look to find:

1. _____ the distance between Bowling Green, Ky., and Cincinnati, Ohio?

2. _____ the coordinates of McMinnville, Tenn.?

3. _____ the best route from Ashland City, Tenn., to Murfreesboro, Tenn.?

4. _____ the location in Nashville of the Country Music Hall of Fame?

5. _____ what the symbol **X** means?

6. _____ how to get to Vanderbilt University in Nashville from Interstate highway 65?

## Map Reading

Use all the information provided on pages 94–97 to do the exercises that follow.

### Exercise 1

*Indicate if each statement below is true (T) or false (F). Work as quickly as you can.*

1. _____ There is a direct route going northwest between Nashville and Clarksville, Tenn.

2. _____ Franklin, located north of Nashville, is in Tennessee.

3. _____ Cincinnati, Ohio, is about 300 miles driving distance from Nashville, Tenn.

4. _____ In southwest Nashville, route 70S will take you directly to the Tennessee Botanical Gardens and Fine Arts Center.

5. _____ There is a passenger service airport near Nashville, Tenn.

6. _____ Going toward downtown Nashville from the southeast, you can get onto route 40 from route 24.

7. _____ Northwest of Nashville, a state highway connects Ashland City and Clarksville.

8. _____ Bellwood, Tenn., is west of Bellsburg, Tenn.

9. _____ Ashland City, Tenn., northwest of Nashville, is less than 15 miles/24 kilometers from Bellsburg.

10. _____ Nashville is the capital of Tennessee.

11. _____ Coming into downtown Nashville from the north on route 431 (Whites Creek Pike), you can exit directly onto route 65.

**Exercise 2**

*If you were to take a trip by car through Kentucky and Tennessee, you would have to solve problems such as the ones posed by the questions in this exercise. Answer each question as completely as possible. Often there is more than one correct answer. Your teacher may ask you to do these orally or in writing.*

1. Could you leave Chattanooga, Tenn., at 8:00 A.M. and get to Bowling Green, Ky., in time for a 12:00 lunch?  How fast would you have to drive?

_____

2. Which route would you take going northeast from Bowling Green to Mammoth Cave National Park?

_____

Can you spend the night at Mammoth Cave National Park? _____

3. Which route would you take from McMinnville, Tenn., to Nashville, Tenn., if you wanted to see the Edgar Evins State Park (northeast of McMinnville) and Cedars of Lebanon State Park (north of Murfreesboro)?

_____

## TENNESSEE CITY AND TOWN INDEX

| | | | | |
|---|---|---|---|---|
| Acton...............R-7 | Auburntown........O-15 | Buckeye...........M-21 | Centertown.........O-15 | Collierville...........R-3 |
| Adair...............O-6 | Austin Sprs........M-27 | Bucksnort.........O-10 | Centerville.........O-10 | Collinwood..........Q-9 |
| Adams..............L-12 | Avoca...............L-28 | Buena Vista........N-8 | Chalk Level........M-25 | Columbia..........P-12 |
| Adamsville..........Q-7 | Bailey...............R-3 | Buffalo............O-9 | Chapel Hill..........P-13 | Comfort............R-16 |
| Aetna..............P-10 | Baileyton...........M-26 | Buffalo Springs....M-23 | Chapmansboro......M-12 | Como...............M-7 |
| Alamo..............O-22 | Bairds Mill.........N-14 | Buffalo Valley......N-16 | Charleys Branch....N-21 | Conasauga..........R-20 |
| Alcoa...............O-5 | Bakerville...........N-9 | Buladeen...........L-28 | Charleston.........Q-19 | Concord............O-13 |
| Alexandria.........N-14 | Bakewell...........Q-18 | Bulls Gap..........M-25 | Charlotte...........N-11 | Cookeville..........N-17 |
| Algood.............N-17 | Banner Hill........N-27 | Bumpus Mill........L-9 | Chattanooga........R-42 | Coopertown........M-12 |
| Allardt.............M-19 | Banner Springs....M-19 | Burke..............O-18 | Cherry..............O-3 | Copperhill..........R-20 |
| Allens..............P-5 | Barefield...........O-14 | Burlison............P-3 | Cherry Valley.......N-15 | Corbin Hill..........N-20 |
| Allisona............O-13 | Bargerton...........O-7 | Burns..............N-11 | Chesney............M-23 | Cordova.............Q-3 |
| Allons.............M-17 | Barkertown.........Q-17 | Burrville...........M-19 | Chesterfield..........P-8 | Cornersville........Q-14 |
| Allred..............M-18 | Barnesville.........Q-11 | Burwood............O-12 | Chestnut Mound....N-16 | Corryton............N-23 |
| Almaville...........O-13 | Barren Plains......L-12 | Butler.............M-28 | Chewalla............R-6 | Cosby...............O-24 |
| Alnwick............O-22 | Bartlett............Q-3 | Bybee..............N-24 | Chic.................N-3 | Cottage Grove......M-7 |
| Alpha..............N-24 | Bath Springs........Q-8 | Byrdstown.........L-18 | Christiana..........O-14 | Cottontown.........M-13 |
| Alpine..............L-18 | Baxter..............N-16 | Cainsville..........N-15 | Christmasville.......N-7 | Cottonwood Grove....M-4 |
| Altamont..........Q-16 | Beacon..............P-8 | Calderwood..........L-26 | Chuckey............M-26 | Coulterville..........P-18 |
| Alto...............P-15 | Beans Creek........R-15 | Calhoun............Q-19 | Church Hill.........L-26 | Counce...............R-8 |
| Anderson..........R-15 | Bean Station.......M-24 | Camden.............N-8 | Churchton...........N-5 | Cove Creek |
| Andersonville......N-23 | Beardstown.........O-9 | Camelot............L-25 | Clairfield...........L-22 |    Cascades........O-23 |
| Annadel............N-19 | Bear Spring........L-10 | Campbellsville......Q-11 | Clarkrange.........N-18 | Covington............P-3 |
| Apison.............R-19 | Beech Bluff.........P-6 | Camp Creek........N-26 | Clarksburg...........O-7 | Cowan..............R-15 |
| Archer.............Q-13 | Beechgrove.........P-15 | Caney Branch......N-25 | Clarksville..........L-10 | Crab Orchard......O-19 |
| Archville...........R-20 | Beersheba Sprgs.....P-16 | Caneyspring........P-13 | Clayton.............L-5 | Crabtree............M-27 |
| Ardmore...........R-12 | Belfast.............Q-13 | Capleville..........R-3 | Cleveland..........R-19 | Craggie Hope.......N-11 |
| Arlington...........Q-3 | Bell Buckle.........P-14 | Carlisle.............M-9 | Clevenger..........N-24 | |
| Armathwaite.......M-19 | Belle Mead.........N-44 | Carter.............M-28 | Clifton.............Q-9 | McMinnville.........O-16 |
| Arp.................O-3 | Belleville...........Q-13 | Carthage...........M-16 | Clifty...............O-18 | |
| Arrington..........O-13 | Bells...............O-5 | Caryville............M-21 | Clinton.............N-21 | Murfreesboro........O-14 |
| Arthur..............L-23 | Bellsburg...........M-11 | Cash Point.........R-12 | Cloverport..........Q-5 | |
| Ashland City.......M-12 | Bell Town...........N-11 | Castalian Springs....M-14 | Coalfield...........N-20 | |
| Ashport.............O-3 | Bellwood...........M-15 | Catlettsburg........O-23 | Coalmont...........Q-16 | |
| Aspen Hill.........R-12 | Belvidere...........R-15 | Cavvia..............O-8 | Coble..............O-10 | |
| Athens.............P-20 | Benton.............R-20 | Cedar Creek........O-25 | Coghill.............Q-20 | |
| Atoka...............P-3 | | Cedar Grove........O-7 | Coldwater..........R-13 | |
| Atwood.............N-7 | | Cedar Hill..........L-12 | Colesburg..........N-11 | |
| | Buchanan...........M-8 | Celina..............L-17 | College Grove......O-13 | |

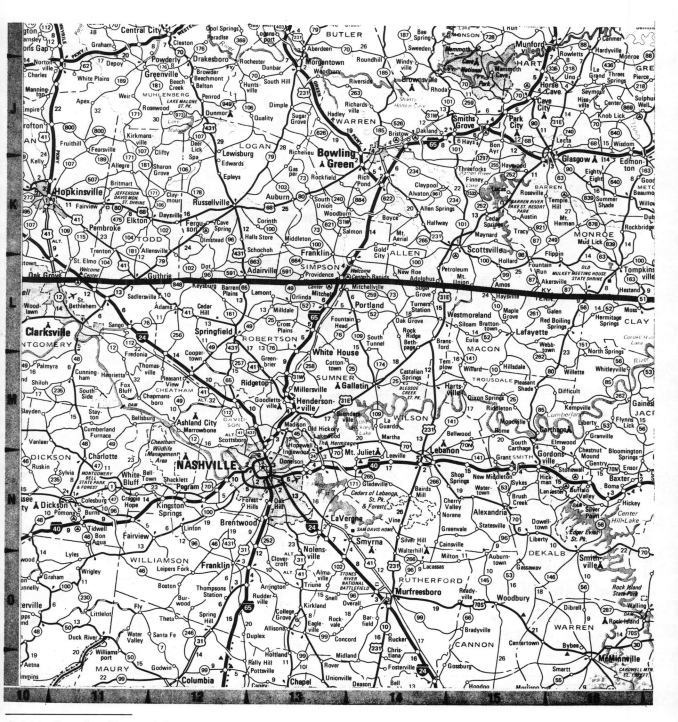

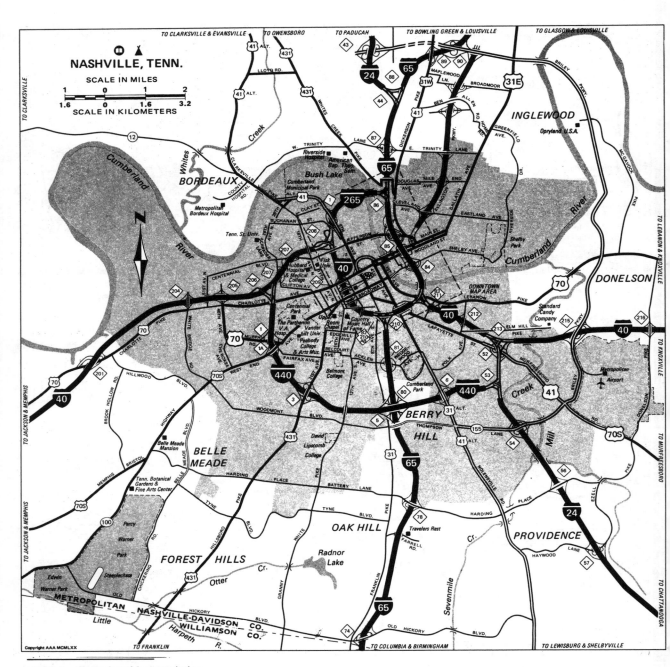

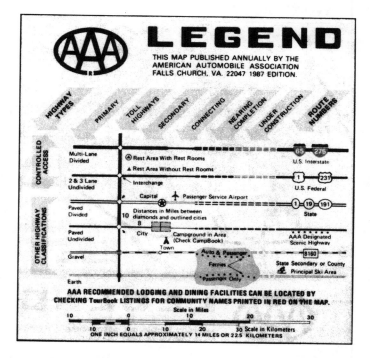

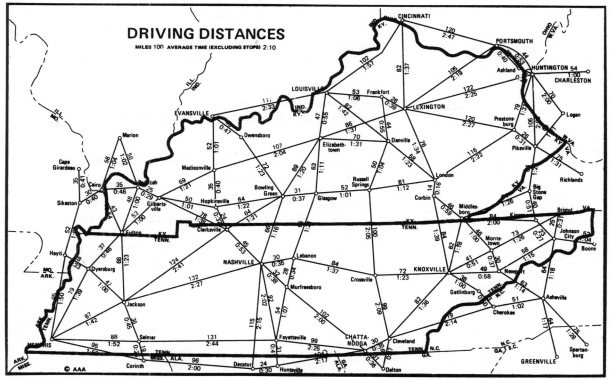

© AAA—Reproduced by permission.

# Word Study

## Context Clues

### Exercise 1

*In the following exercise, do NOT try to learn the italicized words. Concentrate on developing your ability to guess the meaning of unfamiliar words using context clues.\* Read each sentence carefully, and write a definition, synonym, or description of the italicized word on the line provided.*

1. _____  As he reached for the rock above him, his rope broke and he hung *precariously* by one hand as the rescuers ran toward him.

2. _____  The tired soldiers *trudged* through knee-deep mud for hours before they found a dry place to sleep.

3. _____  In the past, the world seemed to run in an orderly way. Now, however, everything seems to be in a state of *turmoil*.

4. _____  Monkeys are well known for their *grooming* habits; they spend hours carefully cleaning bits of dirt and straw from their coats.

5. _____  *Matrimony* doesn't seem to agree with Liz—she's been unhappy ever since she got married.

6. _____  Using a long, slender instrument called a *probe,* doctors are able to locate and remove pieces of metal from a patient's wounds.

7. _____  The following Monday, when the president *convened* the second meeting of the committee, we all sat down quietly and waited for him to begin.

8. _____  We think of plants in general as absorbing water and food; of animals as *ingesting* or "eating it."

9. _____  Robben is considered an *autocratic* administrator because he makes decisions without seeking the opinions of others.

10. _____  There is an element of word magic here: entomology and *limnology* sound more important than merely insect biology and fresh water biology.

_____

\*For an introduction to context clues, see Appendix A.

**Exercise 2**

*This exercise is designed to give you practice using context clues from a passage. Use your general knowledge along with information from the entire text below to write a definition, synonym, or description of the italicized word on the line provided. Read through the entire passage before making a decision. Note that some of the words appear more than once; by the end of the passage you should have a good idea of their meaning. Do not worry if your definition is not exact; a general idea of the meaning will often allow you to understand the meaning of a written text.*

## Major Personality Study Finds That Traits Are Mostly Inherited

*Daniel Goleman*

The *genetic* makeup of a child is a stronger influence on personality than child *rearing*, according to the first study to examine identical twins *reared* in different families. The *findings shatter* a widespread belief among experts and laypeople alike in the *primacy* of family influence and are sure to lead to fierce debate.

The *findings* are the first major results to emerge from a longterm project at the University of Minnesota in which, since 1979, more than 350 pairs of twins have gone through six days of extensive testing that has included analysis of blood, brain waves, intelligence, and allergies.

For most of the traits measured, more than half the variation was found to be due to *heredity,* leaving less than half determined by the influence of parents, home environment and other experiences in life.

The Minnesota *findings* stand in sharp contradiction to standard wisdom on nature vs. *nurture* in forming adult personality. Virtually all major theories since Freud have given far more importance to environment, or *nurture,* than to *genes* or nature.*

genetic/genes _____

rearing/reared _____

findings _____

shatter _____

primacy _____

heredity _____

nurture _____

*From the *New York Times,* December 2, 1986.

## Sentence Study

## Restatement and Inference

This exercise is similar to the one found in Unit 1.* Each sentence below is followed by five statements. The statements are of four types:
1. Some of the statements are restatements of the original sentence. They give the same information in a different way.
2. Some of the statements are inferences (conclusions) that can be drawn from the information given in the original sentence.
3. Some of the statements are false based on the information given.
4. Some of the statements cannot be judged true or false based on the information given in the original sentence.

Put a check (✓) next to all restatements and inferences (types 1 and 2). Note: do not check a statement that is true of itself but cannot be inferred from the sentence given.

1. A favorite definition of joking has long been the ability to find similarity between dissimilar things—that is, hidden similarities.

    _____ a. Joking is the ability to find similarity in dissimilar things.

    _____ b. It takes a long time to develop the ability to tell good jokes.

    _____ c. This definition of joking is a new one in literary theory.

    _____ d. Many people define joking as the ability to find similarity in dissimilar things.

    _____ e. The author agrees with this definition.

2. Since the Romantic period, most modern theory has dealt with the peculiar act of the poet rather than his product or its effect on the audience.

    _____ a. Most modern theory does not deal with the poem itself or its effect on the audience.

    _____ b. Most modern theory of poetry deals with the act of the poet.

    _____ c. Since the Romantic period, literary theory has dealt with the effect of poetry on the reader.

    _____ d. The author believes that literary theory should only deal with the peculiar act of the poet.

    _____ e. Modern theory is considered to begin at the Romantic period.

---

*For an introduction to sentence study, see Appendix D.

3. Although housewives still make up the majority of volunteer groups, male participation is reported on the rise nationwide as traditional distinctions between men's work and women's work begin to fade.

_____ a. As traditional societal roles change, more men are becoming members of volunteer groups.

_____ b. Most members of volunteer groups are women.

_____ c. In the past, volunteer work was done mainly by women.

_____ d. Male participation in volunteer groups is increasing in all cities.

_____ e. The author believes there is a relationship between the changing societal roles and the increasing willingness of men to do work previously done by females.

4. The overall picture of this very early settled Peruvian population is that of a simple, peaceful people living in a small cultivable oasis by the sea, fishing, raising a few food crops, living in small, simple, nonmasonry houses and making the objects necessary for their economic and household life, with slight attention to art.

_____ a. This early Peruvian population had all the basic necessities of life available to it.

_____ b. We can assume that art only exists in very advanced societies.

_____ c. This society moved many times during the year.

_____ d. Because the people worked so hard they had no time for art.

_____ e. The author believes this society provides nothing of interest for historians.

5. Only a small number of scholars can be named who have entered at all deeply into the problems of jokes.

_____ a. Only a few scholars have studied jokes.

_____ b. The area of jokes is so complex that only a small number of people have been able to study it.

_____ c. Few scholars have studied the problem of jokes at all deeply.

_____ d. The author cannot remember the names of scholars who have studied jokes.

_____ e. It is not possible to name all those who have studied jokes at all deeply.

6. There is a question about the extent to which any one of us can be free of a prejudiced view in the area of religion.

   _____ a. Probably everyone is prejudiced in his views on religion.

   _____ b. Any one of us can be free of prejudice in the area of religion.

   _____ c. To some extent we can never be free of prejudice in the area of religion.

   _____ d. A prejudiced view in the area of religion is undesirable.

   _____ e. Because we can't be free of prejudice in the area of religion, we should not practice a religion.

7. Although the November election may significantly change the face of the county Board of Commissioners, the group will still have to confront the same old problems.

   _____ a. The November election may give the Board of Commissioners a new building.

   _____ b. The Board of Commissioners consists of several members.

   _____ c. The November election may change the membership of the Board of Commissioners.

   _____ d. Although board members may change, the problems will remain the same.

   _____ e. The author does not believe that this election will change the difficulties facing the commissioners.

8. If this book begins with a familiar theme—the Indian experience of the last 120 years—the author brings to it great power and deep understanding.

   _____ a. This book was written 120 years ago.

   _____ b. The Indian experience of the last 120 years is a familiar experience, and nothing new can be written about it.

   _____ c. The book lacks understanding of the Indian experience.

   _____ d. The book begins with a familiar theme.

   _____ e. The author of this sentence likes the book.

9. In this part of the world, the political and social changes of the past 20 years have by no means eliminated the old upper class of royalty and friends and advisors of royalty, the holders of state monopolies, the great landlords and lords of commercial fiefs, tribal sheikhs, and village leaders.

_____ a. In this part of the world, political and social changes have eliminated great landlords, lords of commercial fiefs, and village leaders.

_____ b. In this part of the world, the upper class and their friends and advisors have not been eliminated by political and social change.

_____ c. No means can eliminate the old upper class of royalty in this part of the world.

_____ d. The upper class of royalty has not changed in the past 20 years in this part of the world.

_____ e. In this part of the world, village leaders hold as much power as the advisors of royalty.

10. People should and do choose their elected representatives partly on the basis of how well they believe these representatives, once in office, can convince them to do or support whatever needs to be done.

_____ a. It is the author's belief that people should choose representatives whom they believe will convince them to take action.

_____ b. People choose representatives on the basis of whether or not they believe the representatives can be convinced to do what needs to be done.

_____ c. Although people should choose representatives whom they believe will convince them to take action, often they do not.

_____ d. People choose representatives whom they believe will convince them to take action.

_____ e. Representatives are elected only on the basis of their ability to take action.

## Paragraph Analysis

# Reading for Full Understanding

Read each paragraph carefully.* Try to determine the author's main idea while attempting to remember important details. For each of the questions below, select the best answer. You may refer to the passage to answer the questions.

**Paragraph 1**

1     Summers with father were always enjoyable. Swimming, hiking,
2 boating, fishing—the days were not long enough to contain all of our
3 activities. There never seemed to be enough time to go to church,
4 which disturbed some friends and relations. Accused of neglecting this
5 part of our education, my father instituted a summer school for my
6 brother and me. However, his summer course included ancient history,
7 which Papa felt our schools neglected, and navigation, in which we first
8 had a formal examination in the dining room, part of which consisted
9 of tying several knots in a given time limit. Then we were each
10 separately sent on what was grandly referred to as a cruise in my
11 father's 18-foot knockabout, spending the night on board, and loaded
12 down, according to my mother, with enough food for a week. I
13 remember that on my cruise I was required to formally plot our
14 course, using the tide table, even though our goal was an island I
15 could see quite clearly across the water in the distance.†

1. What was the original reason for holding the summer school?
    _____ a. Friends and relatives thought the children should learn religion.
    _____ b. The father wanted the children to learn more about religion.
    _____ c. The children got poor grades in their regular school.
    _____ d. The regular school teachers neglected the children.

2. The purpose of the cruise mentioned in the passage was to _____

    _____ a. have fun.
    _____ b. test the author's sailing ability.
    _____ c. reward the author for completing summer school.
    _____ d. get to the island.

3. Why did the author have to plot the course of her cruise?

    _____ a. She had to demonstrate her ability to do so.
    _____ b. She was afraid of getting lost.
    _____ c. The coast was dangerous.
    _____ d. The tides were strong.

*For an introduction to reading for full understanding, see Appendix G.
†From Sylvia Wright, Introduction to *Islandia*, by Austin Tappan Wright (New York: Rinehart and Co., 1959), pp. vii–viii.

4. How long did the author's cruise last?

_____ a. all summer          _✓_ c. overnight
_____ b. a week              _____ d. one day, morning till night

5. Apparently a knockabout is _____

_____ a. an island.          _✓_ c. a boat.
_____ b. a cruise.           _____ d. a seaman's knot.

---

**Paragraph 2**

1     The cicada exemplifies an insect species which uses a
2  combinatorial communication system. In their life cycle,
3  communication is very important, for only through the exchange of
4  sounds do cicadas know where to meet and when to mate. Three
5  different calls are employed for this purpose. Because of their limited
6  sound producing mechanisms, cicadas can make only ticks and buzzes.
7  The only way they can distinguish between congregation and courtship
8  calls is by varying the rate with which they make ticks and buzzes. The
9  congregation call consists of 12 to 40 ticks, delivered rapidly, followed
10  by a two-second buzz. It is given by males but attracts cicadas of both
11  sexes. Once they are all together, the males use courtship calls. The
12  preliminary call, a prolonged, slow ticking, is given when the male
13  notices a female near him. The advanced call, a prolonged series of
14  short buzzes at the same slow rate, is given when a female is almost
15  within grasp. The preliminary call almost invariably occurs before the
16  advanced call, although the latter is given without the preliminary call
17  occurring first if a female is suddenly discovered very near by. During
18  typical courtship, though, the two calls together result in ticking
19  followed by a buzzing—the same pattern which comprises the
20  congregation call but delivered at a slower rate. In this way, cicadas
21  show efficient use of their minimal sound producing ability, organizing
22  two sounds delivered at a high rate as one call and the same sounds
23  delivered at a slow rate as two more calls.*

---

1. The cicada congregation call _____

_____ a. attracts only males.          _____ c. is given only by males.
_____ b. is given by both sexes.       _____ d. attracts only females.

2. During typical courtship, when a male first notices a female near him, he gives _____

_____ a. the two courtship calls together.   _____ c. 12 to 40 rapid ticks.
_____ b. a series of slow ticks.             _____ d. a two-second buzz.

---

*From David McNeill, *The Acquisition of Language* (New York: Harper and Row, 1970), pp. 48–49.

3. How does the congregation call differ from the two courtship calls together?

_____ a. It is delivered at a slower rate.     _____ c. The ticks precede the buzzes.
_____ b. It is delivered at a faster rate.     _____ d. The buzzes precede the ticks.

4. According to this passage, why is communication so important for cicadas?

_____ a. It helps them defend themselves against other insect species.
_____ b. It warns them of approaching danger.
_____ c. It separates the males from the females.
_____ d. It is necessary for the continuation of the species.

**Paragraph 3**

1    Robert Spring, a 19th century forger, was so good at his profession
2  that he was able to make his living for 15 years by selling false
3  signatures of famous Americans. Spring was born in England in 1813
4  and arrived in Philadelphia in 1858 to open a bookstore. At first he
5  prospered by selling his small but genuine collection of early U.S.
6  autographs. Discovering his ability at copying handwriting, he began
7  imitating signatures of George Washington and Ben Franklin and
8  writing them on the title pages of old books. To lessen the chance of
9  detection, he sent his forgeries to England and Canada for sale and
10  circulation.
11    Forgers have a hard time selling their products. A forger can't
12  approach a respectable buyer but must deal with people who don't
13  have much knowledge in the field. Forgers have many ways to make
14  their work look real. For example, they buy old books to use the aged
15  paper of the title page, and they can treat paper and ink with
16  chemicals.
17    In Spring's time, right after the Civil War, Britain was still fond of
18  the Southern states, so Spring invented a respectable maiden lady
19  known as Miss Fanny Jackson, the only daughter of General
20  "Stonewall" Jackson. For several years Miss Fanny's financial
21  problems forced her to sell a great number of letters and manuscripts
22  belonging to her famous father. Spring had to work very hard to satisfy
23  the demand. All this activity did not prevent Spring from dying in
24  poverty, leaving sharp-eyed experts the difficult task of separating his
25  forgeries from the originals.*

1. Why did Spring sell his false autographs in England and Canada?

_____ a. There was a greater demand there than in America.
_____ b. There was less chance of being detected there.
_____ c. Britain was Spring's birthplace.
_____ d. The prices were higher in England and Canada.

*From the *Michigan Daily,* September 20, 1967.

2. After the Civil War, there was a great demand in Britain for _____

_____ a. Southern money.

_____ b. signatures of George Washington and Ben Franklin.

_____ c. Southern manuscripts and letters.

_____ d. Civil War battle plans.

3. Robert Spring spent 15 years _____

_____ a. running a bookstore in Philadelphia.

_____ b. corresponding with Miss Fanny Jackson.

_____ c. as a forger.

_____ d. as a respectable dealer.

4. According to the passage, forgeries are usually sold to _____

_____ a. sharp-eyed experts.

_____ b. persons who aren't experts.

_____ c. book dealers.

_____ d. owners of old books.

5. Who was Miss Fanny Jackson?

_____ a. the only daughter of General "Stonewall" Jackson

_____ b. a little-known girl who sold her father's papers to Robert Spring

_____ c. Robert Spring's daughter

_____ d. an imaginary person created by Spring

---

**Paragraph 4**

1     In science the meaning of the word "explain" suffers with
2 civilization's every step in search of reality. Science cannot really
3 explain electricity, magnetism, and gravitation; their effects can be
4 measured and predicted, but of their nature no more is known to the
5 modern scientist than to Thales who first speculated on the
6 electrification of amber. Most contemporary physicists reject the notion
7 that human beings can ever discover what these mysterious forces
8 "really" are. Electricity, Bertrand Russell says, "is not a thing, like St.
9 Paul's Cathedral; it is a way in which things behave. When we have
10 told how things behave when they are electrified, and under what
11 circumstances they are electrified, we have told all there is to tell."
12 Until recently scientists would have disapproved of such an idea.
13 Aristotle, for example, whose natural science dominated Western
14 thought for two thousand years, believed that human beings could
15 arrive at an understanding of reality by reasoning from self-evident
16 principles. He felt, for example, that it is a self-evident principle that
17 everything in the universe has its proper place, hence one can deduce
18 that objects fall to the ground because that's where they belong, and
19 smoke goes up because that's where it belongs. The goal of Aristotelian
20 science was to explain *why* things happen. Modern science was born
21 when Galileo began trying to explain *how* things happen and thus
22 originated the method of controlled experiment which now forms the
23 basis of scientific investigation.

1. The aim of controlled scientific experiments is _____

    _____ a. to explain why things happen.
    _____ b. to explain how things happen.
    _____ c. to describe self-evident principles.
    _____ d. to support Aristotelian science.

2. What principles most influenced scientific thought for two thousand years?

    _____ a. the speculations of Thales
    _____ b. the forces of electricity, magnetism, and gravity
    _____ c. Aristotle's natural science
    _____ d. Galileo's discoveries

3. Bertrand Russell's notion about electricity is _____

    _____ a. disapproved of by most modern scientists.
    _____ b. in agreement with Aristotle's theory of self-evident principles.
    _____ c. in agreement with scientific investigation directed toward "how" things happen.
    _____ d. in agreement with scientific investigation directed toward "why" things happen.

4. The passage says that until recently scientists disagreed with the idea _____

    _____ a. that there are mysterious forces in the universe.
    _____ b. that man cannot discover what forces "really" are.
    _____ c. that there are self-evident principles.
    _____ d. that we can discover why things behave as they do.

---

**Paragraph 5**

1    Dice, the plural of die, are small cubes used in games. They are
2  usually made of ivory, bone, wood, bakelite, or similar materials. The
3  six sides are numbered by dots from 1 to 6, so placed that the sum of
4  the dots on a side and the opposite side equals 7.
5    A simple form of play with dice is for each player to throw, or
6  shoot, for the highest sum. However, the most popular dice game in
7  the United States is called craps. It is played with 2 dice and the
8  underlying principle of the game is the fact that the most probable
9  throw is a 7. On the first throw, if a player shoots a 7 or 11 (called a
10  natural), he wins and begins again, but if he shoots 2, 3, or 12 (called
11  craps) on the first throw, he loses. If on the first throw he shoots 4, 5,
12  6, 8, 9, or 10, that number becomes his point. He continues to throw
13  until he shoots that number again (makes his point), in which case he
14  wins and begins again. However, if he shoots a 7 before he makes his
15  point, he loses and relinquishes the dice to the next player. Usually all
16  others in the game bet against the thrower, and in gambling halls bets
17  are made against the house.*

---

*From *Columbia Encyclopedia*, 2d ed. (New York: Columbia University Press, 1950).

1. In craps, a throw of 11 _____

     _____ a. always wins.
     _____ b. sometimes loses.
     _____ c. sometimes wins.
     _____ d. becomes the point.

2. If one side of a die has three dots on it, the opposite side has _____

     _____ a. 6.
     _____ b. 4.
     _____ c. 3.
     _____ d. 7.

3. To shoot the dice means to _____

     _____ a. throw them.
     _____ b. lose.
     _____ c. make a natural.
     _____ d. make one's point.

4. In a game of craps, if a player throws a 5 and then a 3, he _____

     _____ a. wins.
     _____ b. loses.
     _____ c. shoots again.
     _____ d. makes his point.

5. In a game of craps, if a player throws a 6, 3, 4, 4, 6, 11, in that order, he has _____

     _____ a. won twice.
     _____ b. made his point twice.
     _____ c. made two naturals.
     _____ d. shot craps.

6. In a game of craps, if the player throws a 12 on his first throw, _____

     _____ a. he has the highest sum, so he wins.
     _____ b. that number is his point.
     _____ c. he has shot craps.
     _____ d. he has made a natural.

7. What number is most probable on a throw of the dice?

     _____ a. 7 and 11 have equal probabilities
     _____ b. 7
     _____ c. 11
     _____ d. craps

## Discourse Focus

## Prediction

This exercise is similar to the one found in Unit 1. It is designed to give you practice in consciously developing and confirming expectations.

Below is part of an article about the family.* Read the article, stopping to respond to the questions that appear at several points throughout. Remember, you cannot always predict precisely what an author will do, but you can use knowledge of the text and your general knowledge to make good guesses. Work with your classmates on these items, defending your predictions with parts of the text. Do not worry about unfamiliar vocabulary.

# The Changing Family

by Maris Vinovskis

1. Based on the title, what aspect of the family do you think this article will be about? List several possibilities.

_____

_____

_____

Now read the opening paragraph to see what the focus of the article will be.

There is widespread fear among policymakers and the public today that the family is falling apart. Much of that worry stems from a basic misunderstanding of the nature of the family in the past and a lack of appreciation for its strength in response to broad social and economic changes. The general view of the family is that it has been a stable and relatively unchanging institution through history and is only now undergoing changes; in fact, change has always been characteristic of it.

**The Family and Household in the Past**

2. This article seems to be about the changing nature of the family throughout history. Is this what you expected?

3. The introduction is not very specific, so you can only guess what changing aspects of the family will be mentioned in the next section. Using information from the introduction and your general knowledge, check (✔) those topics from the list on page 111 that you think will be mentioned:

---

*From *LSA* 10, no. 3 (Spring 1987).

_____ a. family size
_____ b. relations within the family
_____ c. the definition of a family
_____ d. the role of the family in society
_____ e. different family customs

_____ f. the family throughout the world
_____ g. the economic role of the family
_____ h. sex differences in family roles
_____ i. the role of children
_____ j. sexual relations

Now read the next section, noting which of your predictions is confirmed.

In the last twenty years, historians have been re-examining the nature of the family and have concluded that we must revise our notions of the family as an institution, as well as our assumptions about how children were perceived and treated in past centuries. A survey of diverse studies of the family in the West, particularly in seventeenth- eighteenth- and nineteenth-century England and America shows something of the changing role of the family in society and the evolution of our ideas of parenting and child development. (Although many definitions of _family_ are available, in this article I will use it to refer to kin living under one roof.)

4. Which aspects of the family listed above were mentioned in this section? _____

_____

_____

5. Which other ones do you predict will be mentioned further on in the article? _____

_____

6. What aspects of the text and your general knowledge help you to create this prediction?

_____

_____

7. Below is the topic sentence of the next paragraph. What kind of supporting data do you expect to find in the rest of the paragraph? How do you think the paragraph will continue?

_____

_____

_____

Although we have tended to believe that in the past children grew up in "extended households" including grandparents, parents, and children, recent historical research has cast considerable doubt on the idea that as countries became increasingly urban and industrial, the Western family evolved from extended to nuclear [i.e., parents and children only].

The rest of the paragraph is reprinted below. Read on to see if your expectations are confirmed.

Historians have found evidence that households in pre-industrial Western Europe were already nuclear and could not have been greatly transformed by economic changes. Rather than finding definite declines in household size, we find surprisingly small variations, which turn out to be a result of the presence or absence of servants, boarders, and lodgers, rather than relatives. In revising our nostalgic picture of children growing up in large families, Peter Laslett, one of the foremost analysts of the pre-industrial family, contends that most households in the past were actually quite small (mean household size was about 4.75). Of course, patterns may have varied somewhat from one area to another, but it seems unlikely that in the past few centuries many families in England or America had grandparents living with them.

8. Were your predictions confirmed?

9. Here is the list of topics you saw in question 3. Now *skim* the rest of the article; check (✓) the topics that the author actually discusses

\_\_\_\_\_ a. family size
\_\_\_\_\_ b. relations within the family
\_\_\_\_\_ c. the definition of a family
\_\_\_\_\_ d. the role of the family in society
\_\_\_\_\_ e. different family customs

\_\_\_\_\_ f. the family throughout the world
\_\_\_\_\_ g. the economic role of the family
\_\_\_\_\_ h. sex differences in family roles
\_\_\_\_\_ i. the role of children
\_\_\_\_\_ j. sexual relations

However, as Philip Aries has argued in his well-known *Centuries of Childhood*, the medieval family was nevertheless quite different from its modern counterpart, largely because the boundary between the household and the larger society was less rigidly drawn, and the roles of parents, servants, or neighbors in the socialization of children were more blurred. Relationships within the nuclear family were not much closer, it seems, than those with neighbors, relatives, or other friends.

Another difference, according to Lawrence Stone, was that within property-owning classes, as in sixteenth-century England, for example, marriage was a collective decision, involving not only the immediate family, but also other kin. Protection of long-term interests of lineage and consideration for the needs of the larger kinship group were more important than individual desires for happiness or romantic love. In addition, because the strong sense of individual or family privacy had not yet developed, access to the household by local neighbors was relatively easy. But this type of family gave way in the late sixteenth century to a "restricted patriarchical nuclear family," which predominated from 1580 to 1640, when concern for lineage and loyalty to the local community declined, and allegiances to the State and Church and to kin within the household increased. The authority of the father, as head of the household, was enhanced and bolstered by State and Church support. This drive toward parental dominance over children was particularly characteristic of the Puritans and was not limited to the child's early years; upper-class parents, especially, sought to extend their control to their children's choices of both career and spouse.

By the mid-seventeenth century, the family was increasingly organized around the principle of personal autonomy and was bound together by strong ties of love and affection. The separation, both physical and emotional, between members of a nuclear family and their servants or boarders widened, as did the distance between the household and the rest of society. Physical privacy became more important, and it became more acceptable for individual family members to pursue their own happiness.

Throughout most of the pre-industrial period, the household was the central productive unit of society. Children either were trained for their future occupations in their own homes or were employed in someone else's household. As the economic functions of the household moved to the shop or factory in the late-eighteenth and nineteenth centuries, the household, no longer an economic focal point or an undifferentiated part of neighborhood activities, increasingly became a haven or escape from the outside world. Children growing up in fifteenth-century England were expected and encouraged to interact closely with many adults besides their parents, but by the eighteenth and nineteenth centuries, they had come to rely more and more upon each other and their parents for their emotional needs.

The families that migrated to the New World, especially the Puritans, brought with them the ideal of a close and loving family, and although the economic functions of the American household were altered in the nineteenth century, the overall change was less dramatic than it had been in Western Europe. Thus, although the relationship between parents and children has not remained constant in America during the past three hundred years, the extent of the changes is probably less than it was in Western Europe.

### Changing perceptions and treatment of children

We usually assume that an innate characteristic of human beings is the close and immediate attachment between the newborn child and its parents, especially its mother. Because abandonment or abuse of children seems to defy such beliefs, we are baffled by reports of widespread parental abuse of children. A look at the past may provide a different perspective on the present.

According to some scholars, maternal indifference to infants may have been typical of the Middle Ages. Aries says there is evidence that in the sixteenth and seventeenth centuries parents showed little affection for their children, and Edward Shorter argues that this indifference was probably typical among the ordinary people of Western Europe, even in the eighteenth and nineteenth centuries. The death of young children seems to have been accepted casually, and although overt infanticide was frowned upon, allowing children to die was sometimes encouraged, or at least tolerated. For example, in Western Europe it was common for mothers to leave infants at foundling hospitals or with rural wet nurses, both

## Efforts to prevent cruelty to animals preceded those to accomplish the same ends for children by nearly a half century.

of which resulted in very high mortality rates. Whether these practices were typically the result of economic desperation, the difficulty of raising an out-of-wedlock child, or lack of attachment to an infant is not clear, but the fact that many well-to-do married women casually chose to give their infants to wet nurses, despite the higher mortality risks, suggests that the reasons were not always economic difficulty or fear of social stigma.

While the practice of overt infanticide and child abandonment may have been relatively widespread in parts of Western Europe, it does not seem to have been prevalent in either England or America. Indeed, authorities in both those countries in the sixteenth and seventeenth centuries prosecuted infanticide cases more vigorously than other forms of murder, and the practice of leaving infants with wet nurses went out of fashion in England by the end of the eighteenth century.

By the eighteenth century in Western Europe, parents were expressing more interest in their children and more affection for them, and by the nineteenth century, observers were beginning to criticize parents for being too child-centered. Nevertheless, parents were still not prevented from abusing their own children, as long as it did not result in death. Because the parent-child relationship was regarded as sacred and beyond State intervention, it was not until the late nineteenth century that reformers in England were able to persuade lawmakers to pass legislation to protect children from abusive parents. Ironically, efforts to prevent cruelty to animals preceded those to accomplish the same ends for children by nearly a half century.

Some of the earliest studies of colonial America suggested that at that time childhood was not viewed as a distinct stage: children, these historians said, were expected to think and behave pretty much as adults from an early age. Although a few recent scholars of the colonial American family have supported this view, others have questioned it, pointing out that New England Puritans were well aware that children had different abilities and temperaments and believed that childrearing should be molded to those individual differences.

While young children in colonial America probably were not seen as miniature adults, they *were* thought to be more capable intellectually at a young age than their counterparts generally are today. The Puritans believed that because it was essential for salvation, children should be taught to read the Bible as soon as possible. Indeed, the notion that children could and should learn to read as soon as they could talk was so commonly accepted by educators that they did not think it necessary to justify it in their writings. The infant school movement of the late 1820s reinforced this assumption until it was challenged by Amariah Brigham, a prominent physician who claimed that early intellectual training seriously and permanently weakened growing minds and could lead to insanity later in life.

When the kindergarten movement became popular in the United States, in the 1860s and 70s, intellectual activities such as reading were deliberately avoided. Such examples are a clear indication of how the socialization of children is dependent on our perceptions of children, and one might even speculate that as we become in-

---

Given the recent concern about the "epidemic" of adolescent pregnancies, we might expect more attention to be given to the attitudes of our forebears towards teenage parents.

---

creasingly willing to incorporate the latest scientific and medical findings into our care of the young, shifts in childrearing practices will increase in frequency.

## Youth

Not only young children were perceived and treated differently in the past. Although there is little agreement among scholars either about when "adolescence" came to be viewed as a distinct stage or about the importance of education in the lives of nineteenth-century youths, many family historians have offered their perspectives on these topics. Surprisingly little, however, has been done to explore changes in teenage sexuality, pregnancy, and childbearing. Given the recent concern about the "epidemic" of adolescent pregnancies, we might expect more attention to be given to the attitudes of our forebears towards teenage parents.

Because of the stringent seventeenth-century prohibitions against premarital sexual relations and the low percentage of early teenage marriages, teenage pregnancy seems not to have been a problem in colonial New England. Early Americans were more concerned about pre-marital sexual relations, in general, than about whether teenage or adult women were involved. Not until the late nineteenth and early twentieth centuries did society clearly differentiate between teenage and adult sexual behavior, with a more negative attitude towards the former.

Only in the post-World War II period has the issue of teenage pregnancy and childbearing become a major public concern. But

although the rates of teenage pregnancy and childbearing peaked in the late 1950s, the greatest attention to this phenomenon has come during the late 1970s and early 80s. The controversy over abortion, the great increase in out-of-wedlock births to adolescents, and the growing concern about the long-term disadvantages of early childbearing to the young mother and her child have made this issue more important today than thirty years ago.

## Parent-child relations

Historically, the primary responsibility for the rearing of young children belonged almost exclusively to the parents, especially the father. It was not until the late nineteenth and early twentieth centuries that the State was willing to remove a young child from direct supervision of negligent or abusive parents. Even so, in order to reduce welfare costs to the rest of the community, a destitute family in early America, incapable of supporting its own members, was sometimes broken up and the children placed in other households.

During the eighteenth and nineteenth centuries the mother's role in the upbringing of children was enhanced: women became the primary providers of care and affection; and as men's church membership declined, women also became responsible for the catechizing and educating of young children, even though they often were less literate than men. While childrearing manuals continued to acknowledge the importance of the father, they also recognized that the mother had become the major figure in the care of the young.

Throughout much of Western history, as long as children remained in the home, parents exercised considerable control over them, even to the extent of arranging their marriages and influencing their career choices. Children were expected to be obedient and to contribute to the well-being of the family. And, perhaps more in Western Europe than in America, children were often expected to turn over almost all of their earnings directly to the parents — sometimes even after they had left home.

By the late eighteenth or early nineteenth century some of this control had eroded, and the rights of children as individuals were increasingly recognized and acknowledged. Interestingly, the development of children's rights has proceeded so rapidly and so far that we may now be in the midst of a backlash, as efforts are being made to re-establish parental responsibility in areas such as the reproductive behavior of minor children.

Clearly there have been major changes in the way our society treats children; but it would be very difficult for many of us to agree on the costs and benefits of these trends — whether from the viewpoint of the child, the parents, or society. While many applaud the increasing individualism and freedom of children within the family, others lament the loss of family responsibility and discipline. A historical analysis of parents and children cannot settle such disputes, but it can provide us with a better appreciation of the flexibility and resilience of the family as an institution for raising the young.

This essay was adapted from a longer version, "Historical Perspectives on the Development of the Family and Parent-Child Interactions," in *Parenting Across the Life Span: Biosocial Dimensions*, Jane B. Lancaster, Jeanne Altmann, Alice S. Rossi, and Lonie Sherrod, eds. (New York: Aldine 1987).

# Reading Selection 1

## Textbook

***Before You Begin*** Following is an article from the field of anthropology. What is the task of an anthropologist?

"The Sacred 'Rac' " is adapted from an introductory social anthropology textbook written for students in the United States.* The article describes the customs of a tribe of people studied by the Indian anthropologist Chandra Thapar. Read the passage, and answer the questions that follow. You may want to do the Vocabulary from Context exercise on page 118 before you begin.

### The Sacred "Rac"

*Patricia Hughes*

1    An Indian anthropologist, Chandra Thapar, made a study of foreign cultures which had customs similar to those of his native land. One culture in particular fascinated him because it reveres one animal as sacred, much as the people in India revere the cow. The things he discovered might interest you since you will be studying India as part of this course.

2    The tribe Dr. Thapar studied is called the Asu and is found on the American continent north of the Tarahumara of Mexico. Though it seems to be a highly developed society of its type, it has an overwhelming preoccupation with the care and feeding of the rac—an animal much like a bull in size, strength and temperament. In the Asu tribe, it is almost a social obligation to own at least one if not more racs. People not possessing at least one are held in low esteem by the community because they are too poor to maintain one of these beasts properly. Some members of the tribe, to display their wealth and social prestige, even own herds of racs.

3    Unfortunately the rac breed is not very healthy and usually does not live more than five to seven years. Each family invests large sums of money each year to keep its rac healthy and shod, for it has a tendency to throw its shoes often. There are rac specialists in each

*"The Sacred 'Rac' " by Patricia Hughes, in *Focusing on Global Poverty and Development* by Jayne C. Millar (Washington, D.C.: Overseas Development Council, 1974), pp. 357–58.

community, perhaps more than one if the community is particularly wealthy. These specialists, however, due to the long period of ritual training they must undergo and to the difficulty of obtaining the right selection of charms to treat the rac, demand costly offerings whenever a family must treat an ailing rac.

4    At the age of sixteen in many Asù communities, many youths undergo a puberty rite in which the rac figures prominently. Youths must petition a high priest in a grand temple. They are then initiated into the ceremonies that surround the care of the rac and are permitted to keep a rac.

5    Although the rac may be used as a beast of burden, it has many habits which would be considered by other cultures as detrimental to the life of the society. In the first place the rac breed is increasing at a very rapid rate and the Asu tribe has given no thought to curbing the rac population. As a consequence the Asu must build more and more paths for the rac to travel on since its delicate health and its love of racing other racs at high speeds necessitates that special areas be set aside for its use. The cost of smoothing the earth is too costly for any one individual to undertake; so it has become a community project and each member of the tribe must pay an annual tax to build new paths and maintain the old. There are so many paths needed that some people move their homes because the rac paths must be as straight as possible to keep the animal from injuring itself. Dr. Thapar also noted that unlike the cow, which many people in his country hold sacred, the excrement of the rac cannot be used as either fuel or fertilizer. On the contrary, its excrement is exceptionally foul and totally useless. Worst of all, the rac is prone to rampages in which it runs down anything in its path, much like stampeding cattle. Estimates are that the rac kills thousands of the Asu in a year.

6    Despite the high cost of its upkeep, the damage it does to the land, and its habit of destructive rampages, the Asu still regard it as being essential to the survival of their culture.

## Comprehension

Answer the following questions. Your teacher may want you to answer the questions orally, in writing, or by underlining appropriate parts of the text. True/False items are indicated by a T / F preceding a statement.

1. What society reveres the rac? _____

_____

2. Where is the tribe located? _____

3. T / F   People who don't own racs are not respected in the Asu community.

4. Why does it cost so much to have a rac specialist treat an ailing rac? _____

_____

5. T / F   An Asu must pass through a special ceremony before being permitted to keep a rac.

6. How is the rac helpful to the Asu? _____

_____

7. What effects does the size of the rac population have on the life of the Asu? _____

_____

8. T / F   Rac excrement can be used as fuel or as fertilizer.

9. According to the author, what is the worst characteristic of the rac? _____

10. T / F   The Asu feel that their culture cannot survive without the rac.

11. What is *rac* spelled backward? _____

## Drawing Inferences

What is the author's attitude toward the rac? Why does she choose to present her opinion using this story about the Asu society?

## Discussion/Composition

1. Is the rac essential to the survival of the Asu society? Of your society? What effects is the rac having on your society? Do people in your society revere the rac as much as the Asu do?

2. Describe some aspect of your culture from the point of view of an anthropologist.

## *Vocabulary from Context*

Use the context provided and your knowledge of stems and affixes to determine the meanings of the italicized words. Write a definition, synonym, or description of the italicized vocabulary items in the space provided.

1. _____     Alex has had trouble studying for the final examination because he has been too *preoccupied* with happy thoughts of his summer vacation.

2. _____     Alice's dog is gentle and friendly; unfortunately, my dog doesn't have such a pleasant *temperament*.

3. _____     Peter wants to be a doctor because he feels it is a very *prestigious* occupation, and he has always wanted to hold a high position in society.

4. _____     Do you know a doctor who has experience *treating* children?

5. _____     Instead of complaining to me that you're *ailing,* you should see a doctor to find out what's wrong with you.

6. _____     Many people believe that only primitive societies have a special ceremony to celebrate the time when a child becomes an adult; however, anthropologists say that advanced cultures also have *puberty rites*.

7. _____     The criminal was to be killed at dawn; but he *petitioned* the king to save him and his request was granted.

8. _____     Doctors believe that smoking cigarettes is *detrimental* to your
9. _____     health. They also *regard* drinking as harmful.

# Reading Selection 2
# Essay

An essay is a literary composition on a single subject that usually presents the author's personal opinion. The following essay, written by John V. Lindsay when he was mayor of New York City, is taken from his book, *The City.**

**Before You Begin**    1. What is your attitude toward cities? Do you enjoy them, or do you find them unpleasant?

2. Do you think there is a general attitude toward cities held by most people in your country or community?

Read the passage, then do the exercises that follow. You may want to do Vocabulary from Context exercise 1 on page 124 before you begin reading.

## *The City*

*John V. Lindsay*

1    In one sense, we can trace all the problems of the American city back to a single starting point: we Americans don't like our cities very much.

2    That is, on the face of it, absurd. After all, more than three-fourths of us now live in cities, and more are flocking to them every year. We are told that the problems of our cities are receiving more attention in Washington, and scholarship has discovered a whole new field in urban studies.

3    Nonetheless, it is historically true: in the American psychology, the city has been a basically suspect institution, filled with the corruption of Europe, totally lacking that sense of spaciousness and innocence of the frontier and the rural landscape.

4    I don't pretend to be a scholar on the history of the city in American life. But my thirteen years in public office, first as an officer of the U.S. Department of Justice, then as Congressman, and now as Mayor of the biggest city in America, have taught me all too well the fact that a strong anti-urban attitude runs consistently through the mainstream of American thinking. Much of the drive behind the settlement of America was in reaction to the conditions in European industrial centers—and much of the theory supporting the basis of freedom in America was linked directly to the availability of land and the perfectibility of man outside the corrupt influences of the city.

5    What has this to do with the predicament of the modern city? I think it has much to do with it. For the fact is that the United States,

*Adapted from *The City* by John V. Lindsay (New York: W. W. Norton and Company, 1969).

particularly the federal government, which has historically established our national priorities, has simply never thought that the American city was "worthy" of improvement—at least not to the extent of expending any basic resources on it.

6      Antipathy to the city predates the American experience. When industrialization drove the European working man into the major cities of the continent, books and pamphlets appeared attacking the city as a source of crime, corruption, filth, disease, vice, licentiousness, subversion, and high prices. The theme of some of the earliest English novels—*Moll Flanders* for example—is that of the innocent country youth coming to the big city and being subjected to all forms of horror until justice—and a return to the pastoral life—follow.

7      The proper opinion of Europe seemed to support the Frenchman who wrote: "In the country, a man's mind is free and easy . . . ; but in the city, the persons of friends and acquaintances, one's own and other people's business, foolish quarrels, ceremonies, visits, impertinent discourses, and a thousand other fopperies and diversions steal away the greatest part of our time and leave no leisure for better and necessary employment. Great towns are but a larger sort of prison to the soul, like cages to birds or pounds to beasts."

8      This was not, of course, the only opinion on city life. Others maintained that the city was "the fireplace of civilization, whence light and heat radiated out into the cold dark world." And William Penn planned Philadelphia as the "holy city," carefully laid out so that each house would have the appearance of a country cottage to avoid the density and overcrowding that so characterized European cities.

9      Without question, however, the first major thinker to express a clear antipathy to the urban way of life was Thomas Jefferson. For Jefferson, the political despotism of Europe and the economic despotism of great concentrations of wealth, on the one hand, and poverty on the other, were symbolized by the cities of London and Paris, which he visited frequently during his years as a diplomatic representative of the new nation. In the new world, with its opportunities for widespread landholding, there was the chance for a flowering of authentic freedom, with each citizen, freed from economic dependence, both able and eager to participate in charting the course of his own future. America, in a real sense, was an escape from all the injustice that had flourished in Europe—injustice that was characterized by the big city.

10     This Jeffersonian theme was to remain an integral part of the American tradition. Throughout the nineteenth century, as the explorations of America pushed farther outward, the new settlers sounded most like each other in their common celebration of freedom from city chains.

11     The point is that all this opinion goes beyond ill feelings; it suggests a strong national sense that encouragement and development of the city was to be in no sense a national priority—that our manifest destiny* lay in the untouched lands to the west, in constant movement

---

*The nineteenth-century doctrine that the United States had the right and duty to expand throughout the North American continent

westward, and in maximum dispersion of land to as many people as possible.

12      Thus, the Northwest Ordinance of 1787—perhaps the first important declaration of national policy—explicitly encouraged migration into the Northwest Territory and provided grants of land and free public lands for schools. New York City, by contrast, did not begin a public-education system until 1842—and received, of course, no federal help at all. Similarly, the Homestead Act of 1862* was based on an assumption—supported by generations of American theory—that in the West could be found genuine opportunity and that the eastern-seaboard cities of the United States were simply hopeless collections of vice and deprivation.

13      This belief accelerated after the Civil War, for a variety of reasons. For one thing, the first waves of immigration were being felt around the country as immigrants arrived in urban areas. The poverty of the immigrants, largely from Ireland and Northern Europe, caused many people in rural America to equate poverty with personal inferiority—a point of view that has not yet disappeared from our national thinking. Attacks on the un-American and criminal tendencies of the Irish, the Slavs, and every other ethnic group that arrived on America's shore were a steady part of national thinking, as were persistent efforts to bar any further migration of "undesirables" to our country.

14      With the coming of rapid industrialization, all the results of investigations into city poverty and despair that we think of as recent findings were being reported—and each report served to confirm the beliefs of the Founding Fathers that the city was no place for a respectable American.

15      Is all this relevant only to past attitudes and past legislative history? I don't think so. The fact is that until today, this same basic belief—that our cities ought to be left to fend for themselves—is still a powerful element in our national tradition.

16      Consider more modern history. The most important housing act in the last twenty-five years was not the law that provided for public housing; it was the law that permitted the FHA† to grant subsidized low-interest mortgages to Americans who want to purchase homes. More than anything else, this has made the suburban dream a reality. It has brought the vision of grass and trees and a place for the kids to play within the reach of millions of working Americans, and the consequences be damned. The impact of such legislation on the cities was not even considered—nor was the concept of making subsidized money available for neighborhood renovation in the city so that it might compete with the suburbs. Instead, in little more than a decade 800,000 middle income New Yorkers fled the city for the suburbs and were replaced by largely unskilled workers who in many instances represented a further cost rather than an economic asset.

17      And it was not a hundred years ago but two years ago that a suggested law giving a small amount of federal money for rat control was literally laughed off the floor of the House of Representatives amid

*A law that gave a 160-acre piece of land to anyone who lived on it for five years
†Federal Housing Administration

much joking about discrimination against country rats in favor of city rats.

18      What happened, I think, was not the direct result of a "the city is evil and therefore we will not help it" concept. It was more indirect, more subtle, the result of the kind of thinking that enabled us to spend billions of dollars in subsidies to preserve the family farm while doing nothing about an effective program for jobs in the city; to create government agencies concerned with the interests of agriculture, veterans, small business, labor, commerce, and the American Indian but to create no Department of Urban Development until 1965; to so restrict money that meaningful federal aid is still not possible.

19      In other words, the world of urban America as a dark and desolate place undeserving of support or help has become fixed in the American consciousness. And we are paying for that attitude in our cities today.

## Comprehension

### Exercise 1

*Check (✓) those statements that the author believes accurately reflect Americans' attitudes toward their cities.*

1. _____ Americans don't like their cities very much.

2. _____ Americans have not thought their cities worthy of receiving financial support from the federal government.

3. _____ Americans were suspicious of cities because cities reminded them of the corruption of Europe.

4. _____ Most Americans believe that cities are centers of civilization.

5. _____ Americans believed that the federal government should provide support for establishing public school systems in urban areas.

6. _____ The United States government thought it was more important to develop the American West than to develop the cities.

7. _____ Rural Americans have been sympathetic to the problems of newly arrived immigrants in the city.

8. _____ No one considered the effect on cities of laws to help people build homes in the suburbs.

9. _____ The American attitude toward cities is changing.

10. _____ The American attitude toward cities has been harmful to the United States.

## Exercise 2

*As you read you should be able to differentiate between facts and opinions. Facts are statements of information that can be shown to be true. Opinions are beliefs, conclusions, or judgments not confirmed by positive knowledge or proof.*

*In this essay some of the opinions presented are those of the author; some are those of other people. Read the following sentences carefully. Indicate if each statement is a fact (F) (it could be demonstrated to be true) or an opinion (O) (not everyone would agree with the statement; it probably could not be convincingly proved to be true or false). If the statement is an opinion, indicate whose opinion it is. The number in parentheses indicates the paragraph in which each idea may be found.*

---

**Examples**

F _____ New York City is the largest city in the United States. (4)

O  Founding Fathers _____ Good Americans should not live in cities. (14)

1. ____ _____ More than three-fourths of the American people now live in cities. (2)

2. ____ _____ There is a strong anti-urban attitude in America. (4)

3. ____ _____ When industrialization began, many Europeans went to work in cities. (6)

4. ____ _____ Cities are like prisons. (7)

5. ____ _____ Cities are centers of civilization. (8)

6. ____ _____ Although Thomas Jefferson often visited London and Paris, he did not like these cities. (9)

7. ____ _____ Because of the widespread opportunity to own land, America represented an escape from the injustices of Europe. (9)

8. ____ _____ The Northwest Ordinance gave free land to people. (12)

9. ____ _____ When New York City began its public school system, the federal government did not help. (12)

10. ____ _____ The cities on the east coast of the United States were corrupt. (12)

11. ____ _____ Many of the immigrants who came to America after the Civil War were poor. (13)

12. ____ _____ Poor immigrants are inferior to hard-working Americans. (13)

## Discussion/Composition

This article describes John Lindsay's opinion about cities. What is yours?

## Vocabulary from Context

### Exercise 1

*Use the context provided to determine the meanings of the italicized words. Write a definition, synonym, or description of each of the italicized vocabulary items in the space provided.*

1. _____    The American people have never trusted the city; it has always appeared in literature and history as a *suspect* institution.

2. _____    A high *priority* should be given to providing public transportation; money for highways is less important.

3. _____    It is *absurd* to spend more money on highways. The wise solution for overcrowded roads is public transportation.

4. _____    The government gave money to people to help buy homes outside of the cities. This system of *subsidized* housing caused many people to leave urban areas.

5. _____    Lack of public transportation in the suburbs has caused a terrible *predicament* for poor people who live there; they must either buy a car or depend on friends for transportation.

6. _____    Hotels and restaurants are an *integral* part of the city; without them, the city's tourist industry could not exist.

7. _____    When Governor Holmes was first elected, he was probably an honest man. However, since then, he has become as *corrupt* as all of the dishonest people around him. Now he is as bad as the rest of the state officials.

8. _____    Although Richard Weeks has accomplished many good things during his terms as mayor, the fact that he totally controls the city makes him a *despot,* and he should be forced to give up some of his power.

---

**Exercise 2**

*This exercise is designed to give you additional clues to determine the meaning of unfamiliar vocabulary items from context. In the paragraph indicated by the number in parentheses, find the word that best fits the meaning given. Your teacher may want to read these aloud as you quickly scan the paragraph to find the answer.*

1. (11) Which word means *distribution*?

2. (15) Which word means *provide for; take care of*?

3. (16) Which word means *improvement by repairing*?

---

**Exercise 3**

*This exercise should be done after you have finished reading "The City." The exercise is designed to determine how well you have been able to use context clues to guess the meaning of unfamiliar vocabulary in the essay. Give a definition, synonym, or description of each of the words below. The number in parentheses indicates the paragraph in which the word can be found. Your teacher may want you to do these orally or in writing.*

1. (1)   trace _____

2. (2)   flocking _____

3. (6)   antipathy _____

4. (6)   pastoral _____

5. (9)   charting _____

6. (13) waves _____

7. (13) ethnic _____

8. (13) bar _____

9. (16) fled _____

10. (18) subtle _____

## Reading Selections 3A–3B

# Family Narratives

The two selections that follow present humorous accounts of family life written retrospectively by adults. "Attack on the Family" describes a British family in Greece between the World Wars; "Cheaper by the Dozen" describes an unusual American family growing up in the first quarter of the twentieth century.

*Selection 3A*         **Family Narrative**

**Before You Begin**   1. What is it like to be the youngest child in a family?

2. Below is a picture of a scorpion. What would be the reaction of your family if a child were to bring one home as a pet?

The following selection is taken from Gerald Durrell's book *My Family and Other Animals,* written from the point of view of the youngest child.* The book is an account of the year, during Durrell's childhood, that his family spent on the Greek island of Corfu. As the title indicates, the book is not an ordinary autobiography. In this selection the author's habit of collecting strange and wonderful animal life throws the house into complete confusion.

Read the selection to get a general understanding of the story, then do the exercises that follow. You may want to do Vocabulary from Context exercise 1 on pages 130–31 before you begin reading.

### An Attack on the Family

*Gerald Durrell*

I grew very fond of the scorpions in the garden wall. I found them to be pleasant, unassuming creatures with, on the whole, the most charming habits. Provided you did nothing silly or clumsy (like putting your hand on one) the scorpions treated you with respect, their one desire being to get away and hide as quickly as possible. They must have found me rather a trial, for I was always ripping sections of the plaster away so that I could watch them, or capturing them and making them walk about in jam-jars so that I could see the way their feet moved. By means of my sudden and unexpected assaults on the wall I discovered quite a bit about the scorpions.

2     By crouching under the wall at night with a torch, I managed to catch some brief glimpses of the scorpions' wonderful courtship dances. I saw them standing, claws joined, their bodies raised to the skies, their tails lovingly intertwined; I saw them waltzing slowly in circles, claw in claw. But my view of these performances was all too

*Adapted from *My Family and Other Animals* by Gerald Durrell (New York: Viking, 1956).

short, for almost as soon as I switched on the torch the partners would
stop, pause for a moment, and then, seeing that I was not going to
extinguish the light, they would turn round and walk firmly away, claw
in claw, side by side. They were definitely beasts that believed in
keeping themselves *to* themselves. If I could have kept a colony in
captivity I would probably have been able to see the whole of the
courtship, but the family had forbidden scorpions in the house, despite
my arguments in favour of them.

3      Then one day I found a fat female scorpion in the wall, wearing
what at first glance appeared to be a pale brown fur coat. Closer
inspection proved that this strange garment was made up of a mass of
tiny babies clinging to the mother's back. I was enraptured by this
family, and I made up my mind to smuggle them into the house and up
to my bedroom so that I might keep them and watch them grow up.
With infinite care I manoeuvred the mother and family into a
matchbox, and then hurried to the villa. It was rather unfortunate that
just as I entered the door lunch should be served; however, I placed
the matchbox carefully on the mantelpiece in the drawing-room, so that
the scorpions could get plenty of air, and made my way to the dining-
room and joined the family for the meal. Dawdling over my food,
feeding Roger under the table and listening to the family arguing, I
completely forgot about my exciting new captures. At last Larry,
having finished, brought the cigarettes from the drawing-room, and
lying back in his chair he put one in his mouth and picked up the
matchbox he had brought. Unaware of my impending doom I watched
him interestedly as, still talking glibly, he opened the matchbox.

4      Now, I maintain to this day that the female scorpion meant no
harm. She was agitated and annoyed at being shut up in a matchbox for
so long, and so she seized the first opportunity to escape. She hoisted
herself out of the box with great rapidity, her babies clinging on
desperately, and scuttled on to the back of Larry's hand. There, not
quite certain what to do next, she paused, her sting curved up at the
ready. Larry, feeling the movement of her claws, glanced down to see
what it was, and from that moment things got increasingly confused.

5      He uttered a roar of fright that made Lugaretzia drop a plate and
brought Roger out from beneath the table, barking wildly. With a flick
of his hand he sent the unfortunate scorpion flying down the table, and
she landed midway between Margo and Leslie, scattering babies like
confetti as she thumped on the cloth. Thoroughly enraged at this
treatment, the creature sped towards Leslie, her sting quivering with
anger. Leslie leapt to his feet, overturning his chair, and flicked out
desperately with his napkin, sending the scorpion rolling across the
cloth towards Margo, who promptly let out a scream that any railway
engine would have been proud to produce. Mother, completely
bewildered by this sudden and rapid change from peace to chaos, put
on her glasses and peered down the table to see what was causing the
pandemonium, and at that moment Margo, in a vain attempt to stop the
scorpion's advance, hurled a glass of water at it. The shower missed
the animal completely, but successfully drenched Mother, who, not
being able to stand cold water, promptly lost her breath and sat gasping
at the end of the table, unable even to protest. The scorpion had now

6   gone to ground under Leslie's plate, while her babies swarmed wildly all over the table. Roger, mystified by the panic, but determined to do his share, ran round and round the room, barking hysterically.

"It's that bloody boy again . . ." bellowed Larry.

"Look out! Look out! They're coming!" screamed Margo.

"All we need is a book," roared Leslie; "don't panic, hit 'em with a book."

"What on earth's the *matter* with you all?" Mother kept asking, wiping her glasses.

"It's that bloody boy . . . he'll kill the lot of us . . . Look at the table . . . kneedeep in scorpions . . ."

"Quick . . . quick . . . do something . . . Look out, look out!"

"Stop screeching and get a book, for God's sake . . . You're worse than the dog . . . Shut *up,* Roger."

"By the Grace of God I wasn't bitten . . ."

"Look out . . . there's another one . . . Quick . . . quick . . ."

"Oh, shut up and get me a book or something . . ."

"But *how* did the scorpions get on the table, dear?"

"That bloody boy . . . Every matchbox in the house is a deathtrap . . ."

"Look out, it's coming towards me . . . Quick, quick, do something . . ."

"Hit it with your knife . . . *your knife* . . . Go on, hit it . . ."

7   Since no one had bothered to explain things to him, Roger was under the mistaken impression that the family were being attacked, and that it was his duty to defend them. As Lugaretzia was the only stranger in the room, he came to the logical conclusion that she must be the responsible party, so he bit her in the ankle. This did not help matters very much.

8   By the time a certain amount of order had been restored, all the baby scorpions had hidden themselves under various plates and bits of cutlery. Eventually, after impassioned pleas on my part, backed up by Mother, Leslie's suggestion that the whole lot be killed was defeated. While the family, still simmering with rage and fright, retired to the drawing-room, I spent half an hour collecting the babies, picking them up in a teaspoon, and returning them to their mother's back. Then I carried them outside on a saucer and, with the utmost reluctance, released them on the garden wall. Roger and I went and spent the afternoon on the hillside, for I felt it would be wise to allow the family to have a siesta before seeing them again.

## *Comprehension*

### Exercise 1

*Answer the following questions. Your teacher may want you to answer the questions orally, in writing, or by underlining appropriate parts of the text. True/False items are indicated by a T / F preceding a statement. In many cases you will have to use your own judgment because the answer is not specifically given in the passage.*

1.  T / F   Scorpions are not dangerous.

2.  T / F   The author likes scorpions.

3.  Why wasn't the author able to observe the whole courtship dance? _____

    _____

4.  T / F   The author knew that his family would not allow scorpions in the house.

5.  How did the mother scorpion carry her babies? _____

6.  T / F   The author caught the scorpion family in a jam-jar.

7.  When was the scorpion family discovered? _____

    _____

8.  Why did Margo throw water on Mother? _____

    _____

9.  T / F   The author tried to kill the scorpions with a book.

10. T / F   The author felt that the scorpions were attacking his family.

11. T / F   Mother supported the writer in his attempt to save the scorpions.

12. How were the scorpions removed from the house? _____

    _____

13. T / F   The author stayed outside for the rest of the day because he didn't want to see the
    family until everyone had rested.

---

**Exercise 2**

*To answer the following questions you will have to make decisions about the story based on
careful reading. Many questions do not have clear-cut answers; you will have to decide what you
think the best answer is. Be prepared to defend your choices with portions of the text.*

1.  Who is Roger? _____

2.  Who is Lugaretzia? _____

3.  How many people are in the Durrell family? _____ Name them, and indicate

    if they are male or female. _____

    _____

4. Who keeps yelling for a book? _____

5. Who says that every matchbox in the house is a death-trap? _____

6. Who is "screeching"? _____

7. Who says, "But *how* did the scorpions get on the table, dear?" _____

8. Who is the youngest member of the family? _____

9. In your opinion, who seems the most confused? _____

## Discussion/Composition

Can you describe an incident from your childhood in which one of the children in your family threw the household into confusion?

## Vocabulary from Context

**Exercise 1**

*Use the context provided to determine the meanings of the italicized words. Write a definition, synonym, or description of each of the italicized vocabulary items in the space provided.*

1. _____    Because the light frightened the scorpions away, I wasn't able to observe them for very long. However, by appearing suddenly with my electric torch, I was able to get brief *glimpses* of their behavior.

2. _____    I was completely *enraptured* with the scorpion family. My happiness at finding them was so great that I decided I would keep them in my room for closer study.

3. _____    The members of the family were so angry that I decided to stay away from the house until dinner. Their *rage* truly frightened me.

4. _____    Because she had not seen the scorpions, Mother was completely *bewildered* by the sudden confusion.

5. _____    I begged the family not to kill the scorpions, and they finally listened to my *pleas*.

6. _____    Mr. and Mrs. Firth had a long *courtship*. They dated for nine years before they got married.

7. _____    He *crouched* down to look under the table for his shoes.

8. _____   After the scorpion affair the whole family tried *in vain* to get me to stop collecting animals and insects. They should have known that I wouldn't stop collecting just because of one little scare.

---
### Exercise 2

*This exercise is designed to give you additional clues to determine the meanings of unfamiliar vocabulary items in context. In the paragraph indicated by the number in parentheses, find the word or phrase that best fits the meaning given. Your teacher may want to read these aloud as you quickly scan the paragraph to find the answer.*

1. (1)   Which word means *a bother; an annoyance; a problem*?

2. (3)   Which word in the third sentence means *to bring in secretly*?

3. (3)   Which word at the end of the paragraph means *fate; future problems*?

4. (5)   Which two words in the middle of the paragraph mean *confusion*?

5. (8)   Which word in the first sentence means *peace and quiet; organization*?

---
### Exercise 3

*This exercise should be done after you have finished reading "An Attack on the Family." The exercise is designed to determine how well you have been able to use context clues to guess the meaning of unfamiliar vocabulary in "An Attack on the Family." Give a definition, synonym, or description of each of the words or phrases below. This exercise can be done orally or in writing.*

1. assaults (last sentence, paragraph 1) _____

2. clinging (second sentence, paragraph 3) _____

3. manoeuvred (middle, paragraph 3) _____

4. maintain (paragraph 4) _____

5. hoisted (paragraph 4) _____

6. scuttled (paragraph 4) _____

7. peered (middle, paragraph 5) _____

8. hurled (bottom, paragraph 5) _____

9. drenched (bottom, paragraph 5) _____

10. swarmed (bottom, paragraph 5) _____

11. screeching (middle, paragraph 6) _____

12. reluctance (bottom, paragraph 8) _____

*Selection 3B*

**Before You Begin**   Would you consider a family unusual if:

—all the shopping was done by the children in committees?
—phonographs played constantly in the bathrooms so that everyone could learn foreign languages as they brushed their teeth?
—the mother was a psychologist who became as famous as her engineer husband in the field of scientific management?

All of these statements—and many more just as unusual—apply to the family of John and Lillian Gilbreth. These two remarkable people raised a family in the first quarter of the twentieth century, at a time when the United States was rapidly industrializing, and when large families were becoming less common. Through their research into scientific management, the Gilbreths showed many large companies how to increase profits by saving time and labor. They believed that the principles of good industrial management could also apply to the management of families, and they set out to prove it with their twelve children.

The following selection is taken from *Cheaper by the Dozen,* a book written by two of the Gilbreth children.* Read the passage quickly to appreciate the humor, then do the exercises that follow. You may want to do Vocabulary from Context exercise 1 on page 139 and the Dictionary Study exercise on page 141 before you begin reading.

## Adaptation from
## *Cheaper by the Dozen*

*Frank B. Gilbreth, Jr., and Ernestine Gilbreth Carey*

1       It was an off year that didn't bring a new Gilbreth baby. Both Dad and Mother wanted a large family. And if it was Dad who set the actual goal of an even dozen, Mother as readily agreed.

Dad mentioned the dozen figure for the first time on their wedding day.

"We're going to have a wonderful life, Lillie. A wonderful life and a wonderful family. A great big family."

"We'll have children all over the house," Mother smiled. "From the basement to the attic."

"From the floorboards to the chandelier."

"How many would you say we should have, just an estimate?" Mother asked.

"Just as an estimate, many."

"Lots and lots."

2       "We'll settle for an even dozen," said Dad. "No less. What do you say to that?"

"I say," said Mother, "a dozen would be just right. No less."

"That's the minimum."

"Boys or girls?"

"Well, boys would be fine," Dad whispered. "A dozen boys would be just right.

---

*Adapted from *Cheaper by the Dozen* by Frank B. Gilbreth, Jr., and Ernestine Gilbreth Carey (New York: Thomas Y. Crowell, 1948).

But . . . well, girls would be all right too. Sure, I guess."

3        "I'd like to have half boys and half girls. Do you think it would be all right to have half girls?"

"If that's what you want," Dad said, "we'll plan it that way. Excuse me a minute while I make a note of it." He took out his memorandum book and solemnly wrote: "Don't forget to have six boys and six girls."

They had a dozen children, six boys and six girls, in seventeen years. Somewhat to Dad's disappointment, there were no twins or other multiple births. There was no doubt in his mind that the most efficient way to raise a large family would be to have one huge litter and get the whole business over with at one time.

4        One reason Dad had so many children was that he was convinced anything he and Mother teamed up on was sure to be a success.

Dad always practiced what he preached, and it was just about impossible to tell where his scientific management company ended and his family life began.

Our house at Montclair, New Jersey, was a sort of school for scientific management and the elimination of wasted motions—or "motion study," as Dad and Mother named it.

5        Dad took moving pictures of us children washing dishes, so that he could determine how we could reduce our motions and thus hurry through the task. Irregular jobs, such as painting the back porch or removing a tree stump from the front lawn, were awarded on a low-bid basis. Each child who wanted extra pocket money submitted an offer saying what he would do the job for. The lowest bidder got the contract.

6        Dad put process and work charts in the bathrooms. Every child old enough to write— and Dad expected his offspring to start writing at a tender age—was required to initial the charts in the morning after he had brushed his teeth, taken a bath, combed his hair, and made his bed. At night, each child had to weigh himself, plot the figure on a graph, and initial the process charts again after he had done his homework, washed his hands and face, and brushed his teeth. Mother wanted to have a place on the charts for saying prayers, but Dad said as far as he was concerned prayers were voluntary.

7        It was regimentation, all right. But bear in mind the trouble most parents have in getting just one child off to school, and multiply it by twelve. Some regimentation was necessary to prevent bedlam.

8        Yes, at home or on the job, Dad was always the efficiency expert. He buttoned his vest from the bottom up, instead of from the top down, because the bottom-to-top process took him only three seconds, while the top-to-bottom took seven. He even used two shaving brushes to lather his face, because he found that by so doing he could cut seventeen seconds off his shaving time. For a while he tried shaving with two razors, but he finally gave that up.

9        "I can save forty-four seconds," he grumbled, "but I wasted two minutes this morning putting this bandage on my throat."

It wasn't the slashed throat that really bothered him. It was the two minutes.

10       Mother the psychologist and Dad the motion study man and general contractor decided to look into the new field of the psychology of management, and the old field of psychologically managing a houseful of children. They believed that what would work in the home would work in the factory, and what would work in the factory would work in the home.

Dad put the theory to a test shortly after we moved to Montclair. The house was too big for Tom Grieves, the handyman, and Mrs. Cunningham, the cook, to keep in order. Dad decided we were going to have to help them, and he wanted us to offer the help willingly. He had found that the best way to get cooperation out of employees in a factory was to set up a joint employer-employee board, which would make work assignments on a basis of personal choice and aptitude. He and Mother set up a Family Council, patterned after an employer-employee board. The Council met every Sunday afternoon, immediately after dinner.

*11*        Like most of Dad's and Mother's ideas, the Family Council was basically a good one and, although it verged sometimes on the hysterical, brought results. Family purchasing committees, duly elected, bought the food, clothes, furniture, and athletic equipment. A utilities committee levied one-cent fines on wasters of water and electricity. A projects committee saw that work was completed as scheduled. The amount of money the children were to receive for allowances was decided by the Council, which also determined appropriate rewards and punishments.

*12*        One purchasing committee found a large department store which gave us wholesale rates on everything from underwear to baseball gloves. Another bought canned goods directly from a manufacturer, in truckload lots.

*13*        One Sunday, when Dad convened the meeting of the Council, we sat self-consciously around the table, waiting for the right moment. The chairman knew something was in the air, and it tickled him. He had trouble keeping a straight face when he called for new business.

Martha, who had been carefully instructed in private, arose.

"It has come to the attention of the membership," she began, "that the assistant chairman intends to buy a new rug for the dining room. Since the entire membership will be required to look upon, and sit in chairs resting upon, the rug, I move* that the Council be consulted before any rug is purchased."

"Second the motion," said Anne.

Dad didn't know what to make of this one. "Any discussion?" he asked, in a move designed to kill time while he planned his counter attack.

*14*        "Mr. Chairman," said Lillian. "We have to sweep it. We should be able to choose it."

"We want one with flowers on it," Martha put in. "When you have flowers, the crumbs don't show so easily, and you save motions by not having to sweep so often."

"We want to know what sort of a rug the assistant chairman intends to buy," said Ernestine.

"We want to make sure the budget can afford it," Fred announced.

"I recognize the assistant chairman," said Dad. "This whole Council business was your idea anyway, Lillie. What do we do now?"

*15*        "Well," Mother said doubtfully, "I had planned to get a plain violet-colored rug, and I had planned to spend a hundred dollars. But if the children think that's too much, and if they want flowers, I'm willing to let the majority rule."

"I move," said Frank, "that not more than ninety-five dollars be spent."

Dad shrugged his shoulders. If Mother didn't care, he certainly didn't.

"So many as favor the motion to spend only ninety-five dollars, signify by saying aye."

The motion carried unanimously.

"Any more new business?"

*16*        "I move," said Bill, "that we spend the five dollars we have saved to buy a collie puppy."

"Hey, wait a minute," said Dad. The rug had been somewhat of a joke, but the dog question was serious. We had wanted a dog for years. Dad thought that any pet which didn't lay eggs was an extravagance that a man with twelve children could ill afford. He felt that if he surrendered on the dog question, there was no telling what the Council might vote next. He had a sickening mental picture of a barn full of ponies, a car for Anne, motorcycles, a swimming pool, and, ultimately, the poor house or a debtors' prison, if they still had such things.

---

*"I move," "Second the motion," and "I recognize" are phrases taken from parliamentary procedure. They are generally used only in formal meetings in which each person's participation is rigidly controlled.

17 "Second the motion," said Lillian, yanking Dad out of his dreams.

"A dog," said Jack, "would be a pet. Everyone in the family could pat him, and I would be his master."

"A dog," said Dan, "would be a friend. He could eat scraps of food. He would save us waste and would save motions for the garbage man."

"A dog," said Fred, "would keep burglars away. He would sleep on the foot of my bed, and I would wash him whenever he was dirty."

"A dog," Dad mimicked, "would be an accursed nuisance. He would be our master. He would eat me out of house and home. He would spread fleas from the attic to the garage. He would be positive to sleep on the foot of *my* bed. Nobody would wash his filthy, dirty, flea-bitten carcass."

18 He looked pleadingly at Mother.

"Lillie, Lillie, open your eyes," he begged. "Don't you see where this is leading us? Ponies, cars, trips to Hawaii, silk stockings, rouge, and bobbed hair."

"I think, dear," said Mother, "that we must rely on the good sense of the children. A five-dollar dog is not a trip to Hawaii."

We voted; there was only one negative ballot—Dad's. Mother abstained. In after years, as the collie grew older, shed hair on the furniture, bit the mailman, and did in fact try to appropriate the foot of Dad's bed, the chairman was heard to remark on occasion to the assistant chairman:

19 "I give nightly praise to my Maker that I never cast a ballot to bring that lazy, ill-tempered beast into what was once my home. I'm glad I had the courage to go on record as opposing that illegitimate, shameless fleabag that now shares my bed and board. You abstainer, you!"

---

20 Mother took an active part in church and community work. She didn't teach a class, but she served on a number of committees. Once she called on a woman who had just moved to town, to ask her to serve on a fund-raising committee.

"I'd be glad to if I had the time," the woman said. "But I have three young sons and they keep me on the run. I'm sure if you have a boy of your own, you'll understand how much trouble three can be."

"Of course," said Mother. "That's quite all right. And I do understand."

"Have you any children, Mrs. Gilbreth?"

"Oh, yes."

"Any boys?"

"Yes, indeed."

"May I ask how many?"

"Certainly. I have six boys."

"Six boys!" gulped the woman. "Imagine a family of six!"

"Oh, there're more in the family than that. I have six girls, too."

"I surrender," whispered the newcomer. "When is the next meeting of the committee? I'll be there, Mrs. Gilbreth. I'll be there."

21 One teacher in the Sunday school, a Mrs. Bruce, had the next-to-largest family in Montclair. She had eight children, most of whom were older than we. Her husband was very successful in business, and they lived in a large house about two miles from us. Mother and Mrs. Bruce became great friends.

About a year later, a New York woman connected with some sort of national birth control organization came to Montclair to form a local chapter. Her name was Mrs. Alice Mebane, or something like that. She inquired among her acquaintances as to who in

Montclair might be sympathetic to the birth control movement. As a joke, someone referred her to Mrs. Bruce.

"I'd be delighted to cooperate," Mother's friend told Mrs. Mebane, "but you see I have several children myself."

22    "Oh, I had no idea," said Mrs. Mebane. "How many?"

"Several," Mrs. Bruce replied vaguely. "So I don't think I would be the one to head up any birth control movement in Montclair."

"I must say, I'm forced to agree. We should know where we're going, and practice what we preach."

"But I do know just the person for you," Mrs. Bruce continued. "And she has a big house that would be simply ideal for holding meetings."

"Just what we want," purred Mrs. Mebane. "What is her name?"

"Mrs. Frank Gilbreth. She's community-minded, and she's a career woman."

23    "Exactly what we want. Civic minded, career woman, and—most important of all—a large house. One other thing—I suppose it's too much to hope for—but is she by any chance an organizer? You know, one who can take things over and militantly drive ahead?"

"The description," gloated Mrs. Bruce, "fits her like a glove."

"It's almost too good to be true," said Mrs. Mebane, wringing her hands in ecstasy. "May I use your name and tell Mrs. Gilbreth you sent me?"

"By all means," said Mother's friend. "Please do. I shall be disappointed if you don't."

"And don't think that I disapprove of your having children," laughed Mrs. Mebane. "After all, many people do, you know."

24    "Careless of them," remarked Mrs. Bruce.

The afternoon that Mrs. Mebane arrived at our house, all of us children were, as usual, either upstairs in our rooms or playing in the back yard. Mrs. Mebane introduced herself to Mother.

"It's about birth control," she told Mother.

"What about it?" Mother asked, blushing.

"I was told you'd be interested."

"Me?"

"I've just talked to your friend, Mrs. Bruce, and she was certainly interested."

"Isn't it a little late for her to be interested?" Mother asked.

"I see what you mean, Mrs. Gilbreth. But better late than never, don't you think?"

"But she has eight children," said Mother.

Mrs. Mebane blanched, and clutched her head.

"My God," she said. Not really."

Mother nodded.

25    "How perfectly frightful. She impressed me as quite normal. Not at all like an eight-child woman."

"She's kept her youth well," Mother agreed.

"Ah, there's work to be done, all right," Mrs. Mebane said. "Think of it, living right here within eighteen miles of our national birth control headquarters in New York City, and her having eight children. Yes, there's work to be done, Mrs. Gilbreth, and that's why I'm here."

"What sort of work?"

"We'd like you to be the moving spirit behind a Montclair birth control chapter."

26    Mother decided at this point that the situation was too ludicrous for Dad to miss, and that he'd never forgive her if she didn't deal him in.

"I'll have to ask my husband," she said. "Excuse me while I call him."

Mother stepped out and found Dad. She gave him a brief explanation and then led him into the parlor and introduced him.

27 "It's a pleasure to meet a woman in such a noble cause," said Dad.

"Thank you. And it's a pleasure to find a man who thinks of it as noble. In general, I find the husbands much less sympathetic with our aims than the wives. You'd be surprised at some of the terrible things men have said to me."

"I love surprises," Dad leered. "What do you say back to them?"

"If you had seen, as I have," said Mrs. Mebane, "relatively young women grown old before their time by the arrival of unwanted young ones. And population figures show . . . Why Mr. Gilbreth, what are you doing?"

28 What Dad was doing was whistling assembly. On the first note, feet could be heard pounding on the floors above. Doors slammed, there was a landslide on the stairs, and we started skidding into the parlor.

"Nine seconds," said Dad pocketing his stopwatch. "Three short of the all-time record."

"God's teeth," said Mrs. Mebane. "What is it? Tell me quickly. Is it a school? No. Or is it . . .? For Lord's sakes. It is!"

"It is what?" asked Dad.

"It's your family. Don't try to deny it. They're the spit and image of you, and your wife, too!"

"I was about to introduce you," said Dad. "Mrs. Mebane, let me introduce you to the family—or most of it. Seems to me like there should be some more of them around here someplace."

29 "God help us all."

"How many head of children do we have now, Lillie, would you say off hand?"

"Last time I counted, seems to me there was an even dozen of them," said Mother. "I might have missed one or two of them, but not many."

"I'd say twelve would be a pretty fair guess," Dad said.

"Shame on you! And within eighteen miles of national headquarters."

30 "Let's have tea," said Mother.

But Mrs. Mebane was putting on her coat. "You poor dear," she clucked to Mother. "You poor child." Then turning to Dad. "It seems to me that the people of this town have pulled my leg on two different occasions today."

"How revolting," said Dad. "And within eighteen miles of national headquarters, too."

## Comprehension

Indicate if each statement is true (T) or false (F) according to your understanding of the passage. Use information in the passage and inferences that can be drawn from the passage to make your decisions.

1. _____ Mr. Gilbreth had difficulty convincing his wife to have twelve children.

2. _____ Mr. Gilbreth would have liked to have a family of twelve boys.

3. _____ Mr. Gilbreth made every effort to separate his professional life from his family life.

4. _____ The Gilbreth Company showed other businesses how to save time.

5. _____ At the Gilbreth home, jobs that were performed regularly were studied so that they could be performed without wasted motion.

6. _____ Irregular jobs were assigned to the child who had the necessary amount of knowledge and free time.

7. _____ Each Gilbreth child was expected to perform certain duties before leaving for school.

8. _____ Mr. Gilbreth set up the Family Council to make sure that the household chores would be distributed among the family members.

9. _____ Apparently, the Gilbreth family had been run for a number of years without the Family Council.

10. _____ A cow is the type of pet Mr. Gilbreth would have liked.

11. _____ The Council voted 12 to 2 in favor of getting a dog.

12. _____ Although the Council was set up as a democracy, Mr. Gilbreth had complete control, and would defeat decisions he did not like.

13. _____ The children hoped that they would soon be able to buy ponies and cars.

14. _____ Mr. Gilbreth finally began to like the dog.

15. _____ Because of her large family, Mrs. Gilbreth was not able to participate in community affairs.

16. _____ Birth control organizations are in favor of small families.

17. _____ Mrs. Bruce and Mrs. Gilbreth were recommended to Mrs. Mebane because both women were very active in the community.

18. _____ Mrs. Bruce was correct when she recommended Mrs. Gilbreth as a good organizer.

19. _____ Mr. Gilbreth whistled to assemble the family.

20. _____ Mrs. Mebane apparently felt that the closer one got to the national birth control headquarters, the smaller families should be.

## Discussion/Composition

Do you find the Gilbreth family odd? Describe a day in the life of your family. You may be serious or humorous.

## Vocabulary from Context

**Exercise 1**

*Use the context provided to determine the meanings of the italicized words. Write a definition, synonym, or description of each word in the space provided.*

1. _____   Although dogs and cats often have large families, rabbits are famous for the size of their *litters,* which sometimes number more than twelve bunnies at one time.

2. _____   By putting his fingers in his mouth and blowing hard through his teeth and fingers, Mr. Gilbreth produced a loud *whistle.*

3. _____   Richard organized his staff with a rigid schedule of jobs and responsibilites which often occupied them twelve hours a day, seven days a week. Many people, unable to tolerate this *regimentation,* quit their jobs after the first week.

4. _____   In order to discover who had a natural ability to learn languages, the students were given tests to determine their language *aptitude.*

5. _____   His behavior became more and more unusual until, just as his family was on the *verge* of sending him to a mental hospital, he recovered.

6. _____   Mark became *hysterical* when his basketball team won, and he did not calm down for several days.

7. _____   Pets are a *nuisance*; if you have one, you can't go anywhere or do anything without making arrangements for them to stay behind or accompany you.

8. _____   That horse won't work without some reward, but it is remarkable how much he can accomplish with a carrot as an *incentive.*

9. _____   Some of the jobs around the house were required, while others were done on a *voluntary* basis.

10. _____   With mud from head to toe, flowers still clutched in his hand, John looked so *ludicrous* that we couldn't help laughing.

**Exercise 2**

*This exercise should be done after you have finished reading the selection from* Cheaper by the Dozen. *The exercise is designed to determine how well you have been able to use context clues to guess the meaning of unfamiliar vocabulary in the story. Give a definition, synonym, or description of each of the words below. The number in parentheses indicates the paragraph in which the word can be found. Your teacher may want you to do these orally or in writing.*

1. (6)   offspring _____

2. (6)   tender _____

3. (9)   slashed _____

4. (14)  sweep _____

5. (17)  mimicked _____

6. (18)  abstained _____

## Figurative Language and Idioms

In the paragraph indicated by the number in parentheses, find the phrase that best fits the meaning given. Your teacher may want to read these aloud as you quickly scan the paragraph to find the answer.

1. (4)    What phrase in the second sentence means *do what he says others should do*?

2. (16)   What phrase means *impossible to predict*?

3. (17)   What phrase means *cost a great deal to support; cost too much to support*?

4. (23)   What phrase means *fits exactly; is exactly correct or appropriate*?

5. (26)   What phrase in the first sentence means *include him*?

6. (30)   What phrase means *played a joke on*?

## Dictionary Study

Many words have more than one meaning. When you use the dictionary* to discover the meaning of an unfamiliar word, you need to use the context to determine which definition is appropriate. Use the portions of the dictionary provided on page 142 to select the best definition for each of the italicized words below.

1. "It was an *off* year that didn't bring a new Gilbreth baby."

   _____

2. "Some regimentation was necessary to prevent *bedlam*."

   _____

3. The Family Council determined the amount of the children's *allowances*.

   _____

4. Mr. Gilbreth knew that the children had planned a surprise and it *tickled* him.

   _____

5. He had trouble keeping a *straight face* when he asked for suggestions.

   _____

6. "They're all your children. Don't try to deny it. They're the *spit and image* of you, and

   your wife, too!" _____

7. "How many head of children do we have now, Lillie, would you say *off hand*?"

   _____

*For an introduction to dictionary use, see Appendix B.

**al·low·ance** (ə-[ou'əns), *n.* 1. an allowing. 2. something allowed. 3. an amount of money, food, etc. given regularly to a child, dependent, soldier, etc. 4. a reduction in the price of something in consideration of a large order or of turning in a used article, etc. 5. the amount by which something is allowed to be more or less than stated, as to compensate for the weight of the container, inaccuracy of machining, etc. *v.t.* [ALLOWANCED (-ənst), ALLOWANCING], 1. to put on an allowance or a ration. 2. to apportion economically.
  **make allowance** (or **allowances**), to take circumstances, limitations, etc. into consideration.
  **make allowance** (or **allowances**) **for**, 1. to forgive or excuse because of mitigating factors. 2. to leave room, time, etc. for; allow for.

**bed·lam** (bed'ləm), *n.* [ME. *Bedlem, Bethlem* < the London hospital of St. Mary of *Bethlehem*]. 1. [B-], a famous old London hospital for the mentally ill. 2. any similar hospital. 3. any noisy, confused place or situation. 4. noise and confusion; uproar. *adj.* full of noise and confusion.

**off** (ôf), *adv.* [a Late ME. variant spelling of *of*, later generalized for all occurrences of *of* in stressed positions; *off* is thus merely *of* stressed], 1. so as to be away, at a distance, to a side, etc.: as, he moved *off* toward the door. 2. so as to be no longer on, attached, united, in contact, etc.: as, he took *off* his coat, he tore a sheet *off*. 3. (a specified distance) away: *a*) in space: as, the road is 200 yards *off*. *b*) in time: as, my vacation is only two weeks *off*. 4. *a*) so as to be no longer in operation, function, continuance, etc.: as, he turned the motor *off*. *b*) to the point of completion or exhaustion: as, drink it *off*. 5. so as to be less, smaller, fewer, etc.: as, the number of customers dropped *off*. 6. away from one's work or usual activity: as, let's take the week *off*. **prep.** 1. (so as to be) no longer (or not) on, attached, united, etc.: as, it rolled *off* the table, the car is *off* the road. 2. from the substance of; on: as, he lived *off* the fat of the land. 3. coming or branching out from: as, an alley *off* Main Street. 4. free or relieved from: as, *off* duty. 5. not up to the usual level, standard, etc. of: as, badly *off* one's game. 6. [Colloq.], no longer using, engaging in, supporting, etc.; abstaining from: as, he's *off* liquor for life. 7. in *nautical usage*, away from (shore): as, a mile *off* shore. *adj.* 1. not on, attached, united, etc.: as, his hat is *off*. 2. not in operation, function, continuance, etc.: as, the motor is *off*. 3. gone away; on the way: as, the children are *off* to school. 4. less, smaller, fewer, etc.: as, profits are *off* this year. 5. away from work, etc.; absent: as, the office force is *off* today. 6. not up to the usual level, standard, etc.: as, an *off* season. 7. more remote; further: as, on the *off* chance, *off* side. 8. on the right: said of a horse in double harness, etc. 9. in (specified) circumstances: as, they are well *off*. 10. wrong; in error: as, you are *off* in your calculations. 11. in *cricket*, designating the side of the field facing the batsman. 12. in *nautical usage*, toward the sea; seaward. *n.* 1. the fact or condition of being off: as, I've had my *off*s and ons. 2. in *cricket*, the off side. *interj.* go away! stay away! *Off* is also used in various idiomatic expressions, many of which are entered in this dictionary under the key words. Abbreviated *o.*
  **be** (or **take**) **off**, to go away; depart.
  **off and on**, now and then; intermittently.
  **off with**, put off! take off! remove!
  **off with you!** go away! depart!
**off.,** 1. office. 2. officer. 3. official. 4. officinal.
**off·cast, off-cast** (ôf'kast', ôf'käst'), *adj. & n.* castoff.
**off-chance** (ôf'chans', ôf'chäns'), *n.* a slight chance.
**off-col·or** (ôf'kul'ẽr), *adj.* 1. varying from the usual, standard, or required color. 2. not quite proper; in rather poor taste; risqué: as, an *off-color* joke.
**off·hand** (ôf'hand'), *adv.* without prior preparation or study; at once; extemporaneously. *adj.* 1. said or done offhand; extemporary; unpremeditated; hence, 2. casual, curt, informal, brusque, etc.
**off·hand·ed** (ôf'han'did), *adj.* offhand.

**spit** (spit), *n.* [ME. *spite*; AS. *spitu*; akin to OHG. *spizzi*, a point; IE. base *spei-*, a point (cf. SPIRE)]. 1. a thin, pointed rod or bar on which meat is impaled and held to be broiled or roasted over a fire. 2. a narrow point of land extending into a body of water. 3. a long, narrow reef, shoal, or sandbank extending from the shore. *v.t.* [SPITTED (-id), SPITTING], to thrust a pointed rod through; fix or impale on or as on a spit.

**spit** (spit), *v.t.* [SPAT (spat) or SPIT, SPITTING], [ME. *spitten*; AS. *spittan*; akin to Dan. *spytte*; IE. echoic base *sp(h)jēu-*, etc., as also in L. *sputum*, Eng. *spew*], 1. to eject from within the mouth. 2. to eject, throw out, emit, or utter explosively: as, the man *spat* an oath. 3. to light (a fuse). *v.i.* 1. to eject saliva from the mouth; expectorate. 2. to rain or snow lightly or briefly. 3. to make an explosive hissing noise, as an angry cat. *n.* 1. the act of spitting. 2. saliva. 3. something like saliva, as the frothy secretion of certain insects. 4. a light, brief shower of rain or fall of snow. 5. [Colloq.], the likeness or counterpart, as of a person.
  **spit and image**, [Colloq.], perfect likeness; exact image.
  **spit on** (or **at**), to express contempt for, hatred of, etc. by or as if by ejecting saliva on or at.

**straight** (strāt), *adj.* [ME. *streght* (pp. of *strecchen*, to stretch, used as *adj.*); AS. *streht*, pp. of *streccan*, to stretch; cf. STRETCH], 1. having the same direction throughout its length; having no curvature or angularity: as, a *straight* line. 2. not crooked, bent, bowed, wavy, curly, etc.; upright; erect: as, a *straight* back, *straight* hair. 3. with all cylinders in a direct line: said of some internal-combustion engines. 4. direct; undeviating; continuous; uninterrupted, etc.: as, a *straight* course. 5. following strictly the principles, slate of candidates, etc. of a political party: as, he votes a *straight* ticket. 6. following a direct or systematic course of reasoning, etc.; methodical; accurate. 7. in order; properly arranged, etc.: as, put your room *straight*. 8. *a*) honest; sincere; upright. *b*) [Colloq.], reliable, as information. 9. outspoken; frank. 10. unmixed; undiluted: as, *straight* whisky. 11. unqualified; unmodified: as, a *straight* answer. 12. at a fixed price per unit regardless of the quantity bought or sold: as, the apples are ten cents *straight*. 13. in *card games*, consisting of cards in sequence: as, a *straight* flush. *adv.* 1. in a straight line; unswervingly. 2. upright; erectly. 3. without deviation, detour, circumlocution, etc.; directly. *n.* 1. the quality or condition of being straight. 2. something straight; specifically, *a*) the straight part of a racecourse between the last turn and the winning post. *b*) in *poker*, a series of five cards in sequence.
  **straight away** (or **off**), at once; without delay.
**straight angle**, an angle of 180 degrees.
**straight-arm** (strāt'ärm'), *v.t.* in *football*, to push away (a tackler) with the arm outstretched. *n.* the act of straight-arming.
**straight·a·way** (strāt'ə-wā'), *adj.* extending in a straight line. *n.* a track, or part of a track, that extends in a straight line.
**straight·edge** (strāt'ej'), *n.* a piece or strip of wood, etc. having a perfectly straight edge used in drawing straight lines, testing plane surfaces, etc.
**straight·en** (strāt'n), *v.t. & v.i.* to make or become straight.
**straight-faced** (strāt'fāst'), *adj.* showing no amusement or other emotion.
**straight·for·ward** (strāt'fôr'wẽrd), *adj.* 1. moving or leading straight ahead; direct. 2. honest; frank; open. *adv.* in a straightforward manner; directly.
**straight·for·wards** (strāt'fôr'wẽrdz), *adv.* straightforward.
**straight-line** (strāt'līn'), *adj.* 1. composed of straight lines. 2. having the parts arranged in a straight line or lines. 3. designating a linkage or similar device (*straight-line motion*) used to produce or copy motion in straight lines.
**straight man**, in the *theater*, an actor who serves as a foil for a comedian.
**straight-out** (strāt'out'), *adj.* [Colloq.], 1. straightforward; direct. 2. unrestrained; outright. 3. thoroughgoing; unqualified.
**straight·way** (strāt'wā'), *adv.* at once; without delay.

**tick·le** (tik''l), *v.t.* [TICKLED (-'ld), TICKLING], [ME. *tikelen*; akin to G. dial. *zickeln*; for the base see TICK (insect)], 1. to please; gratify: as, this dessert will *tickle* the palate. 2. to amuse; delight: as, the story *tickled* him. 3. to excite the surface nerves of by touching or stroking lightly with the finger, a feather, etc. so as to cause involuntary twitching, laughter, etc. 4. to rouse, stir, move, get, etc. by or as by touching lightly. *v.i.* 1. to have an itching or tingling sensation: as, my palm *tickles*. 2. to be affected by excitation of the surface nerves; be ticklish. *n.* 1. a tickling or being tickled. 2. a tickling sensation.
  **tickle one pink**, [Slang], to please one greatly.
**tick·ler** (tik'lẽr), *n.* 1. a person or thing that tickles. 2. a memorandum pad, file, or other device for aiding the memory. 3. an irritating problem; puzzle. 4. an account book showing notes due and the dates of these.
**tick·lish** (tik'lish), *adj.* 1. sensitive to tickling. 2. easily upset; unstable; unsteady; touchy; fickle. 3. needing careful handling; precarious; delicate.

---

From *Webster's New World Dictionary,* College Edition (New York: World Publishing Company, 1966).

142

# 7

# Longer Reading

## Psychology

This unit addresses issues of obedience to authority. Before you begin the longer reading in this unit, you will need to complete the Attitude Questionnaire and discuss The Question of Obedience. These selections will provide an introduction to the longer reading, "The Milgram Experiment."

### Attitude Questionnaire

In the following questionnaire you are asked to predict your behavior in particular situations and to predict the behaviors of others. Specifically, you are asked to indicate three things:
1. What you, yourself, would do in the situations. Indicate your opinion on the scale marked *S* (for self).
2. What you think would be the reactions of people from your native culture. Indicate this opinion on the scale marked *C* (for native culture).
3. What you think would be the reactions of people in the United States. Indicate this opinion on the scale marked *U* (for U.S. native).

**Example**

The following item was marked by a college student from Japan.

You are a department head in a company that has very strict rules concerning punctuality. One of your most talented and productive employees is habitually late for work in the mornings. Company policy is to reduce latecomers' wages. Do you obey the company rule?

Definitely Yes ⟷ Definitely No

S   ___ ___ ✔ ___ ___ ___

C   ✔ ___ ___ ___ ___ ___

U   ___ ___ ___ ___ ___ ✔

*Explanation*

The checks on the scale indicate that the student believes that there is some difference between her and her fellow citizens, and substantial difference between her and U.S. natives. She indicates that she would probably follow the company rule, while she thinks that most of the people from her native culture would definitely follow the rule, and that most U.S. natives would definitely not follow the rule.

In the questionnaire that follows you will be asked to respond to a number of items such as the one preceding. Remember, there are no right answers. What matters is your honest opinion.

After you have responded to all of the items, your teacher may want you to discuss your answers in small groups.

1. You travel on business a great deal with all expenses paid by your company. On one trip a waiter offers to leave the space blank on your receipt so that you can fill in whatever amount you wish. Do you accept his offer?

| | Definitely Yes ←——————→ Definitely No |
|---|---|
| S | —— —— —— —— —— —— |
| C | —— —— —— —— —— —— |
| U | —— —— —— —— —— —— |

2. You have been attending a course regularly. An acquaintance, who rarely comes to class, asks for help with the take-home exam. Do you agree to help?

| | Definitely Yes ←——————→ Definitely No |
|---|---|
| S | —— —— —— —— —— —— |
| C | —— —— —— —— —— —— |
| U | —— —— —— —— —— —— |

3. The police ask you for information about a friend who has strong political views. Do you give it to them?

| | Definitely Yes ←——————→ Definitely No |
|---|---|
| S | —— —— —— —— —— —— |
| C | —— —— —— —— —— —— |
| U | —— —— —— —— —— —— |

4. You are in love with a person who is a devout follower of a different religion. What do you do?

| | Continue to see the person, hoping your differences in religion will not matter. | Change your religion. | Attempt to change the religion of your lover. | End the relationship. |
|---|---|---|---|---|
| S | —— | —— | —— | —— |
| C | —— | —— | —— | —— |
| U | —— | —— | —— | —— |

5. You are the manager of a grocery store. You notice a woman stealing food. She is an acquaintance whom you know to be the unemployed single mother of three small children. What do you do?

| | Report her to the police. | Speak to her privately; allow her to replace the food. | Ignore the situation. | Secretly pay for the food she took. |
|---|---|---|---|---|
| S | —— | —— | —— | —— |
| C | —— | —— | —— | —— |
| U | —— | —— | —— | —— |

6. In a high-level meeting with all of the bosses in your company, a superior takes credit for work of a colleague who is not present. Do you correct the information?

| | Definitely Yes ←——————→ Definitely No |
|---|---|
| S | —— —— —— —— —— —— |
| C | —— —— —— —— —— —— |
| U | —— —— —— —— —— —— |

7. The police have captured a man who they say is a dangerous criminal and whom they hope to convict of a series of violent crimes. You have been brought in to see if he is the same person who robbed you recently in the park. He is not the man who robbed you, but the police are pressing you to testify against him. Do you identify him as the robber?

| | Definitely Yes ←——————→ Definitely No |
|---|---|
| S | —— —— —— —— —— —— |
| C | —— —— —— —— —— —— |
| U | —— —— —— —— —— —— |

8. Your boss is about to fire a woman for a mistake which you know she did not make. You think the woman is not a very good employee. Do you correct your boss?

Definitely Yes ←——→ Definitely No

S ____ ____ ____ ____ ____ ____
C ____ ____ ____ ____ ____ ____
U ____ ____ ____ ____ ____ ____

9. You discover that your brother is selling important information to a foreign power. What do you do?

|   | Report him to the police. | Try to convince him to stop. | Ignore the situation. |
|---|---|---|---|
| S | ____ | ____ | ____ |
| C | ____ | ____ | ____ |
| U | ____ | ____ | ____ |

10. Your company is about to sign an extremely important contract. Your boss asks you to not mention a production problem you have been trying to solve because knowlege of the problem might cause the client to go to a different company. In a meeting with the client you are asked if there are any production problems. Do you tell the truth?

Definitely Yes ←——→ Definitely No

S ____ ____ ____ ____ ____ ____
C ____ ____ ____ ____ ____ ____
U ____ ____ ____ ____ ____ ____

11. Your boss is having marital difficulties with her husband. She decides to take a weekend vacation with another man. She instructs you to tell her husband that she is at a business meeting. Do you follow her instructions?

Definitely Yes ←——→ Definitely No

S ____ ____ ____ ____ ____ ____
C ____ ____ ____ ____ ____ ____
U ____ ____ ____ ____ ____ ____

12. You work for a large firm that owns many apartment buildings. You have been instructed to evict all tenants who are behind in their rent. Mr. and Mrs. Jones are hardworking people who have always paid on time. They have five children to support. They have both just lost their jobs and are unable to pay the rent. Do you evict them?

Definitely Yes ←——→ Definitely No

S ____ ____ ____ ____ ____ ____
C ____ ____ ____ ____ ____ ____
U ____ ____ ____ ____ ____ ____

13. You are taking a college psychology class. The professor asks you to participate in an experiment that requires you to lie to your friends. Do you do as you are told?

Definitely Yes ←——→ Definitely No

S ____ ____ ____ ____ ____ ____
C ____ ____ ____ ____ ____ ____
U ____ ____ ____ ____ ____ ____

Examine your answers to the questionnaire. Did you tend to see yourself as agreeing more with citizens of your country or with citizens of the U.S.? Do you see yourself as a "member of the group" or as an "individualist"? Did your answers differ markedly from those of other members of your class? What kinds of evidence did people give to support their points of view?

## The Question of Obedience

The preceding questionnaire and the longer reading in the next section raise the question of obedience to authority. There are times when we must follow the orders of people in authority and times when we must follow our own conscience. Use the items below to guide your discussion of this conflict between authority and conscience.

1. The following individuals are authority figures in most cultures. Indicate the extent to which they should be obeyed. Compare your responses to those of others in your class.

   Most Obedience ←——→ Least Obedience

   a. employer        ___  ___  ___  ___  ___  ___

   b. police officer  ___  ___  ___  ___  ___  ___

   c. friend          ___  ___  ___  ___  ___  ___

   d. grandmother     ___  ___  ___  ___  ___  ___

   e. mother          ___  ___  ___  ___  ___  ___

   f. teacher         ___  ___  ___  ___  ___  ___

   g. judge           ___  ___  ___  ___  ___  ___

   h. father          ___  ___  ___  ___  ___  ___

   i. military officer ___  ___  ___  ___  ___  ___

   j. religious leader ___  ___  ___  ___  ___  ___

   k. grandfather     ___  ___  ___  ___  ___  ___

2. T /F  Authority figures should be obeyed even when they order you to do something you disagree with.

3. What do you mean when you use the word obedience?

   a. Are there situations when one should unquestioningly obey an authority? List occasions when this is true.

   _____

   _____

   b. Can you obey someone without doing *exactly* what that person tells you to do? _____

   c. Are there times when children should not obey their elders? _____

   _____

*The Milgram Experiment*

During the 1960s Yale psychologist Stanley Milgram conducted a study to determine the extent to which ordinary people would obey clearly immoral orders. The results were disturbing and led Milgram to conclude that "ordinary people, simply doing their jobs, and without any hostility on their part, can become agents in a terrible destructive process."

The article that follows summarizes the experiment conducted by Milgram.* Your teacher may want you to do the Vocabulary from Context exercises on pages 154–55 before you begin reading. Read the first eight paragraphs to understand the design of the experiment, then answer the questions that follow. Your teacher may want you to discuss your answers before continuing with the reading.

# THE MILGRAM EXPERIMENT
### *Ronald E. Smith, Irwin G. Sarason, and Barbara Sarason*

1   After World War II the Nuremberg war trials were conducted in order to try Nazi war criminals for the atrocities they had committed. In many instances the defense offered by those on trial was that they had "only followed orders." During the Vietnam War American soldiers accused of committing atrocities in Vietnam gave basically the same explanation for their actions.

2   Most of us reject justifications based on "obedience to authority" as mere rationalizations, secure in our convictions that we, if placed in the same situation, would behave differently. However, the results of a series of ingenious and controversial investigations performed in the 1960s by psychologist Stanley Milgram suggest that perhaps we should not be so sure of ourselves.

3   Milgram wanted to determine the extent to which people would obey an experimenter's commands to administer painful electric shocks to another person. Pretend for a moment that you are a subject in one of his studies. Here is what would happen. On arriving at a university laboratory in response to a classified ad offering volunteers $4 for one hour's participation in an experiment on memory, you meet another subject, a pleasant, middle-aged man with whom you chat while awaiting the arrival of the experimenter. When the experimenter arrives, dressed in a laboratory coat, he pays you and then informs you and the other person that one of you will be the subject in the experiment and that the other will serve as his assistant. You are chosen by lot to be the assistant, but in reality you are the subject.

4   The experimenter explains that the study is concerned with the effects of punishment on learning. Accompanied by you, the "subject" is conducted into a room and strapped into a chair, and a large electrode is attached to his wrist. He is told that he is to learn a list of word pairs and that whenever he makes an error he will receive electric shocks of increasing intensity. On hearing this, the "subject" responds, "When I was at the West Haven V.A. Hospital a few years

*Ronald E. Smith, Irwin G. Sarason, and Barbara R. Sarason, "Blind Obedience to Authority" (pp. 19–22 sans table, figure, and quotes by Milgram) from *Psychology: The Frontiers of Behavior* by Ronald E. Smith, Irwin G. Sarason, and Barbara R. Sarason (New York: Harper and Row, 1978).

ago, they detected a slight heart condition. Nothing serious, but are these shocks dangerous?" The experimenter replies in an unconcerned manner that although the shocks may be painful, they will cause no permanent tissue damage.

5      You and the experimenter then proceed to an adjoining room connected by an intercom so that the "subject's" responses can be heard. You are seated in front of an apparatus with 30 toggle switches ranging from 15 volts to 450 volts. (See Figure 1.) Your task is to administer the learning task to the "subject." Whenever he gives an incorrect answer, you must give him an electric shock, starting at the lowest level (15 volts) and increasing the level by 15 volts each time. You are given a sample shock of 45 volts and find it moderately painful.

6      What you are unaware of at this point is that you are in a carefully contrived situation. The learner is actually an actor who receives no shock at all, and the responses you hear over the intercom are tape-recorded so that they will be exactly the same for each "assistant." The experimenter's actions are also carefully programmed.

7      As the experiment proceeds, the learner makes error after error. You increase the shock level steadily until he is clearly experiencing pain. The tape-recorded responses are programmed to correspond to the shock intensities as follows:

| | |
|---|---|
| 75 volts | Ugh! |
| 90 volts | Ugh! |
| 105 volts | Ugh! (*louder*) |
| 120 volts | Ugh! Hey, *this* really hurts. |
| 135 volts | Ugh!! |
| 150 volts | Ugh!!! Experimenter! That's all. Get me out of here. I told you I had heart trouble. My heart's starting to bother me now. Get me out of here. I told you I had heart trouble. My heart's starting to bother me. I refuse to go on. Let me out. |
| 165 volts | Ugh! Let me out. (*shouting*) |
| 180 volts | Ugh! I can't stand the pain. Let me out of here! (*shouting*) |
| 195 volts | Ugh! Let me out of here. Let me out of here. My heart's bothering me. Let me out of here! You have no right to keep me here! Let me out! Let me out of here! My heart's bothering me. Let me out! Let me out! |
| 210 volts | Ugh!! Experimenter! *Get* me out of here. I've had enough. I won't be in the experiment any more. |
| 225 volts | Ugh! |
| 240 volts | Ugh! |
| 255 volts | Ugh! Get me *out* of here. |
| 270 volts | (*Agonized scream*). Let me out of here. Let me out of here. Let me out of here. Let me out. Do you hear? Let me out of here. |
| 285 volts | (*Agonized scream*). |
| 300 volts | (*Agonized scream*). I absolutely refuse to answer any more. Get me out of here. You can't hold me here. Get me out. Get me out of here. |
| 315 volts | (*Intensely agonized scream*). *I told you I refuse to answer.* I'm no longer part of this experiment. |

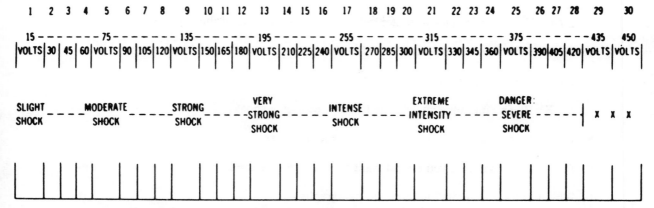

**Figure 1** The control panel of the shocking apparatus used in the Milgram research. Copyright © 1974 by Stanley Milgram. Reprinted by permission of Harper & Row, Publishers, Inc.

330 volts (*Intense and prolonged agonized scream*). Let me out of here. Let me out of here. My heart's bothering me. Let me out, I tell you. (*Hysterically*) Let me out of here. Let me out of here. You have no right to hold me here. Let me out! Let me out! Let me out of here! Let me out! Let me out!

345 volts (*At 345 volts and thereafter, there was only silence.*)[1]

8      But supposing you express unwillingness at some point to continue shocking the learner? In that event the experimenter, sitting at a nearby desk, would respond in one of the following ways:

"Please continue" or "Please go on."
"The experiment requires that you continue."
"It is absolutely essential that you continue."
"You have no other choice. You must go on."

---

## Comprehension

---

### Exercise 1

*Pretend you have volunteered to participate in Milgram's experiment as you answer the following questions. True/False items are indicated by a T / F preceding the item.*

1. T / F   The person you first meet at the laboratory is the experimenter.

2. T / F   You have an equal chance of being the person giving the shocks (the assistant) or the person receiving the shocks (the learner).

3. T / F   You are told you will be the assistant.

---

[1]Stanley Milgram, *Obedience to Authority* (New York: Harper and Row, 1975).

4. T / F  The experimenter does not tell you the true purpose of the experiment.

5. T / F  In reality, the experiment studies the effects of punishment in learning.

6. T / F  The shocks are not dangerous.

7. T / F  When you pull a switch, the learner receives a shock.

8. T / F  Some learners make more mistakes than others.

9. T / F  If you say that you do not want to continue, the experimenter stops the experiment.

10. Why is *subject* in quotation marks in paragraphs 4 and 5? _____

    _____

11. If you were a participant in this experiment, at what point would you stop administering

    "shocks"? _____

    _____

12. What results would you predict for the experiment?

    a. Do you think most people would continue pulling the switches? How long do you think
       most people would continue?

       _____

    b. Do you think there would be different results depending on the subject's age, education,
       nationality, sex?

       _____

Now, read the rest of the article and answer the questions that follow.

9    Having now experienced the Milgram situation at least in your imagination, how long do you think you would continue to administer shocks? Most of our students maintain that they would not go beyond 105 volts before refusing to continue the experiment. A panel of psychiatrists predicted before the experiment that perhaps only 1 percent of the subjects would proceed to the 450-volt level.

10    In fact, however, the "shock" produced by the results of this study was much more startling than the simulated shocks in the experiment. Forty men ranging in age from 20 to 50 and representing a cross section of the population, participated in the investigation. The maximum shock levels they administered are shown in Table 1. Nearly two-thirds of them administered the 450-volt maximum shock, and the average maximum shock they administered was 368 volts.

**Table 1** Maximum shock levels administered by subjects in the Milgram experiment.

| Shock level | Verbal designation and voltage level | Number of subjects giving each maximum shock level |
|---|---|---|
| | Slight Shock | |
| 1 | 15 | |
| 2 | 30 | |
| 3 | 45 | |
| 4 | 60 | |
| | Moderate Shock | |
| 5 | 75 | |
| 6 | 90 | 1 |
| 7 | 105 | |
| 8 | 120 | |
| | Strong Shock | |
| 9 | 135 | |
| 10 | 150 | 6 |
| 11 | 165 | |
| 12 | 180 | 1 |
| | Very Strong Shock | |
| 13 | 195 | |
| 14 | 210 | |
| 15 | 225 | |
| 16 | 240 | |
| | Intense Shock | |
| 17 | 255 | |
| 18 | 270 | 2 |
| 19 | 285 | |
| 20 | 300 | 1 |
| | Extreme-Intensity Shock | |
| 21 | 315 | 1 |
| 22 | 330 | 1 |
| 23 | 345 | |
| 24 | 360 | |
| | Danger: Severe Shock | |
| 25 | 375 | 1 |
| 26 | 390 | |
| 27 | 405 | |
| 28 | 420 | |
| | XXX | |
| 29 | 435 | |
| 30 | 450 | 26 |
| | Average maximum shock level | 368 volts |
| | Percentage of obedient subjects | 65.0% |

11    Virtually all the people who administered high levels of shock exhibited extreme discomfort, anxiety, and distress. Most verbally refused to continue on one or more occasions. But continue they did when ordered to do so by the experimenter, who assured them that what happened in the experiment was his responsibility.

12    By contriving a situation with many real-life elements, Milgram succeeded in demonstrating that a high percentage of "normal" people will obey an authority figure even when the destructive effects of

their obedience are obvious. The conclusions that he draws from his work are chilling indeed:

13       A commonly offered explanation is that those who shocked the victim at the most severe level were monsters, the sadistic fringe of society. But if one considers that almost two-thirds óf the participants fall into the category of "obedient" subjects, and that they represented ordinary people drawn from working, managerial, and professional classes, the argument becomes very shaky. . . . After witnessing hundreds of ordinary people submit to the authority in our own experiments, I must conclude that [Hannah] Arendt's conception of the *banality of evil* comes closer to the truth than one might dare imagine. The ordinary person who shocked the victim did so out of a sense of obligation — a conception of his duties as a subject — and not from any peculiarly aggressive tendencies.

14       This is, perhaps, the most fundamental lesson of our study: ordinary people, simply doing their jobs, and without any particular hostility on their part, can become agents in a terrible destructive process. Moreover, even when the destructive effects of their work become patently clear, and they are asked to carry out actions incompatible with fundamental standards of morality, relatively few people have the resources needed to resist authority. A variety of inhibitions against disobeying authority come into play and successfully keep the person in his place. (Milgram, 1974, pp. 5–6) [2]

15   Milgram's method of investigation also generated shock waves among psychologists. Many questioned whether it was ethical to expose subjects without warning to experiments that were likely to generate considerable stress and that might conceivably have lasting negative effects on them. But supporters of Milgram's work argue that adequate precautions were taken to protect participants. There was an extensive debriefing at the conclusion of the experiment, and participants were informed that they had not actually shocked anyone. They had a friendly meeting with the unharmed "subject." The purpose of the experiment was explained to them, and they were assured that their behavior in the situation was perfectly normal. Further, supporters argue, the great societal importance of the problem being investigated justified the methods the experimenters used. Finally, they cite follow-up questionnaire data collected by Milgram from his subjects after they received a complete report of the purposes and results. Eighty-four percent of the subjects stated that they were glad to have been in the experiment (and several spontaneously noted that their participation had made them more tolerant of others or otherwise changed them in desirable ways). Fifteen percent expressed neutral feelings, and only 1.3 percent stated that they were sorry to have participated.

16   The controversy over the ethics of Milgram's research has raged for over a decade. In combination with other controversial issues, it has prompted a deep and abiding concern for protecting the welfare of subjects in psychological research. Because of such concerns, it is most unlikely that Milgram's research could be conducted today.

---

[2]Stanley Milgram, *Obedience to Authority* (New York: Harper and Row, 1975).

---

**Exercise 2**

*Answer the following questions. Your teacher may want you to do this exercise orally, in writing, or by underlining appropriate parts of the text. True/False items are indicated by a T / F preceding a statement.*

1. What was the purpose of Milgram's experiment? _____

   _____

2. T / F   Most of the subjects continued to shock the learners when the shock level reached the danger level.

3. T / F   The subjects appeared to enjoy the opportunity to hurt other people.

4. T / F   The people who shocked the learners at the most severe level were mentally disturbed or in other ways antisocial.

5. T / F   Today we are far more sophisticated than we were in the 1960s and therefore we do not have to worry about people submitting to an immoral authority.

6. T / F   Most professionals, school teachers for example, are incapable of inflicting pain on others while following a superior's orders.

7. The authors state that the subjects were visibly shaken by the experience, and that many refused to continue. Why *did* they continue if it was so painful for the learner and so upsetting for them? Why didn't they just refuse to go on?

   _____

   _____

8. Follow-up studies indicated that the subjects' opinions of the experiment were generally positive.

   a. T / F   These positive evaluations could be attributed to the subjects' respect for the experimenter, and their obedience to his authority.

   b. T / F   The results of the experiment should cause us to doubt the validity of the follow-up study.

9. T / F   If Stanley Milgram participated in such an experiment, he would probably agree to push the shocks above the comfort level.

## *Vocabulary from Context*

### Exercise 1

*Use the context provided to determine the meanings of the italicized words. Write a definition, synonym, or description of each of the italicized items in the space provided.*

1. _____ Many people, when forced to justify poor behavior, come up with *rationalizations* that seem convincing but are really just excuses.

2. _____ The experiment was cleverly organized to appear as if it were real, but in fact it was merely a *simulation* in which all of the participants were actors.

3. _____ Extraordinary evil is very frightening, but when it appears as if evil has a common, everyday quality about it, its *banality* is even more frightening.

4. _____ Scientists cannot agree on the value of the Milgram study. Heated debate and angry disagreement have surrounded the *controversial* research ever since the first experiment was completed.

5. _____ We are all comforted by the thought that society is governed by a system of moral principles and human values. It is, in fact, our confidence in the *ethical* nature of the common person that gives us peace of mind.

### Exercise 2

*This exercise is designed to give you additional clues to determine the meanings of unfamiliar words in context. In the paragraph indicated by the number in parentheses, find the word that best fits the meaning given. Your teacher may want to read these aloud as you quickly scan the paragraph to find the answer.*

1. (1)  Which word means *extremely wicked or cruel acts*?

2. (2)  Which word means *very clever*?

3. (3)  Which word means *give*?

4. (3)  Which word means *person studied in an experiment*?

5. (6)  Which word means *constructed, designed*?

6. (11) Which word means *almost*?

7. (13) Which word means *cruel; experiencing pleasure from others' suffering*?

8. (15) Which word means *a session provided to give information to an experimental subject after the experiment*?

## Figurative Language and Idioms

In the paragraph indicated by the number in parentheses, find the phrase that best fits the meaning given. Your teacher may want to read these aloud as you quickly scan the paragraph to find the answer.

1. (3)   What phrase means *by chance, at random*?

2. (10) What phrase means *a wide variety*?

3. (12) What word means *frightening*?

4. (13) What phrase means *the edges of normal society*?

5. (16) What phrase means *has occurred energetically and violently*?

## Discussion/Composition

1. What is the correct balance between individual conscience and one's obedience to authority? How do we protect ourselves against evil leaders and immoral authority figures?

2. Some scientists argue that experiments such as this violate basic human rights of the subjects because they deceive the participants. Others claim that the deception is justified because of the importance of the findings. What do you think?

   a. In what ways are the subjects deceived?

   b. What might be the negative effects upon the subjects of having participated in the study?

   c. What is the importance of this sort of study? What do you know now about society that you did not know before reading the article?

# 8

## Longer Reading

## Anthropology

The author of this selection, Jane van Lawick-Goodall, spent six years observing chimpanzees at the Gombe Stream Chimpanzee Reserve on the shores of Lake Tanganyika in Tanzania before she wrote *In the Shadow of Man.** In this selection, a chapter from that book, she compares chimpanzees and people in five areas: brain development, tool-using and toolmaking, communicatory gestures, speech, and awareness of self. As you read, look for the similarities and differences.

You may want to do the Vocabulary from Context exercise on pages 162–63 before you begin reading.

### In the Shadow of Man

*Jane van Lawick-Goodall*

1    The amazing success of humans as a species is the result of the evolutionary development of our brains which has led, among other things, to tool-using, toolmaking, the ability to solve problems by logical reasoning, thoughtful cooperation, and language. One of the most striking ways in which chimpanzees biologically resemble humans lies in the structure of their brains. The chimpanzee, with the capacity for primitive reasoning, exhibits a type of intelligence more like that of humans than does any other mammal living today. The brain of the modern chimpanzee is probably not too dissimilar to the brain that so many millions of years ago directed the behavior of the first ape man.

2    For a long time, the fact that prehistoric people made tools was considered to be one of the major criteria distinguishing them from other creatures. As I pointed out earlier, I have watched chimpanzees modify grass stems in order to use them to probe for termites. It is true that the chimpanzee does not fashion tools to "a regular and set pattern"—but then, prehistoric people, before their development of stone tools, undoubtedly poked around with sticks and straws, at which stage it seems unlikely that they made tools to a set pattern either.

3    It is because of the close association in most people's minds of tools with humans that special attention has always been focused upon any animal able to use an object as a tool; but it is important to realize that this ability, on its own, does not necessarily indicate any special intelligence in the creature concerned. The fact that the Galápagos woodpecker finch uses a cactus spine or twig to probe insects from crevices in the bark is indeed a

---

*Adapted from *In the Shadow of Man* by Jane van Lawick-Goodall (Boston: Houghton Mifflin Company, 1971).

fascinating phenomenon, but it does not make the bird more intelligent than a genuine woodpecker that uses its long beak and tongue for the same purpose.

4    The point at which tool-using and toolmaking, as such, acquire evolutionary significance is surely when an animal can adapt its ability to manipulate objects to a wide variety of purposes, and when it can use an object spontaneously to solve a brand-new problem that without the use of a tool would prove insoluble.

5    At the Gombe Stream alone we have seen chimpanzees use objects for many different purposes. They use stems and sticks to capture and eat insects, and, if the material picked is not suitable, then it is modified. They use leaves to sop up water they cannot reach with their lips—and first they chew on the leaves and thus increase their absorbency. We have seen them use handfuls of leaves to wipe dirt from their bodies or to dab at wounds.

6    In captivity chimpanzees often use objects as tools quite spontaneously. One group that was studied intensively by Wolfgang Köhler used sticks to try to pry open box lids and dig in the ground for roots. They wiped themselves with leaves or straw, scratched themselves with stones and poked straws into columns of ants in order to eat the insects much like the Gombe Stream chimpanzees probe for termites. They often used sticks and stones as weapons during aggressive encounters. Extensive tests have been carried out in laboratory settings in order to find out more about the tool*making* ability of chimpanzees. Results show that they can pile up to five boxes one on top of the other in order to climb to hanging food, that they can fit up to three tubes together to reach food placed outside the bars of their cages, and that they can unwind part of a length of wire for the same purpose. So far, however, no chimpanzee has succeeded in using one tool to make another. Even with teaching, one chimpanzee, the subject of exhaustive tests, was not able to use a stone hand ax to break a piece of wood into splinters suitable for obtaining food from a narrow pipe. She could do this when the material was suitable for her to break off pieces with her teeth but, although she was shown how to use the hand ax on tougher wood many times, she never even attempted to make use of it when trying to solve the problem. However, many other chimpanzees must be tested before we say that the chimpanzee as a species is unable to perform this act. Some humans are mathematicians—others are not.

7    When the performance of chimpanzees in the field is compared with their actual abilities in test situations, it would seem that, in time, they might develop a more sophisticated tool-culture. After all, primitive people continued to use their early stone tools for thousands of years, virtually without change. Then we find a more sophisticated type of stone tool-culture suddenly appearing widespread across the continents. Possibly a stone-age genius invented the new culture and others, who undoubtedly learned from and imitated each other, copied the new technique.

8    If chimpanzees are allowed to continue living they, too, might suddenly produce a race of chimp superbrains and evolve an entirely new tool-culture. For it seems almost certain that, although the ability to manipulate objects is innate in a chimpanzee, the actual tool-using patterns practiced by the Gombe Stream chimpanzees are learned by the infants from their elders. We saw one very good example of this. It happened when a female had diarrhea: she picked a large handful of leaves and wiped her messy bottom. Her two-year-old infant watched her closely and then twice picked leaves and wiped his own clean bottom.

9    To Hugo and me, and assuredly to many scientists interested in human behavior and evolution, one significant aspect of chimpanzee behavior lies in the close similarity of many of their communicatory gestures and postures to those of humans. Not only are the actual positions and movements similar to our own but also the contexts in which they often occur.

10    When a chimpanzee is suddenly frightened it frequently reaches to touch or embrace a chimpanzee nearby, much like a child watching a horror film may seize a companion's

hand. Both chimpanzees and humans seem reassured in stressful situations by physical contact with another individual. Once David Graybeard caught sight of his reflection in a mirror. Terrified, he seized Fifi, then only three years old. Even such contact with a very small chimp appeared to reassure him; gradually he relaxed and the grin of fear left his face. Humans may sometimes feel reassured by holding or stroking a dog or some other pet in moments of emotional crisis.

11    This comfort, which chimpanzees and humans alike appear to derive from physical contact with each other, probably originates during the years of infancy, when for so long the touch of the mother, or the contact with her body, serves to calm the frights and soothe the anxieties of both ape and human infants. So, when the child grows older and its mother is not always close at hand, it seeks the next best thing—close physical contact with another individual. If its mother is around, however, it may deliberately pick her out as its comforter. Once when Figan was about eight years old he was threatened by Mike. He screamed loudly and hurried past six or seven other chimps nearby until he reached Flo; then he held his hand toward her and she held it with hers. Calmed, Figan stopped screaming almost at once. Young human beings, too, continue to unburden their hearts to their mothers long after the days of childhood have passed—provided, of course, that an affectionate relationship exists between them.

12    When chimpanzees are overjoyed by the sight of a large pile of bananas they pat and kiss and embrace one another as two friends might embrace when they hear good news, or as a child may leap to hug its mother when told of a special treat. We all know those feelings of intense excitement or happiness which cause people to shout and leap around, or to burst into tears. It is not surprising that chimpanzees, if they feel anything like this, should seek to calm themselves by embracing their companions.

13    Chimpanzees, after being threatened or attacked by a superior, may follow the aggressor, screaming and crouching to the ground or holding out their hands. They are, in fact, begging a reassuring touch from the other. Sometimes they will not relax until they have been touched or patted, kissed or embraced. Figan several times flew into a tantrum when such contact was withheld, hurling himself about on the ground, his screams cramping in his throat until the aggressor finally calmed him with a touch. I have seen a human child behaving in the same sort of way, following his mother around the house after she has told him off, crying, holding on to her skirt, until finally she picked him up and kissed and cuddled him in forgiveness. A kiss or embrace or some other gesture of endearment is an almost inevitable outcome once a matrimonial disagreement has been resolved, and in many cultures the clasping of hands occurs to demonstrate renewal of friendship and forgiveness after a quarrel.

14    When one human begs forgiveness from or gives forgiveness to another there are, however, moral issues involved; it is when we consider these that we get into difficulties in trying to draw parallels between chimpanzees and human behavior. In chimpanzee society the principle involved when a subordinate seeks reassurance from a superior, or when a high-ranking individual calms another, is in no way concerned with the right or wrong of an aggressive act. A female who is attacked for no reason other than she happens to be standing too close to a charging male is quite as likely to approach the male and beg a reassuring touch as is the female who is bowled over by a male while she attempts to take a fruit from his pile of bananas.

15    Again, while we may make a direct comparison between the effect on an anxious chimpanzee or human of a touch or embrace of reassurance, the issue becomes complicated if we probe into the motivation that directs the gesture of the ape or the human who is doing the reassuring. Human beings are capable of acting from purely unselfish motives; we can be genuinely sorry for others and try to share in their troubles in an effort to offer comfort. It is unlikely that a chimpanzee acts from feelings quite like these; I doubt whether even members of one family, united as they are by strong mutual

affections, are ever motivated by pure altruism in their dealings with one another.

16     On the other hand, there may be parallels in some instances. Most of us have experienced sensations of extreme discomfort and unease in the presence of an abject, weeping person. We may feel compelled to try to calm the person, not because we feel compassion in the altruistic sense, but because the behavior disturbs our own feeling of well-being. Perhaps the sight—and especially the sound—of a crouching, screaming subordinate similarly makes a chimpanzee uneasy; the most efficient way of changing the situation is to calm the other with a touch.

17     Another area of similarity between chimpanzees and humans is greeting behavior. When two chimpanzees greet each other after a separation, their behavior often looks amazingly like that shown by two humans in the same context. Chimpanzees may bow or crouch to the ground, hold hands, kiss, embrace, touch, or pat each other on almost any part of the body, especially the head and face. A male may chuck a female or an infant under the chin. Humans in many cultures, show one or more of these gestures.

18     In human societies much greeting behavior has become ritualized. People who smile when greeting a friend, or who incline their heads when passing an acquaintance in the street, are not necessarily acknowledging that the other has a superior social status. Yet the nod undoubtedly derives from submissive bowing or prostration and the smile from a nervous grin. Often, though, human greetings still do serve to clarify the relative social status of the individuals concerned, particularly on formal occasions.

19     A greeting between two chimpanzees nearly always serves such a purpose—it reestablishes the dominance status of the one relative to the other. When nervous Olly greets Mike she may hold out her hand toward him, or bow to the ground, crouching submissively with downbent head. She is, in effect, acknowledging Mike's superior rank. Mike may touch or pat or hold her hand, or touch her head, in response to her submission. A greeting between two chimps is usually more demonstrative when the individuals concerned are close friends, particularly when they have been separated for days rather than hours. Goliath often used to fling his arms around David, and the two would press their lips to each other's faces or necks when they met; whereas a greeting between Goliath and Mr. Worzle seldom involved more than a casual touch even when the two had not seen each other for some time.

20     If we survey the whole range of the communication signals of chimpanzees on the one hand and humans on the other, we find striking similarities in many instances. It would appear, then, that human and chimp either have evolved gestures and postures along a most remarkable parallel or that we share with the chimpanzees an ancestor in the dim and very distant past; an ancestor, moreover, who communicated by means of kissing and embracing, touching and patting and holding hands.

21     One of the major differences between humans and our closest living relative is, of course, that the chimpanzee has not developed the power of speech. Even the most intensive efforts to teach young chimps to talk have met with almost no success. Verbal language represents a truly gigantic step forward in human evolution.

22     Chimpanzees do have a wide range of calls, and these certainly serve to convey some types of information. When a chimp finds good food it utters loud barks; other chimps in the vicinity instantly become aware of the food source and hurry to join in. An attacked chimpanzee screams and this may alert its mother or a friend, either of whom may hurry to its aid. A chimpanzee confronted with an alarming and potentially dangerous situation utters a spine-chilling *wraaaa*—again, other chimps may hurry to the spot to see what is happening. A male chimpanzee, about to enter a valley or charge toward a food source, utters his pant-hoots—and other individuals realize that another member of the group is arriving and can identify which one. To our human ears each chimpanzee is characterized more by its pant-hoots than by any other type of call. This is significant since the pant-hoot in particular is the call that serves to maintain contact between the separated groups

of the community. Yet the chimps themselves can certainly recognize individuals by other calls; for instance, a mother knows the scream of her offspring. Probably a chimpanzee can recognize the calls of most of its acquaintances.

23       While chimpanzee calls do serve to convey basic information about some situations and individuals, they cannot for the most part be compared to a spoken language. Humans by means of words can communicate abstract ideas; they can benefit from the experiences of others without having to be present at the time; they can make intelligent cooperative plans.

24       Recently it has been proved that the chimpanzee is capable of communicating with people in quite a sophisticated manner. There are two scientists in America, R. Allen and Beatrice Gardner, who have trained a young chimpanzee in the use of the approved sign language of the deaf. The Gardners felt that, since gesture and posture formed such a significant aspect of *chimpanzee* communication patterns, such a sign language might be more appropriate than trying to teach vocal words.

25       Washoe was brought up from infancy constantly surrounded by human companions. These people from the start communicated in sign language with Washoe and also with each other when in the chimp's presence. The only sounds they made were those approximating chimpanzee calls such as laughter, exclamations, and imitations of Washoe's own sounds.

26       Their experiment has been amazingly successful. At five years of age Washoe can understand some three hundred and fifty different symbols, many of which signify clusters of words rather than just a single word, and she can also use about one hundred and fifty of them correctly.

27       I have not seen Washoe; but I have seen some film demonstrating her level of performance and, strangely enough, I was most impressed by an error she made. She was required to name, one after the other, a series of objects as they were drawn from a sack. She signed off the correct names very fast—but even so, it could be argued that an intelligent dog would ultimately learn to associate the sight of a bowl with a correct response. And then a brush was shown to Washoe, and she made the sign for a comb. That to me was very significant. It is the sort of mistake a small child might make, calling a shoe a slipper or a plate a saucer—but never calling a shoe a plate.

28       Perhaps one of the Gardners' most fascinating observations concerns the occasion when for the first time Washoe was asked (in sign language) "Who is that?" as she was looking into a mirror. Washoe, who was very familiar with mirrors by that time, signaled back, "Me, Washoe."

29       This is, in a way, a scientific proof of a fact we have long known—that, in some way, the chimpanzee has a primitive awareness of Self. Undoubtedly there are people who would prefer not to believe this, since even more firmly rooted than the old idea that humans alone are the only toolmaking beings is the concept that humans alone in the animal kingdom are Self-conscious. Yet, this should not be disturbing. It has come to me, quite recently, that it is only through a real understanding of the ways in which chimpanzees and humans show similarities in behavior that we can reflect with meaning on the ways in which humans and chimpanzees *differ*. And only then can we really begin to appreciate, in a biological and spiritual manner, the full extent of our uniqueness.

30       Yes, human beings definitely overshadow the chimpanzee. The chimpanzee is, nevertheless, a creature of immense significance to the understanding of humans. Just as they are overshadowed by us, so the chimpanzees overshadow all other animals. They have the ability to solve quite complex problems, they can use and make tools for a variety of purposes, their social structure and methods of communication with each other are elaborate, and they show the beginnings of Self-awareness. Who knows what the chimpanzees will be like forty million years hence? It should be of concern to us all that we permit them to live, that we at least give them the chance to evolve.

# Comprehension

## Exercise 1

*Indicate if each statement below is true (T) or false (F) according to your understanding of the passage. Use information in the passage and inferences that can be drawn from the passage to make your decisions.*

1. _____ The brain structure of the chimpanzee probably resembles that of early humans.

2. _____ Toolmaking distinguishes humans from all other animals.

3. _____ Using a familiar tool to solve an unfamiliar problem is common among animals.

4. _____ No chimp can learn to use one tool to make another tool.

5. _____ In the future there might be chimpanzee geniuses.

6. _____ Baby chimpanzees learn how to use tools by watching older chimpanzees.

7. _____ Hugo, mentioned in paragraph 9, is apparently one of the Gombe Stream chimpanzees.

8. _____ Chimpanzee gestures are very different from human gestures.

9. _____ A touch or embrace is reassuring to both anxious chimpanzees and anxious humans.

10. _____ Both apes and humans comfort an upset individual for unselfish reasons.

11. _____ The greeting behavior of chimpanzees serves to distinguish social position.

12. _____ Chimpanzees can recognize each other by their calls.

13. _____ Washoe has learned to speak.

14. _____ Washoe's mistakes in using language seem to indicate that chimp language learning proceeds similarly to the language learning of the human child.

## Exercise 2

*Check (✓) those statements with which you think the author would agree.*

1. _____ Prehistoric people were similar to the modern chimpanzee in several ways.

2. _____ Chimpanzees, like humans, may have varying abilities.

3. _____ Chimpanzee society has different social ranks.

4. _____ Issues of morality seem to enter into chimpanzee behavior.

5. _____ Physical contact plays an important part in the security of chimpanzees throughout their lives.

6. _____ Humans are the only animals with self-awareness.

7. _____ Chimps have reached the height of their development.

8. _____ The similarities between humans and chimpanzees prove that humans are not unique.

## Vocabulary from Context

Both the ideas and the vocabulary in the sentences below are taken from "In the Shadow of Man." Use the context provided to determine the meanings of the italicized words. Give a definition, synonym, or description of each italicized vocabulary item.

1. _____  Chimpanzees in the wild use simple objects as tools, but in laboratory situations they can use more *sophisticated* items.

2. _____  A chimpanzee is born with the ability to handle objects, but the actual tool-using patterns are not *innate;* the infants learn them by observing their elders.

3. _____  Some people believe that one's *posture* tells us a lot about one's self-confidence. They claim that people who stand up straight are generally more self-confident than people who stand bent over.

4. _____  The baby chimp *hurled* himself to the ground, screaming and crying, until his mother picked him up.

5. _____  Humans may sometimes feel reassured by touching and *stroking* a dog or some other pet in moments of emotional crisis.

6. _____  When chimps are angry, they may raise their arms rapidly and wave them wildly. These *gestures* are similar to those of an angry human.

7. _____  Most troubles can be avoided, but death and taxes are *inevitable*.

8. _____  Whereas humans are able to offer help unselfishly, chimpanzees do not seem to help each other for purely *altruistic* reasons.

9. _____  A chimp gets reassurance from touching another chimp just as a person *derives* comfort from touching another person.

10. _____  Some chimps are very independent and appear to be the superior members of a group; others seem to be ruled by the leaders and are quite *submissive*.

11. _____  For chimpanzees, the use of tools is learned behavior that is limited to familiar tasks. They have not demonstrated an ability to use tools *spontaneously* to solve new problems.

12. _____  Hungry chimpanzees have demonstrated their intelligence by using sticks to *probe* for insects in narrow spaces.

## Stems and Affixes

The words in the left column are taken from "In the Shadow of Man." Using your knowledge of stems and affixes, match each word on the left with its synonym or definition on the right. The number in parentheses indicates the paragraph in which the word can be found.

1. ____ dissimilar (1)       a. unable to be solved

2. ____ prehistoric (2)      b. in a lower or inferior class

3. ____ manipulate (4)       c. unlike; different

4. ____ insoluble (4)        d. to free or relieve from trouble

5. ____ reassure (10)        e. occurring before written history

6. ____ unburden (11)        f. to control by skilled use of the hands

7. ____ overjoyed (12)       g. to give confidence or assurance again

8. ____ endearment (13)      h. delighted; filled with joy

9. ____ uneasy (16)          i. restless; without ease or comfort

10. ____ subordinate (16)    j. a loving word; an expression of affection

## Figurative Language and Idioms

In the paragraph indicated by the number in parentheses find the word or phrase that best fits the meaning given. Your teacher may want to read these aloud as you quickly scan the paragraph to find the answer.

1. (4)  Which word means *without an external cause; arising out of the individual*?

2. (12)  What phrase means *to begin to cry suddenly*?

3. (13)  What phrase in sentence four means *became violently angry*?

4. (13)  What phrase in sentence five means *scolded; spoke angrily with*?

5. (14)  What phrase in sentence one means *to find similarities*?

6. (14)  What phrase means *is knocked down*?

## *Discussion/Composition*

Each of the quotations below is taken from "In the Shadow of Man." They are intended to focus your attention on specific aspects of the author's point of view.

**Quotation 1**

It would appear, then, that human and chimp either have evolved gestures and postures along a most remarkable parallel or that we share with the chimpanzees an ancestor in the dim and very distant past; an ancestor, moreover, who communicated by means of kissing and embracing, touching and patting and holding hands.

What are the two possibilities suggested to explain the similarities between human and chimpanzee behavior? Do you agree with either of these explanations? Why or why not?

**Quotation 2**

Yes, human beings definitely overshadow the chimpanzee. The chimpanzee is, nevertheless, a creature of immense significance to the understanding of humans.

Do you think that we can reach an understanding of the human race by studying animals?

**Quotation 3**

Recently it has been proved that the chimpanzee is capable of communicating with people in quite a sophisticated manner.

Is it important that humans attempt to communicate with animals? Why? What animals other than chimpanzees can humans communicate with? What kind of information can animals convey to people?

**Quotation 4**

In human societies much greeting behavior has become ritualized. People who smile when greeting a friend, or who incline their heads when passing an acquaintance in the street, are not necessarily acknowledging that the other has a superior social status. . . . Often, though, human greetings still do serve to clarify the relative social status of the individuals concerned, particularly on formal occasions.

What greetings are you familiar with that indicate social rank? What differences are there in the way you greet your teacher, your parents, and your best friend? What special greetings are used on formal occasions?

**Quotation 5**

The author concludes her essay with the following thought:

Just as they are overshadowed by us, so the chimpanzees overshadow all other animals. They have the ability to solve quite complex problems, they can use and make tools for a variety of purposes, their social structure and methods of communication with each other are elaborate, and they show the beginnings of Self-awareness. Who knows what the chimpanzees will be like forty million years hence?

What does the author suggest about the chimpanzee's potential for development? Do you believe that chimpanzees will continue to develop? Do you think that chimpanzees will ever have the same abilities as humans?

## Vocabulary Review

Place the appropriate word or phrase from the following list in each of the blanks below. Do not use any word or phrase more than once.

| | | |
|---|---|---|
| flew into a tantrum | submissive | altruism |
| draw parallels | sophisticated | inevitable |
| burst into tears | posture | hurled |
| spontaneously | gestured | derived |
| innate | probes | stroking |

1. Unlike the simple machines of the early 1900s, today's automobiles are quite

   _____.

2. "Have a seat," said the professor kindly as she _____ toward a chair.

3. People today are fond of saying that only two things are _____: death and taxes.

4. Some scientists believe that the ability to learn a language is _____ rather than learned.

5. The little girl picked up a stone and _____ it at the letter carrier.

6. The children were so saddened by the death of their pet that they _____ .

7. _____ is encouraged by many religions. Some even suggest that a certain percentage of one's income be given to the poor.

8. My mother always advised me, "Be firm but not aggressive; be polite but not _____ ."

9. When the little boy was told to go to bed, he _____ . His mother had to carry him, kicking and screaming, into the house.

10. A good scientist _____ into all aspects of a problem in order to find solutions.

11. Children are often told to stand up straight so that when they grow up they will have good

    _____ .

12. A person who is truly kind does thoughtful things for others _____ , without having to be asked or reminded.

13. The political situation is so different in the two countries that it is foolish to try to

    _____ between them.

14. The children loved their pet dog and would spend hours _____ it and talking to it.

15. The ritualized greetings used today are probably _____ from the primitive gestures of prehistoric human beings.

# Appendixes

# Appendix A

## Context Clues

Efficient reading requires the use of various problem-solving skills. For example, it is impossible for you to know the exact meaning of every word you read, but by developing your guessing ability, you will often be able to understand enough to arrive at the total meaning of a sentence, paragraph, or essay. Context Clues exercises are designed to help you improve your ability to guess the meaning of unfamiliar words by using clues from the sentence and paragraph in which the words occur. In using the context to decide the meaning of a word you have to use your knowledge of grammar and your understanding of the author's ideas. Although there is no formula that you can memorize to improve your ability to guess the meaning of unfamiliar words, you should keep the following points in mind:

1. Use the meanings of the other words in the sentence (or paragraph) and the meaning of the sentence as a whole to reduce the number of possible meanings.
2. Use grammar and punctuation clues that point to the relationships among the various parts of the sentence.
3. Be content with a general idea about the unfamiliar word; the exact definition or synonym is not always necessary.
4. Learn to recognize situations in which it is not necessary to know the meaning of the word.

---

**Example**

*Each of the sentences in this example contains a blank in order to encourage you to look only at the context provided as you attempt to determine the possible meanings of the missing word. Read each sentence quickly and supply a word for each blank. There is no single correct answer. You are to use context clues to help you provide a word that is appropriate in terms of grammar and meaning.*

1. I removed the _____ from the shelf and began to read.

2. Harvey is a thief; he would _____ the gold from his grandmother's teeth and not feel guilty.

3. Our uncle was a _____, an incurable wanderer who never could stay in one place.

4. Unlike his brother, who is truly a handsome person, Hogartty is quite _____.

5. The Asian _____, like other apes, is specially adapted for life in trees.

6. But surely everyone knows that if you step on an egg, it will _____.

7. Tom got a new _____ for his birthday. It is a sports model, red, with white interior and bucket seats.

*Explanation*

1. I removed the _____
   from the shelf and began
   to read.

   *book*
   *magazine*
   *paper*
   *newspaper*

   The number of things that can be taken
   from a shelf and read is so few that the
   word *book* probably jumped into your
   mind at once. Here, the association
   between the object and the purpose for
   which it is used is so close that you have
   very little difficulty guessing the right
   word.

2. Harvey is a thief; he
   would _____ the gold
   from his grandmother's
   teeth and not feel guilty.

   *steal*
   *take*
   *rob*

   Harvey is a thief. A thief steals. The
   semicolon (;) indicates that the sentence
   that follows contains an explanation of
   the first statement. Further, you know
   that the definition of *thief* is: a person
   who steals.

3. Our uncle was
   a _____,
   an incurable wanderer
   who never could stay in
   one place.

   *nomad*
   *roamer*
   *traveler*
   *drifter*

   The comma (,) following the blank
   indicates a phrase in apposition, that is, a
   word or group of words that could be
   used as a synonym of the unfamiliar
   word. The words at the left are all
   synonyms of *wanderer*.

4. Unlike his brother, who is
   truly a handsome person,
   Hogartty is quite
   _____.

   *ugly*
   *homely*
   *plain*

   Hogartty is the opposite of his brother,
   and since his brother is handsome,
   Hogartty must be ugly. The word *unlike*
   signals the relationship between Hogartty
   and his brother.

5. The Asian _____, like
   other apes, is specially
   adapted for life in trees.

   *gibbon*
   *monkey*
   *chimp*
   *ape*

   You probably didn't write *gibbon,* which
   is the word the author used. Most native
   speakers wouldn't be familiar with this
   word either. But since you know that the
   word is the name of a type of ape, you
   don't need to know anything else. This is
   an example of how context can teach you
   the meaning of unfamiliar words.

6. But surely everyone
   knows that if you step on
   an egg, it will _____.

   *break*

   You recognized the cause and effect
   relationship in this sentence. There is
   only one thing that can happen to an egg
   when it is stepped on.

7. Tom got a new _____
   for his birthday. It is a
   sports model, red, with
   white interior and bucket
   seats.

   *car*

   The description in the second sentence
   gave you all the information you needed
   to guess the word *car.*

# Appendix B

## Dictionary Use

The dictionary is a source of many kinds of information about words. Look at this sample entry* carefully; notice how much information the dictionary presents under the word *prefix*.

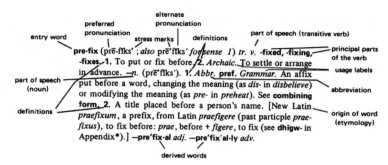

Your dictionary may use a different system of abbreviations or different pronunciation symbols. It is important for you to become familiar with your English dictionary and with the symbols that it uses. Look up *prefix* in your dictionary, and compare the entry to the sample entry.

The following information is provided in Book 1 of *Reader's Choice, International Edition.* We present it here along with the sample dictionary page (page 173) for review.

1. When the dictionary gives more than one spelling or pronunciation, very often the first one is preferred. This varies, however, from dictionary to dictionary, so you will want to check the key to decide if this is true for your dictionary.

2. Dictionaries show how a word is divided into syllables. In the sample dictionary used in this book, syllables are separated by raised dots: pre•fix.

3. The primary reason you might want to know where to divide words into syllables is to hyphenate words at the ends of lines.

4. In the sample dictionary entries in this book, accented syllables are indicated by ' for primary stress and ' for secondary stress.

5. Every dictionary has a pronunciation guide—a list of symbols with common words that illustrate the sound represented by the symbol. In *Reader's Choice,* the sample dictionary provides a pronunciation key at the bottom of each page. Where is the pronunciation key in your dictionary? Note that the entry word that shows you how to pronounce the *u* in *ruse* is *boot.* What is the key word for this sound in your dictionary?

6. You have no doubt noticed that dictionaries do not list all forms of a word separately. For example, *runt* is the entry in the sample dictionary page, but *runty* and *runtiness* are also listed in this entry. These two words are "derived words," words that have the same general meaning as the entry word but are variations. You have to remember this or you will waste time looking up words that do not appear as entry words in the dictionary. For example, what word would you look up if you wanted to know the definition of *ruralism*?

---

*From *The American Heritage Dictionary of the English Language* (Boston: Houghton Mifflin, 1976).

7. Note that dictionaries also provide historical information about words. For example, *runt* probably developed from the Dutch word, *rund,* which means small ox. Knowing this will help you understand the meaning of the word. Can you think of English words that developed from your language? Are there words you use in your native language that come from English?

8. Dictionaries also include "usage labels" to give you information about how common a word is or under what conditions you might want to use a word. Some examples of usage labels are *archaic* and *obsolete* (used to indicate words that are not commonly used today); *slang, informal,* and *colloquial* (words that are used in informal conversation but usually not in formal speech or writing); *poetic* (words used in poetry); and *regional* (words used in particular parts of the English-speaking world).

**runcinate**
Runcinate leaf of dandelion

**rune**

f u th a r k
g w h n i j e
p z s t b e
m l ng o d

basic Germanic runic alphabet

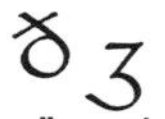
edh yogh

two later runes used in English

**run·a·gate** (rŭn′ə-gāt′) *n. Archaic.* **1.** A renegade or deserter. **2.** A vagabond. [Variant of RENEGADE (influenced by RUN).]
**run-a·round** (rŭn′ə-round′) *n.* Also **run·round** (rŭn′round′). **1.** Deception, usually in the form of evasive excuses. **2.** *Printing.* Type set in a column narrower than the body of the text, as on either side of a picture.
**run·a·way** (rŭn′ə-wā′) *n.* **1.** One that runs away. **2.** An act of running away. **3.** *Informal.* An easy victory. —*adj.* **1.** Escaping or having escaped from captivity or control. **2.** Of or done by running away. **3.** Easily won, as a race. **4.** Of or pertaining to a rapid price rise.
**run·back** (rŭn′băk′) *n.* **1.** The act of returning a kickoff, punt, or intercepted forward pass. **2.** The distance so covered.
**run·ci·ble spoon** (rŭn′sə-bəl). A three-pronged fork, as a pickle fork, curved like a spoon and having a cutting edge. [*Runcible,* a nonsense word coined by Edward Lear.]
**run·ci·nate** (rŭn′sə-nāt′, -nĭt) *adj. Botany.* Having saw-toothed divisions directed backward: *runcinate leaves.* [Latin *runcinātus,* past participle of *runcināre,* to plane, from *runcina,* carpenter's plane (formerly taken also to mean a saw), from Greek *rhukanē*†.]
**run down.** **1. a.** To slow down and stop, as a machine. **b.** To exhaust or wear out. **c.** To lessen in value. **2.** To pursue and capture. **3.** To hit with a moving vehicle. **4.** To disparage; decry. **5.** To give a brief or summary account of. **6.** *Baseball.* To put out a runner after trapping him between two bases.
**run-down** (rŭn′doun′) *n.* **1.** A summary or résumé. **2.** *Baseball.* A play in which a runner is put out when he is trapped between bases. —*adj.* **1.** In poor physical condition; weak or exhausted. **2.** Unwound and not running.
**rune** (rōōn) *n.* **1.** One of the letters of an alphabet used by ancient Germanic peoples, especially by the Scandinavians and Anglo-Saxons. **2.** Any poem, riddle, or the like written in runic characters. **3.** Any occult characters. **4.** A Finnish poem or canto. [In sense 4, from Finnish *runo.* In other senses, Middle English *roun, rune,* secret writing, rune, from Old Norse *rūn* (unattested). See **rūno-** in Appendix.*] —**run′ic** *adj.*
**rung**[1] (rŭng) *n.* **1.** A rod or bar forming a step of a ladder. **2.** A crosspiece supporting the legs or back of a chair. **3.** The spoke in a wheel. **4.** *Nautical.* One of the spokes or handles on a ship's steering wheel. [Middle English *rung, rong,* Old English *hrung,* akin to Old High German *runga,* Gothic *hrugga*†.]
**rung**[2]. Past tense and past participle of **ring.** See Usage note at **ring.**
**run in.** **1.** To insert or include as something extra. **2.** *Printing.* To make a solid body of text without a paragraph or other break. **3.** *Slang.* To take into legal custody.
**run-in** (rŭn′ĭn′) *n.* **1.** A quarrel; an argument; a fight. **2.** *Printing.* Matter added to a text. —*adj.* Added or inserted in text.
**run·let** (rŭn′lĭt) *n.* A rivulet. [Diminutive of RUN (stream).]
**run·nel** (rŭn′əl) *n.* **1.** A rivulet; a brook. **2.** A narrow channel or course, as for water. [Middle English *rynel,* Old English *rynel,* from *rinnan,* to run, flow. See **er-**[1] in Appendix.*]
**run·ner** (rŭn′ər) *n.* **1.** One who or that which runs, as: **a.** One that competes in a race. **b.** A fugitive. **c.** A messenger or errand boy. **2.** An agent or collector, as for a bank or brokerage house. **3.** One who solicits business, as for a hotel or store. **4.** A smuggler. **5.** A vessel engaged in smuggling. **6.** One who operates or manages something. **7.** A device in or on which a mechanism slides or moves, as: **a.** The blade of a skate. **b.** The supports on which a drawer slides. **8.** A long narrow carpet. **9.** A long narrow tablecloth. **10.** A roller towel. **11.** *Metallurgy.* A channel along which molten metal is poured into a mold; gate. **12.** *Botany.* **a.** A slender, creeping stem that puts forth roots from nodes spaced at intervals along its length. **b.** A plant, such as the strawberry, having such a stem. **c.** A twining vine, such as the **scarlet runner** *(see).* **13.** Any of several marine fishes of the family Carangidae, such as the blue runner, *Caranx crysos,* of temperate waters of the American Atlantic coast.
**run·ner-up** (rŭn′ər-ŭp′) *n.* One that takes second place.
**run·ning** (rŭn′ĭng) *n.* **1.** The act of one that runs. **2.** The power or ability to run. **3.** Competition: *in the running.* **4.** An operating: *the running of a machine.* **5. a.** That which runs or flows. **b.** The amount that runs. —*adj.* Continuous: *a running commentary.* —*adv.* Consecutively: *four years running.*
**running board.** A narrow footboard extending under and beside the doors of some automobiles and other conveyances.
**running gear.** **1.** The working parts of an automobile, locomotive, or other vehicle. **2.** **Running rigging** *(see).*
**running hand.** Writing done rapidly without lifting the pen from the paper.
**running head.** *Printing.* A title printed at the top of every page or every other page. Also called "running title."
**running knot.** A **slipknot** *(see).*
**running light.** **1.** One of several lights on a boat or ship kept lighted between dusk and dawn. **2.** One of several similar lights on an aircraft; a navigation light.
**running mate.** **1.** A horse used to set the pace in a race for another horse. **2.** The candidate or nominee for the lesser of two closely associated political offices.
**running rigging.** The part of a ship's rigging that comprises the ropes with which sails are raised, lowered, or trimmed, booms and gaffs are operated, etc. Also called "running gear."
**running stitch.** One of a series of small, even stitches.
**run·ny** (rŭn′ē) *adj.* **-nier, -niest.** Inclined to run or flow.
**Run·ny·mede** (rŭn′ĭ-mēd). A meadow on the Thames, 19 miles west of London, where King John is thought to have signed the Magna Carta in 1215. [Middle English *Runimede,* "meadow on the council island" : Old English *Rūnieg,* council island : *rūn,* secret, secret council (see **rūno-** in Appendix*) + *īeg, īg,* island (see **akwā-** in Appendix*) + *mede,* MEAD (meadow).]
**run off.** **1.** To print, duplicate, or copy. **2.** To run away; elope. **3.** To spill over; to overflow. **4.** To decide a contest or competition by a run-off.
**run-off** (rŭn′ôf′, -ŏf′) *n.* **1. a.** The overflow of a fluid from a container. **b.** Rainfall that is not absorbed by the soil. **2.** Eliminated waste products from manufacturing processes. **3.** An extra competition held to break a tie.
**run-of-the-mill** (rŭn′əv-*thə*-mĭl′) *adj.* Ordinary; not special; average. See Synonyms at **average.** [From *run of (the) mill,* products of a mill that are not graded for quality.]
**run on.** **1.** To continue on and on. **2.** *Printing.* To continue a text without a formal break.
**run-on** (rŭn′ŏn′, -ôn′) *n. Printing.* Matter that is appended or added without a formal break. —*adj.* Being run on.
**run·round.** Variant of **run-around.**
**runt** (rŭnt) *n.* **1.** An undersized animal; especially, the smallest animal of a litter. **2.** A person of small stature. Often used disparagingly. [Possibly from Dutch *rund,* small ox. See **ker-**[1] in Appendix.*] —**runt′i·ness** *n.* —**runt·y** *adj.*
**run through.** **1.** To pierce. **2.** To use up (money, for example) quickly. **3.** To examine or rehearse quickly.
**run-through** (rŭn′thrōō′) *n.* A complete but rapid review or rehearsal of something, such as a theatrical work.
**run·way** (rŭn′wā′) *n.* **1.** A path, channel, or track over which something runs. **2.** The bed of a water course. **3.** A chute down which logs are skidded. **4.** *Bowling.* A narrow track on which balls are returned after they are bowled. **5.** A smooth ramp for wheeled vehicles. **6.** A narrow walkway extending from a stage into an auditorium. **7.** A strip of level ground, usually paved, on which aircraft take off and land.
**Run·yon** (rŭn′yən), **(Alfred) Damon.** 1884–1946. American journalist and author of short stories.
**ru·pee** (rōō-pē′, rōō′pē) *n. Abbr.* **Re., r., R.** **1. a.** The basic monetary unit of Ceylon and Mauritius, equal to 100 cents. **b.** The basic monetary unit of India, equal to 100 paise. **c.** The basic monetary unit of Nepal, equal to 100 pice. **d.** The basic monetary unit of Pakistan, equal to 100 paisas. See table of exchange rates at **currency.** **2.** A coin worth one rupee. [Hindi *rupaīyā,* from Sanskrit *rūpya,* wrought silver, from *rūpa*†, shape, image.]
**Ru·pert** (rōō′pərt). A river of Quebec, Canada, flowing 380 miles westward from Mistassini Lake to James Bay.
**Ru·pert** (rōō′pərt), **Prince.** 1619–1682. German-born English military, naval, and political leader; supporter of Charles I; inventor.
**Ru·pert's Land** (rōō′pərts). The Canadian territory granted the Hudson's Bay Company in 1670, most of which was incorporated in The Northwest Territories after its purchase by Canada in 1870.
**ru·pi·ah** (rōō-pē′ä) *n., pl.* **rupiah** or **-ahs.** **1.** The basic monetary unit of Indonesia, equal to 100 sen. See table of exchange rates at **currency.** **2.** A note worth one rupiah. [Hindi *rupaīyā,* RUPEE.]
**rup·ture** (rŭp′chər) *n.* **1. a.** The act of breaking open or bursting. **b.** The state of being broken open or burst. **2.** A break in friendly relations between individuals or nations. **3.** *Pathology.* **a.** A **hernia** *(see),* especially of the groin or intestines. **b.** A tear in bodily tissue. —*v.* **ruptured, -turing, -tures.** —*tr.* To break open; burst. —*intr.* To undergo or suffer a rupture. —See Synonyms at **break.** [Middle English *ruptur,* from Old French *rupture,* from Latin *ruptūra,* from *rumpere* (past participle *ruptus*), to break. See **reup-** in Appendix.*] —**rup′tur·a·ble** *adj.*
**ru·ral** (rŏŏr′əl) *adj.* **1.** Of or pertaining to the country as opposed to the city; rustic. **2.** Of or pertaining to people who live in the country. **3.** Of or relating to farming; agricultural. Compare **urban.** [Middle English, from Old French, from Latin *rūrālis,* from *rūs* (stem *rūr-*), country. See **rewe-** in Appendix.*] —**ru′ral·ism′** *n.* —**ru′ral·ist** *n.* —**ru′ral·ly** *adv.*
***Synonyms:*** *rural, arcadian, bucolic, rustic, pastoral, sylvan.* These adjectives are all descriptive of existence or environment which is close to nature; those with a literary flavor are often used facetiously. *Rural* applies to sparsely settled or agricultural country, as distinct from settled communities. *Arcadian* implies ideal or simple country living. *Bucolic* is often used derisively of country people or manners. *Rustic,* sometimes uncomplimentary, applies to country people who seem unsophisticated, but may also apply favorably to living conditions or to natural environments which are pleasingly primitive. *Pastoral* implies the supposed peace of rural living and the shepherd's life, with a suggestion of artificiality. *Sylvan* refers to wooded as opposed to cultivated country, and carries the sense of unspoiled beauty.
**rural free delivery.** *Abbr.* **R.F.D., RFD** Free government delivery of mail in rural areas.
**ru·ral·i·ty** (rōō-răl′ə-tē) *n., pl.* **-ties.** **1.** The state or quality of being rural. **2.** A rural trait or characteristic.
**ru·ral·ize** (rŏŏr′əl-īz′) *v.* **-ized, -izing, -izes.** —*tr.* To make rural. —*intr.* To live or visit in the country. —**ru′ral·i·za′tion** *n.*
**rural route.** *Abbr.* **R.R.** A rural mail route.
**Ru·rik** (rŏŏ′rĭk). Died A.D. 879. Scandinavian warrior; founder of the dynasty that ruled Russia until 1598.
**Rus.** Russia; Russian.
**Ru·se** (rōō′sā). *Turkish* **Rus·chuk** (rōōs′chŏŏk). A Danubian port in northeastern Bulgaria. Population, 118,000.
**ruse** (rōōz) *n.* An action or device meant to confuse or mislead. See Synonyms at **artifice.** [Middle English, detour of a hunted animal, from Old French, from *ruser,* to repulse, detour. See **rush** (to dash off).]

# Appendix C

## Stems and Afixes

Using context clues is one way to discover the meaning of an unfamiliar word. Another way is word analysis, that is, looking at the meanings of parts of words. Many English words have been formed by combining parts of older English, Greek, and Latin words. If you know the meanings of some of these word parts, you can often guess the meaning of an unfamiliar English word, particularly in context.

For example, *report* is formed from *re*, which means back, and *port*, which means carry. *Scientist* is derived from *sci*, which means know, and *ist*, which means one who. *Port* and *sci* are called stems. A stem is the basic part on which groups of related words are built. *Re* and *ist* are called affixes, that is, word parts that are attached to stems. Affixes like *re*, which are attached to the beginning of stems, are called prefixes. Affixes attached to the end, like *ist*, are called suffixes. Generally, prefixes change the meaning of a word and suffixes change its part of speech. Here is an example:

| Stem | pay (verb) | honest (adjective) |
| --- | --- | --- |
| Prefix | *re*pay (verb) | *dis*honest (adjective |
| Suffix | repay*ment* (noun) | dishonest*ly* (adverb) |

Word analysis is not always enough to give you the precise definition of a word you encounter in a reading passage, but often along with context it will help you to understand the general meaning of the word so that you can continue reading without stopping to use a dictionary.

Below is a list of the stems and affixes that appear in *Reader's Choice, International Edition: Books 1 and 2*. The numbers in parentheses indicate the book and unit in which an item appears.

### Prefixes

(1:5) **a-, an-**  without, lacking, not

(1:3) **ante-**  before

(1:5) **bene-**  good

(1:5) **bi-**  two

(2:3) **by-**  aside or apart from the common, secondary

(1:3) **circum-**  around

(1:1) **com-, con-, col-, cor-, co-**  together, with

(1:3) **contra-, anti-**  against

(2:3) **de-**  down from, away

(2:3) **dia-**  through, across

(2:3) **epi-**  upon, over, outer

(2:3) **hyper-**  above, beyond, excessive

(2:3) **hypo-**  under, beneath, down

(1:1) **in-, im-, il-, ir-**  in, into, on

(1:1) **in-, im-, il-, ir-**  not

(1:3) **inter-**  between

(1:3) **intro-, intra-**  within

(1:1) **micro-**  small

(1:5) **mis-**  wrong

(1:5) **mono-**  one, alone

(2:1) **multi-**  many

(2:1) **peri-**  around

(1:5) **poly-**  many

(1:3) **post-**  after

(1:1) **pre-**  before

(1:1) **re-, retro-**  back, again

(2:1) **semi-**  half, partly

(1:3) **sub-, suc-, suf-, sug-, sup-, sus-**  under

(1:3) **super-**  above, greater, better

(1:5) **syn-, sym-, syl-**  with, together

(1:3) **trans-**  across

(2:1) **tri-**  three

(2:1) **ultra-** beyond, excessive, extreme
(2:1) **uni-** one

## Stems

(1:5) **-anthro-, -anthropo-** human
(1:5) **-arch-** first, chief, leader
(2:1) **-aster-, astro-, stellar-** star
(1:1) **-audi-, audit-** hear
(2:1) **-auto-** self
(2:1) **-bio-** life
(2:3) **-capit-** head, chief
(1:3) **-ced-** go, move, yield
(1:1) **-chron-** time
(2:3) **-corp-** body
(2:1) **-cycle-** circle
(2:3) **-derm-** skin
(1:1) **-dic-, -dict-** say, speak
(1:3) **-duc-** lead
(1:5) **-fact-, -fect-** make, do
(1:3) **-flect-** bend
(1:5) **-gam-,** marriage
(2:3) **-geo**-earth
(1:1) **-graph-, -gram-** write, writing
(1:5) **-hetero-** different, other
(1:5) **-homo-** same
(2:3) **-hydr-, -hydro-** water
(1:1) **-log-, -ology-** speech, word, study
(1:5) **-man-, -manu-** hand
(2:1) **-mega-** great, large
(1:3) **-mit-, -miss-** send
(1:5) **-morph-** form, structure
(2:1) **-mort-** death
(1:5) **-onym-, -nomen-** name
(2:3) **-ortho-** straight, correct
(1:5) **-pathy-** feeling, disease

(2:1) **-phil-** love
(1:1) **-phon-** sound
(2:3) **-pod-, -ped-** foot
(1:3) **-pon-, -pos-** put, place
(2:1) **-polis-** city
(1:3) **-port-** carry
(2:1) **-psych-** mind
(1:1) **-scrib-, script-** write
(1:3) **-sequ-, -secut-** follow
(2:3) **-son-** sound
(1:1) **-spect-** look at
(1:3) **-spir-** breathe
(2:1) **-soph-** wise
(1:3) **-tele-** far
(1:5) **-theo-, -the-** god
(2:3) **-therm-, -thermo-** heat
(1:3) **-ven-, -vene-** come
(2:3) **-ver-** true
(1:1) **-vid-, -vis-** true
(1:3) **-voc-, -vok-** call

## Suffixes

(1:3) **-able, -ible, -ble** capable of, fit for
(2:3) **-ate** to make
(1:1) **-er, -or** one who
(2:3) **-fy** to make
(1:5) **-ic, -al** relating to, having the nature of
(1:5) **-ism** action or practice, theory or doctrine
(1:1) **-ist** one who
(2:1) **-ity** condition, quality, state of being
(2:3) **-ize** to make
(2:1) **-ness** condition, quality, state of being
(1:5) **-oid** like, resembling
(1:3) **-ous, ious, -ose** full of, having the qualities of
(1:1) **-tion, -ation** condition, the act of

# Appendix D

## Sentence Study

The exercises in this book provide you with practice in using a number of reading skills and strategies to understand an author's message. Context Clues, Stems and Affixes, and Dictionary Use exercises teach you strategies for discovering the meanings of unfamiliar vocabulary items. Scanning exercises provide you with practice in quickly finding specific pieces of information in a passage. Skimming exercises allow you to focus on reading a passage quickly for a general idea of its meaning.

When you have difficulty understanding a passage, just reading further will often make the passage clearer. Sometimes, however, comprehension of an entire passage depends on your being able to understand a single sentence. Sentences that are very long, sentences that have more than one meaning, or sentences that contain difficult grammatical patterns often cause comprehension problems for readers. The sentence study exercise that follows as well as similar ones in later units gives you the opportunity to develop strategies for attacking complicated sentences.

Although there is no easy formula that will help you to arrive at an understanding of a difficult sentence, you should keep the following points in mind.

1. Try to determine what makes the sentence difficult:

   a. If the sentence contains a lot of difficult vocabulary it may be that the sentence can be understood without knowing the meaning of every word. Try crossing out unfamiliar items:

   > The West had sent armies to ~~capture and~~ hold Jerusalem; instead they themselves fell ~~victim~~ to ~~a host of~~ new ideas and ~~subtle~~ influences which left their mark on the development of European literature, ~~chivalry,~~ warfare, ~~sanitation,~~ commerce, political institutions, medicine, ~~and the papacy itself.~~

   b. If the sentence is very long, try to break it up into smaller parts:

   > The West had sent armies to capture and hold Jerusalem. The West fell victim to a host of new ideas and subtle influences. These ideas and influences left their mark on the development of European literature, chivalry, warfare, sanitation, commerce, political institutions, medicine, and the papacy.

   c. Also, if the sentence is very long, try to determine which parts of the sentence express specific details supporting the main idea. Often clauses which are set off by commas, or introduced by words like *which, who,* and *that,* are used to introduce extra information or to provide supporting details. Try crossing out the supporting details in order to determine the main idea:

   > These ideas, ~~which left their mark on the development of European literature, chivalry, warfare, sanitation, commerce, political institutions, medicine, and the papacy,~~ greatly changed Western culture.

*Be careful! A good reader reads quickly but accurately.*

2. Learn to recognize the important grammatical and punctuation clues that can change the meaning of a sentence.

   a. Look for single words and affixes that can change the entire meaning of a sentence:

      Summery weather is *not un*common.
      The *average* daytime *high* temperature is *approximately* 56°.

   b. Look for punctuation clues:

      Wally ⌣sings☺ at all of his friends' parties.
      Barry said, "George has been elected president⑦"

Note that all of the italicized words or affixes and the circled punctuation above are essential to the meaning of the sentences; if any of these are omitted, the meaning of the sentence changes significantly.

   c. Look for key words that tell you of relationships within a sentence:

      The school has grown *from* a small building holding 200 students *to* a large institute that educates 4,000 students a year.

      *From . . . to* indicates the beginning and end points of a period of change.

      Many critics have proclaimed Doris Lessing as *not only* the best writer of the postwar generation, *but also* a penetrating analyst of human affairs.

      *Not only . . . but also* indicates that both parts of the sentence are of equal importance.

      *In order to* graduate on time, you will need to take five courses each semester.

      *In order to* is like *if*; it indicates that some event must occur before another event can take place.

      The West had sent armies to capture and hold Jerusalem; *instead* they themselves fell victim to new ideas and subtle influences.

      *Instead* indicates that something happened contrary to expectations.

      *As a result of* three books, a television documentary, and a special exposition at the Library of Congress, the mystery has aroused considerable public interest.

      *As a result of* indicates a cause and effect relationship. The clause that follows *as a result of* is the cause of some event. The three books, television program, and exposition are the *cause*; the arousal of public interest is the *effect*.

      *Because* of the impact of these ideas, *which* had been introduced originally to Europe by soldiers returning from the East, the West was greatly changed.

      *Because of* indicates a cause and effect relationship. The West was changed as a result of these ideas. The information between the word *which* and the final comma (,) refers to *these ideas*.

# Appendix E

## Main Idea

Being able to determine the main idea of a passage is one of the most useful reading skills you can develop. It is a skill you can apply to any kind of reading. For example, when you read for enjoyment or to obtain general information, it is probably not important to remember all the details of a selection. Instead, you want to quickly discover the general message—the main idea of the passage. For other kinds of reading, such as reading textbooks or articles in your own field, you need both to determine the main ideas and to understand the way in which these are developed.

The main idea of a passage is the thought that is present from the beginning to the end. In a well-written paragraph, most of the sentences support, describe, or explain the main idea. It is sometimes stated in the first or last sentence of the paragraph. Sometimes the main idea is only implied. In a poem, the main idea is often implied rather than stated explicitly.

In order to determine the main idea of a piece of writing, you should ask yourself what idea is common to most of the text. What is the idea that relates the parts to the whole? What opinion do all the parts support? What idea do they all explain or describe?

Main Idea exercises are designed to teach you how to read quickly to determine the general message without worrying about details.

---

**Example**

By the time the first European travelers on the American continent began to record some of their observations about Indians, the Cherokee people had developed an advanced culture that probably was exceeded only by the civilized tribes of the Southwest: Mayan and Aztec groups. The social structures of the Cherokee people consisted of a form of clan kinship in which there were seven recognized clans. All members of a clan were considered blood brothers and sisters and were bound by honor to defend any member of that clan from wrong. Each clan, the Bird, Paint, Deer, Wolf, Blue, Long Hair, and Wild Potato, was represented in the civil council by a councillor or councillors. The chief of the tribe was selected from one of these clans and did not inherit his office from his kinsmen. Actually, there were two chiefs, a Peace chief and War chief. The Peace chief served when the tribe was at peace, but the minute war was declared, the War chief was in command.*

---

*Select the statement that best expresses the main idea of the paragraph.*

_____ a. The Cherokee chief was different in war time than in peace time.

_____ b. Before the arrival of the Europeans the Cherokees had developed a well-organized society.

_____ c. The Mayans and the Aztecs were part of the Cherokee tribe.

_____ d. Several Indian cultures had developed advanced civilizations before Europeans arrived.

---

*From Tim B. Underwood, *The Story of the Cherokee People* (S. B. Newman Printing Co., 1961), p. 13.

*Explanation*

_____ a. This is not the main idea. Rather, it is one of several examples the author uses to support his statement that the Cherokee people had developed an advanced culture.

_✓_ b. This statement expresses the main idea of the paragraph. All other sentences in the paragraph are examples supporting the idea that the Cherokees had developed an advanced culture by the time Europeans arrived on the continent.

_____ c. This statement is false, so it cannot be the main idea.

_____ d. This statement is too general. The paragraph describes the social structure of the Cherokee people only. Although the author names other advanced Indian cultures, he does this only to strengthen his argument that the Cherokees had developed an advanced culture.

# Appendix F

## Restatement and Inference

Restatement and Inference exercises are designed to sharpen your critical reading skills. They· give you practice in recognizing different ways of stating the same information and in identifying conclusions that are implied but not stated.

In the exercises each paragraph is followed by five statements. The statements are of four types:

1. Some of the statements are *restatements* of ideas in the original paragraph. They give the same information in a different way.
2. Some of the statements are *inferences* (conclusions) that can be drawn from the information given in the paragraph.
3. Some of the statements are not true based on the information given.
4. Some of the statements cannot be judged true or false based on the information given in the original paragraph.

Sentences that are restatements or inferences (types 1 or 2) should be checked ( ✓ ). Statements that are true generally but cannot be inferred from the paragraph should not be checked.

---

**Example**

> Often people who hold higher positions in a given group overestimate their performance, while people in the lowest levels of the group underestimate theirs. While this may not always be true, it does indicate that often the actual position in the group has much to do with the feeling of personal confidence a person may have. Thus, members who hold higher positions in a group or feel that they have an important part to play in the group will probably have more confidence in their own performance.

---

_____ a. If people have confidence in their own performance, they will achieve high positions in a group.

_____ b. If we let people know they are an important part of a group, they will probably become more self-confident.

_____ c. People who hold low positions in a group often overestimate their performance.

_____ d. People in positions of power in a group may feel they do better work than they really do.

_____ e. People with higher positions in a group do better work than other group members.

*Explanation*

_____ a. This cannot be inferred from the paragraph. We know that people who hold high positions have more self-confidence than those who don't. However, we don't know that people with more confidence will achieve higher status. Confidence may come only *after* one achieves a higher position.

✔ b. This is an inference that can be drawn from the last sentence in the paragraph. We know that if people feel they have an important part to play in a group, they will probably have more self-confidence. We can infer that if we let people know (and therefore make them feel) that they have an important part to play, they will probably become more self-confident.

___ c. This is false. The first sentence states that the people in the lowest levels of a group underestimate, not overestimate, their performance.

✔ d. This is a restatement of the first sentence. People who hold higher positions tend to overestimate their performance: they may feel they do better work than they really do.

___ e. We do not know this from the paragraph. We now that people who hold higher positions often *think* they do better work than others in a group. (They "overestimate their performance.") We do not know that they actually do better work.

# Appendix G

## Reading for Full Understanding

Exercises in Reading for Full Understanding require very careful reading. Each selection is followed by a number of questions. The questions are designed to give you practice in:
1. determining the main idea
2. understanding supporting details
3. drawing inferences
4. guessing vocabulary items from context
5. using syntactic and stylistic clues to understand selected portions of the paragraphs

In Reading for Full Understanding exercises read each paragraph carefully. Try to determine the author's main idea while attempting to remember important details. For each of the questions, select the *best* answer. You may refer to the passage to answer the questions.

*Example*

1     It is not often realized that women held a high place in southern
2 European societies in the 10th and 11th centuries. As a wife, the
3 woman was protected by the setting up of a dowry or *decimum*.
4 Admittedly, the purpose of this was to protect her against the risk of
5 desertion, but in reality its function in the social and family life of the
6 time was much more important. The *decimum* was the wife's right to
7 receive a tenth of all her husband's property. The wife had the right to
8 withhold consent, in *all* transactions the husband would make. And
9 more than just a right: the documents show that she enjoyed a real
10 power of decision, equal to that of her husband. In no case do the
11 documents indicate any degree of difference in the legal status of
12 husband and wife.
13     The wife shared in the management of her husband's personal
14 property, but the opposite was not always true. Women seemed
15 perfectly prepared to defend their own inheritance against husbands
16 who tried to exceed their rights, and on occasion they showed a
17 fine fighting spirit. A case in point is that of María Vivas, a Catalan
18 woman of Barcelona. Having agreed with her husband Miró to sell a
19 field she had inherited, for the needs of the household, she insisted on
20 compensation. None being offered, she succeeded in dragging her
21 husband to the scribe to have a contract duly drawn up assigning her a
22 piece of land from Miró's personal inheritance. The unfortunate
23 husband was obliged to agree, as the contract says, "for the sake of
24 peace." Either through the dowry or through being hot-tempered, the
25 Catalan wife knew how to win herself, within the context of the family,
26 a powerful economic position.*

---

*From Sylvia L. Thrupp, ed., *Early Medieval Society* (New York: Appleton-Century-Crofts, 1967), p. 120.

1. A *decimum* was _____

  _____ a.  the wife's inheritance from her father.
  _____ b.  a gift of money to the new husband.
  _____ c.  a written contract.
  _____ d.  the wife's right to receive one-tenth of her husband's property.

2. In the society described in the passage, the legal standing of the wife in marriage was _____

  _____ a.  higher than that of her husband.
  _____ b.  lower than that of her husband.
  _____ c.  the same as that of her husband.
  _____ d.  higher than that of a single woman.

3. What compensation did María Vivas get for the field?

  _____ a.  some of the land Miró had inherited
  _____ b.  a tenth of Miró's land
  _____ c.  money for household expenses
  _____ d.  money from Miró's inheritance

4. Could a husband sell his wife's inheritance?

  _____ a.  no, under no circumstances
  _____ b.  yes, whenever he wished to
  _____ c.  yes, if she agreed
  _____ d.  yes, if his father-in-law agreed

5. Which of the following is NOT mentioned as an effect of the dowry system?

  _____ a.  The husband had to share the power of decision in marriage.
  _____ b.  The wife was protected from desertion
  _____ c.  The wife gained a powerful economic position.
  _____ d.  The husband was given control over his wife's property.

*Explanation*

1. (d)  This is a restatement of a part of the passage. If you did not remember the definition of the word *decimum,* you could have scanned for it quickly and found the answer in lines 6 and 7.

2. (c)  This is the main idea of the paragraph. The high place of women in the society is introduced in the first sentence. In lines 9 and 10 the author states that a woman enjoyed a legal power of decision equal to that of her husband. The last sentence tells us that, within the context of the home, women held a powerful economic position.

3. (a)  This tests your understanding of details. In lines 20, 21, and 22 the author states that María Vivas forced her husband to agree to a contract giving her a piece of land from his inheritance.

4. (c) This is an inference. In lines 7 and 8 the author states that the wife could refuse to agree to any business agreements the husband might want to make. Thus, we can infer that a husband could only sell his wife's inheritance if she agreed. Furthermore, in lines 18 and 19, the fact that María Vivas allowed her husband to sell a field she had inherited indicates that her agreement was necessary.

5. (d) Items a, b, and c serve as a summary of the ideas of the passage.

   (a) Lines 9 and 10 tell us that wives enjoyed a real power of decision; lines 13 and 14 state that a wife shared in the management of her husband's estate.

   (b) Lines 4 and 5 state that the purpose of the dowry was to protect wives from desertion.

   (c) The final sentence states that, within the context of the family, the wife was able to win a powerful economic position.

   (d) Nowhere does it state that a husband was given control over a wife's property, and in several instances the opposite is stated (see questions 3 and 4).

# Appendix H

## Scanning

We read differently depending on our goal for reading. Sometimes we only need to locate a particular piece of information. For example, we might read the newspaper to discover the final score of a sports event, or to find out when and where a lecture will be held. To scan is to read quickly in order to locate specific information. The steps involved in scanning are the following:

1. Decide exactly information you are looking for, and think about the form it may take. For example, if you want to know when something happened, you would look for a date. If you want to find out who did something, you would look for a name.
2. Next, decide where you need to look to find the information you want. You probably would not look for sports scores on the front page of the newspaper, nor look under the letter *S* for the telephone number of Sam Potter.
3. Move your eyes as quickly as possible down the page until you find the information you need. Read it carefully.
4. When you find what you need, do not read further.

# Appendix I

## Skimming

It is sometimes useful to obtain a general impression of a book, article, or story before deciding whether or not to read more carefully. *To skim* is to read quickly in order to get a general idea of a passage. Unlike scanning,* which involves searching for details or isolated facts, skimming requires you to note only information and clues that provide an idea of the central theme or topic of a piece of prose.

When you skim, it is necessary to read only selected sentences in order to get the main idea. You should also use textual clues such as italicized or underlined words, headlines or subtitles, spacing, paragraphing, etc. Do not read every word or sentence.

Once you have a general idea about an article, you may decide to read the entire selection carefully, or only to scan for specific pieces of information in order to answer questions that have occurred to you.

The following partial entry from an encyclopedia is from a biography of a famous person. Preceding the selection is a question concerning a research topic. You must skim the passage to decide if a careful reading would provide information on the topic given. Indicate your answer by checking *Yes* or *No*.

---

**Example**

In one minute, skim this passage and indicate if the selection should be read carefully.

Would you do more research on Jane Addams if you were interested in women's contribution to modern elementary education?

\_\_\_\_\_ Yes
\_\_\_\_\_ No

---

ADDAMS, JANE (1860–1935), American social worker who founded the Chicago social welfare center known as Hull House. She was born in Cedarville, Ill., on Sept. 6, 1860, the daughter of a prosperous merchant. She graduated from Rockford College (then Rockford Seminary) in 1881. Traveling in Europe, she was stirred by the social reform movement in England and especially by a visit to Toynbee Hall, the first university settlement. In 1889, with her college classmate Ellen Gates Starr, she founded Hull House in the slums of Chicago.

Hull House grew rapidly and soon became the most famous settlement house in America. Many reformers came there, not so much to serve as to learn. Jane Addams was the leader and dominant personality. Hull House pioneered in child labor reform and in the fight for better housing, parks, and playgrounds. It initiated steps toward progressive education and attempts to acclimatize immigrants to America.

Jane Addams was a practical idealist and an activist. She favored prohibition and woman suffrage, and she campaigned for the Progressive party in 1912. She went beyond politics, however, for politics to her was part of a larger movement to humanize the industrial city.

She had always been a pacifist, and when World War I broke out in 1914, she became chairman of the Woman's Peace party and president of the International Congress of Women. In 1915 she visited many countries in Europe, urging the end of the war through mediation. She remained a pacifist when the United States entered the war in 1917, and as a result she was denounced by many Americans. In 1931 she was awarded the Nobel Peace Prize (sharing the award with Nicholas Murray Butler).

Jane Addams continued to be in the vanguard of social reform movements until her death in Chicago on May 21, 1935. She wrote ten books (including her famous *Twenty Years at Hull House*) and more than 400 articles. The influence that had begun at Hull House continued to spread around the world.†

*Explanation*

You should have checked *No*. The first sentence identifies Jane Addams as an ". . . American social worker who founded the Chicago social welfare center known as Hull House." A brief glance at the second and fourth paragraphs indicates that she worked for child labor reform, that

---

*For an introduction to scanning, see Appendix H.
†From *The Encyclopedia Americana*, 1983 ed. (Danbury, Conn.: Grolier, 1983).

she was a pacifist, and that she was chair of the Women's Peace party. Her publications, mentioned at the end of the article, do not deal with elementary education. Note that it is necessary to read only selected parts of each paragraph in order to obtain the main idea.

# Answer Key

The processes involved in arriving at an answer are often more important than the answer itself. It is expected that students will not use the Answer Key until they have completed the exercises and are prepared to defend their answers. If a student's answer does not agree with the Key, it is important for the student to return to the exercise to discover the source of the error. No answer is provided where the students have been asked to express their own opinions or when there is no one best answer.

## Unit 1

### Nonprose Reading: Poetry

**Comprehension Clues (page 4)**

"Living Tenderly": a turtle
1. rounded
2. a short snake
3. F
4. T
5. F

"Southbound on the Freeway": a highway with motorists and a police car
1. The tourist is parked in the air.
2. They are made of metal and glass.
   a. Their feet are round.
   b. They have four eyes; the two in back are red.
3. the road on which they travel
4. a. They have a fifth turning red eye on top.
   b. The others go slowly when it is around.
5. a large roadway

"By Morning": snow
1. fresh, daintily, airily
2. transparent
3. a covering
4. They become like fumbling sheep.
5. snow

### Word Study: Context Clue

**Exercise 1 (page 5)**
1. attributes: qualities; talents; abilities
2. to confer: to grant; to give to
3. plump: fat; chubby
4. pedantic: bookish; boring; giving attention to small, unimportant, scholarly details
5. aloof: above; apart from
6. to refrain: to hold back; to control oneself
7. ineffectual: not effective; not producing the intended effect
8. marigolds: a (type of) flower
9. drab: uninteresting; dull; cheerless; lacking in color or brightness
10. skin/cortex/membrane: outside cover of a body or organ; boundary

**Exercise 2 (page 6)**
babbling: meaningless sounds that babies make before they learn to talk
sequence: related group; series; the coming of one thing after another
hearing impaired: deaf; having problems hearing
myth: untruth; an untrue story or belief

### Word Study: Stems and Affixes

**Exercise 1 (pages 7–8)**
1. b
2. c
3. d
4. d
5. b
6. b
7. c
8. a
9. An astronaut is a person who sails (travels) to the stars (outer space). (*astro*: star)

10. All the clothes look the same.
11. birth rate

**Exercise 2 (page 9)**
1. biographies: life histories
2. triplets: three children born at a single birth
3. multimillionaire: person who is worth many millions of dollars
4. metropolitan: a population area consisting of a central city and smaller surrounding communities
5. semiprivate: partly, but not completely private; a room with more than one person
6. multivolume: several-volume; consisting of more than one book
7. peripheral: (vision) away from the center, at the sides; having good peripheral vision means having the ability to see things on either side
8. semiprecious: of lesser value; semiprecious stones have lower value than "precious stones"
9. mortal wound: injury that causes death
10. periodontist: dentist concerned with diseases of the bone and tissue around the teeth
11. popularity: the state or quality of being popular; being liked by the general population

**Exercise 3 (page 10)**
1. f
2. e
3. a
4. d
5. c
6. b
7. c
8. a
9. f
10. e
11. d
12. b
13. a
14. f
15. d
16. b
17. e
18. c

### Sentence Study: Restatement and Inference (pages 12–14)

1. c, e
2. b, c, e
3. b, e
4. b, c
5. b, d
6. d
7. b, c
8. b, d, e
9. a, c, d
10. b, e

### Paragraph Reading: Main Idea (pages 15–20)

Paragraph 1: c
Paragraph 2: d
Paragraph 3: d
Paragraph 4: a
Paragraph 5: c
Paragraph 6: A summit is a meeting between leaders of enemy Great Powers trying to reach agreements in order to avoid future conflict.
Paragraph 7: The ideals that children hold have important implications for their school experiences. Belief in the value of hard work, the importance of personal responsibility, and the importance of education itself contributes to greater success in school.
Poem: Our photo albums show our lives as we want to believe they were.

### Discourse Focus: Prediction (pages 22–24)

There are no single correct responses to the items in this exercise. Students should work interactively: interacting with each other and the text in order to form predictions, then reading to see if these are confirmed. The answers, therefore, are available by further reading.

3. While there is no single correct answer, *a* and *d* are the most likely. The inset suggests that the

191

author will *begin* by reviewing the current troubled state of calculus instruction.

4–5. These questions require a personal response.

6. This paragraph presents calculus instruction in a negative light: calculus is described as a *barrier*; students have *no choice* but to take it; calculus brings back *painful memories*. This very *general* introductory description might lead us to expect that the author will go on to describe *specific* aspects of the current state of calculus instruction.

7. This question is intended for discussion.

8. The final, transition sentence of the previous paragraph states that "participants brought worthwhile suggestions." One might expect that suggestions for change will follow.

9. This question requires a personal response.

10. This question is intended for discussion.

11. This question requires a personal response.

12. The rest of the article discusses suggestions for change and issues involved in implementing that change. Suggestions for change include utilizing the potential of handheld calculators to eliminate routine problems, thus concentrating on the central ideas of calculus. Other suggestions are to reinforce the important role of approximation and to streamline courses by eliminating much specialized material. In terms of implementation, issues discussed are the need for change in high school math curricula, for new textbooks, and for smaller university calculus classes.

## Unit 2

### Selection 1A: Magazine Article
### "Crowded Earth—Billions More Coming"

**Comprehension (pages 25–26)**

| | | | | | | | | | |
|---|---|---|---|---|---|---|---|---|---|
| 1. F | 4. T | 7. T | 10. F | 13. T | 16. F |
| 2. T | 5. T | 8. T | 11. T | 14. F | 17. T |
| 3. F | 6. F | 9. F | 12. T | 15. F | 18. F |

19. decline in infant mortality; increased life spans
20. greater likelihood of violence and upheaval
21. It is based on the 1972 rate of increase. Factors include medical advances, birth control education, natural disasters, etc.

### Selection 1B: Magazine Article
### "The Global Community: On the Way to 9 Billion"

**Comprehension (page 28)**

| | | | | |
|---|---|---|---|---|
| 1. T | 2. T | 3. F | 4. T | 5. T |

### Selection 1C: Magazine Article
### "The Stork Has a Busier Time, but—"

**Comprehension (pages 30–32)**

| | | | | |
|---|---|---|---|---|
| 1. F | 5. T | 9. T | 13. T | 17. T |
| 2. T | 6. T | 10. F | 14. T | 18. F |
| 3. F | 7. F | 11. T | 15. F | |
| 4. a | 8. F | 12. T | 16. T | |

19. the changing role of women (women entering the work force; the fact that women are having their first babies later in life than before)

### Reading Selection 2: Magazine Article
### "Why We Laugh"

## Comprehension

### Exercise 1 (pages 34–36)

| | | | | |
|---|---|---|---|---|
| 1. T | 4. T | 7. F | 10. T | 13. T |
| 2. T | 5. F | 8. T | 11. T | 14. F |
| 3. T | 6. F | 9. T | 12. F | |

### Exercise 2 (page 36)

| | | | | | |
|---|---|---|---|---|---|
| 1. 3 (4) | 2. 4 | 3. 12 | 4. 8 | 5. 1 | 6. 2 |

(Other answers are possible for these questions.)

## Critical Reading

### Exercise 1 (pages 36–37)

1. Bergson: essayist
2. Grotjahn: psychiatrist
3. Levine: professor of psychology
4. Plato: philosopher

### Exercise 2 (page 37)

| | | |
|---|---|---|
| 1. Freud | 3. author | 5. author |
| 2. author | 4. Grotjahn | 6. author |

## Vocabulary from Context

### Exercise 1 (pages 38–39)

1. anxiety: uneasiness; worry; nervousness, tension
2. to resent: to feel displeasure; to feel injured or offended
3. conscious: aware; knowing what one is doing and why
4. tension: nervousness; anxiety; mental or physical strain
5. to disguise: to hide; to cover up; to make unrecognizable
6. aggressive: attacking; bold; energetic; active
7. butt: the object of joking or criticism; target
8. target: the object of verbal attack or criticism; butt
9. to master: to control; to conquer; to overcome
10. factor: any circumstance or condition that brings about a result; a cause; an element
11. crucial: of extreme importance; decisive; critical; main
12. to suppress: to keep from appearing or being known; to hide; to repress
13. to repress: to prevent unconscious ideas from reaching the level of consciousness; to suppress
14. drive: basic impulse or urge; desire; pressure
15. to discharge: to release; to get rid of; to emit; to relieve oneself of a burden
16. to trigger: to initiate an action; to cause a psychological process to begin
17. cue: a stimulus that triggers a behavior; a trigger
18. crisis: an emergency; a crucial or decisive situation whose outcome decides whether possible bad consequences will follow
19. guilty: having done wrong; feeling responsible for wrongdoing
20. integral: essential; basic; necessary for completeness

### Exercise 2 (pages 39–40)

1. to intersperse: to put among things; to interrupt
   to avert: to avoid; to miss; to prevent
2. to inhibit: to suppress; to hide
3. foible: weakness; fault; minor flaw in character
4. to ogle: to keep looking at with fondness or desire
   dowdy: not neat or fashionable

## Vocabulary Review (page 40)

| | | |
|---|---|---|
| 1. cue | 3. resent | 5. aggression |
| 2. trigger | 4. conscious | |

## Reading Selection 3: Short Story "The Lottery"

### Comprehension

#### Exercise 1 (pages 44–45)

| | | | | |
|---|---|---|---|---|
| 1. T | 3. F | 5. F | 7. T | 9. T |
| 2. F | 4. T | 6. F | 8. F | |

#### Exercise 2 (page 45)

| | | | |
|---|---|---|---|
| 1. T | 3. T | 5. T | 7. F |
| 2. F | 4. T | 6. F | |

### Drawing Inferences (page 45)

1. Answers might include such things as the following:
   People were nervous.
   Tessie didn't want to win the lottery.
2. Answers might include such things as the following:
   *Normal Lottery*
   a. The whole village was present.
   b. Tessie's arrival was good-humored.
   c. Mr. Summers conducted square dances, teen clubs, and the lottery.
   d. The slips of paper and the initial ritual of the lottery seemed typical.
   *Strange Lottery*
   a. Piles of rocks were prepared.
   b. People hesitated to volunteer to hold the box.
   c. Some villages had already stopped having a lottery.
   d. Mr. Warner considered such villages barbaric.
   e. A girl whispered, "I hope it's not Nancy."
   f. Tessie didn't want to win; she wanted to include her married children in the second drawing.
   *Double Meaning*
   a. There was no place to leave the box during the year.
   b. The Watson boy blinked his eyes "nervously."
   c. There were continual references to tension, nervousness, and humorless grins.
   d. Mrs. Dunbar said to "get ready to run tell Dad."
3. They had to take part so that everyone would be responsible, so that everyone would have to take part next year.
4. Mr. Warner felt that giving up the lottery would bring bad luck and would be uncivilized. He represents the older, more conservative members of a society who resist change.
5. Tessie wanted more people to be included in the final drawing so that her chances of "winning" would be reduced.
6. *Changes in the Lottery*
   a. The original paraphernalia had been lost.
   b. The box had changed.
   c. Slips of paper had replaced wooden chips.
   d. There used to be a recital and ritual salute.
   *Unchanged Elements of the Lottery*
   a. The list of names was checked in the same way.
   b. The black box was made with wood from the original box.
   c. There were two drawings and the result of the lottery had remained the same.

### Vocabulary from Context

#### Exercise 1 (page 46)

1. ritual: any formal, customary observance or procedure; ceremony; rite

2. paraphernalia: equipment; any collection of things used in some activity
3. drawing: a lottery; the act of choosing a winner in a lottery
4. gravely: seriously; soberly; somberly; solemnly
5. soberly: seriously; gravely; solemnly; sedately
6. murmur: a low, indistinct, continuous sound
7. to discard: to throw away, abandon, or get rid of something that is no longer useful
8. to disengage: to release oneself; to get loose; to leave

#### Exercise 2 (page 47)

| | | |
|---|---|---|
| 1. boisterous | 3. gossip | 5. interminably |
| 2. reprimands | 4. fussing | |

#### Exercise 3 (page 47)

1. to devote: to give
2. stirred up: moved; shook; displaced
3. to fade off: to slowly disappear or end; to die out
4. shabbier: older; more broken down; worn out; showing more wear
5. to lapse: to fall away; to slip from memory; to return to former ways
6. craned: raised or moved
7. tapped: hit lightly
8. consulted: looked at; checked; referred to; sought information from

## Unit 3

### Nonprose Reading: Bus Schedule

#### Exercise 1 (page 49)

1. 20th Avenue
2. The schedule does not list the university; however, if you knew that the university was in downtown Denver, you would know that the bus goes near the university. The bus does go by the museum.
3. "Peak hours" are when the most traffic is on the road: 6–9 A.M. and 4–6 P.M. weekdays. Because the traffic moves more slowly, your ability to get to work on time may depend on this knowledge. Also, it costs more to ride the bus during peak hours.
4. $1.40 (round-trip: 35 cents per adult each way; children 5 or under may ride free)
5. Yes, you must have exact change or use tokens.
6. 573-2288
7. 778-6000 or 753-9405 (for hearing impaired)
8. Five cents

#### Exercise 2 (page 50)

| | | |
|---|---|---|
| 1. Yes | 2. Yes | 3. F |

4. During selected trips only (on days of Bronco football games)
5. Yes (on selected trips only)

#### Exercise 3 (page 50)

1. T
2. All 20th Avenue buses are accessible to wheelchairs.
3. The 8:55 A.M. bus will get you there 40 minutes early. The 9:57 bus will get you there 22 minutes late. You decide which bus to take.
4. The 6:07 P.M. bus
5. None
6. F
7. F
8. T or F. You might answer true if you believe that the amount of Spanish written on this schedule is sufficient to enable a speaker of Spanish to use it. You would answer false if you believe the amount of Spanish is insufficient.

### Word Study: Stems and Affixes

*Exercise 1 (pages 53–54)*

1. hydroelectric (plant): a plant that uses water power to produce electricity
2. thermometer: an instrument that measures heat and indicates temperature
3. hyperactive: overactive; too active; abnormally active
4. to verify: to make sure it is true; to confirm
5. pedals: the parts of the bicycle moved by the feet to make the wheels turn
6. dehydration: loss of water from the body
7. tripod: a three-legged stand used to hold a camera
8. hypersensitive: overly sensitive; too easily hurt
9. hypodermic: a needle used to inject substances under the skin
10. orthodontics: a type of dentistry concerned with straightening teeth
11. deported: made (him) leave the country
12. per capita: individual; for each person
13. dermatologist: a doctor who treats skin diseases
14. geothermal: heat of the earth
15. bipedal: walked on two feet
16. veracity: truth
17. supersonic: faster than (above) the speed of sound

*Exercise 2 (pages 54–55)*

| | | | |
|---|---|---|---|
| 1. d | 6. e | 12. c | 18. a |
| 2. a | 7. f | 13. a | 19. c |
| 3. e | 8. d | 14. d | 20. e |
| 4. c | 9. b | 15. f | 21. d |
| 5. b | 10. a | 16. b | 22. b |
| | 11. c | 17. e | |

### Sentence Study: Comprehension (pages 56–57)

| | | | | |
|---|---|---|---|---|
| 1. d | 3. a | 5. c | 7. b | 9. b |
| 2. b | 4. c | 6. a | 8. d | |

### Paragraph Reading: Restatement and Inference (pages 58–60)

Paragraph 1: e          Paragraph 4: a (c)
Paragraph 2: a, b, c, d      Paragraph 5: a, d
Paragraph 3: b

### Discourse Focus: Careful Reading/Drawing Inferences (pages 61–63)

1. "Murder on Board": Nathan Cohen was held because it would have been impossible for him to have written in small, precise handwriting during a violent storm.
2. "Death in the Mountains": It was a dark, starless, moonless night. No animal's eyes shine unless there is a light that can be reflected from them. A human's eyes NEVER shine under any circumstances.
   Wylie could not possibly have seen eyes shining at him in the dark. It was clearly murder.
3. "Case #194": If the newspaper account was correct, Mayer was lying. He could not possibly have been in the water, walked half a mile through ten below zero weather, and then shaken water from his clothes. Had the tragedy happened as he described it, the water on his clothes would have been frozen.
4. "The Break": Before ascertaining the killer's identity we will find out who is the mob leader.
   The leader is not Louis Segal (2). And he is not Anton Kroll or Sam Chapin (3), therefore the leader is Dan Morgan. Dan Morgan (the leader) is not the killer. The killer is not Louis Segal (2 and 4) and

in (5) we learn Anton Kroll is not the murderer. Hence the man who killed Trooper Burton is Sam Chapin.

## Unit 4

### Selection 1A: Feature Article "Japanese Style in Decision-Making"

**Comprehension**

*Exercise 1 (page 66)*

| | | | | |
|---|---|---|---|---|
| 1. J | 3. J | 5. US | 7. US | 9. US |
| 2. US | 4. US | 6. US | 8. J | |

*Exercise 2 (page 66)*

1. In Japan the most important thing is what organization you work for; in the United States one's position in a company defines one's professional identity.
2. See paragraphs 10 and 11, page 191, for explanations of the "I to you" and "you to you" approaches.
   See paragraph 16, page 191, for an explanation of Western versus Japanese decision-making.
3. a. The Japanese try to formulate a rather broad direction.
   b. Westerners like to take time for in-depth planning.
4. Employees stay at work after hours, until the job is completed.
5. The author is Yoshio Terasawa, President of Nomura Securities International, Inc. The article was adapted from a speech before the Commonwealth Club of San Francisco.

**Vocabulary from Context**

*Exercise 1 (pages 67–68)*

1. to formulate: to form; to express in a systematic way
2. reliance: dependence
3. adroit: skillful; clever
4. confrontation: a face-to-face meeting, as of antagonists, competitors, or enemies
5. harmony: agreement of feeling, action, ideas, interests, etc.; peaceful or friendly relations
6. consensus: agreement in opinion; agreement among all parties
7. mutual: done, felt, etc., by two or more people for each other; reciprocal
8. literate: able to read and write; educated
9. articulate: able to express oneself clearly
10. stability: resistance to change; permanence
11. mobility: movement; change
12. exasperated: angered; irritated; frustrated; annoyed
13. deadline: a time limit
14. dedication: seriousness; loyalty; faithfulness; devotion to some duty
15. unanimous: showing complete agreement; united in opinion
16. homogeneous: composed of similar elements or parts; similar; identical; uniform
17. inflexible: not flexible; rigid; not adjustable to change; not capable of modification
18. unilateral: done or undertaken by one side only; not reciprocal
19. firm: company; business

*Exercise 2 (page 68)*

1. vocational: professional; relating to one's job
2. forthrightly: directly
3. densely: with many people in a small area; with the parts crowded together

4. consult: to seek information
5. impact: effect; influence
6. converted: changed

### Figurative Language and Idioms (page 69)

1. "coming to grips with"
2. "for a living"
3. "sounding out"
4. "keeping (your) finger on the pulse"
5. "falls through"
6. "paper logjam"
7. "pitch in"

### Vocabulary Review

#### Exercise 1 (pages 69–70)

| | | |
|---|---|---|
| 1. adroit | 4. exasperated | 7. reliance |
| 2. articulate | 5. deadlines | 8. formulate |
| 3. transactions | 6. dedicated | |

#### Exercise 2 (page 70)

| | | |
|---|---|---|
| 1. unilaterally | 3. heterogeneous | 5. inflexible |
| 2. confrontation | 4. mobility | 6. unilateral |

### Selection 1B: Feature Article
### "Happy Customers Matter of Honor among Japanese"

#### Critical Reading

#### Exercise 1 (page 72)
1. T     2. T     3. F     4. F     5. T

#### Exercise 2 (pages 72–73)
Apparently the author assumes the following to be typical of the United States:

1. *shopping for food:* Check-out counters typically have only one or two people ringing up and bagging food; stores do not deliver food to your home.
2. *purchasing a T.V.:* Customers install their own T.V. sets; technicians do not come to your home.
3. *getting a haircut:* In the U.S. barbers only give haircuts; they do not give massages or clean glasses.
4. *buying gas for a car:* In the U.S., the popular self-service gas stations do not provide the services available in Japan: putting gasoline in the car, wiping the windshield, emptying ash trays, stopping traffic to let the motorist back on the road.
5. *shopping in a department store:* Apparently the author finds fewer salespeople in department stores, and finds it unusual for purchases to be wrapped and for shopping to be done at home.
6. *staying at a hotel:* The author finds more personalized service in U.S. hotels: he expects to be personally greeted and, after a long stay, he expects the staff to know who he is.

#### Vocabulary from Context (page 73)

1. luxury: something adding to pleasure or comfort but not absolutely necessary
2. staff: group of workers; force
3. proprietor: owner
4. fuss: unnecessary bother
5. demeaning: degrading; making your status lower
6. ingredients: parts; constituents; things that a mixture is made of
7. treacherous: disloyal; untrustworthy
8. upscale: rich
9. courtesies: polite acts
10. on a national scale: nationally; throughout the country
11. proliferation: rapid growth; rapid increase in the number

### Reading Selection 2: Satire
### "Pockety Women Unit?"

#### Comprehension

#### Exercise 1 (page 76)
1. They hold better positions because they are men; cultural traditions and social conditioning have worked together to give them a special place in the world order.
2. 9
3. none
4. There is a positive correlation between pockets and power.
5. Pockets hold all the equipment necessary for running the world; they are necessary for efficiency, order, confidence.
6. It is difficult to organize one's belongings in a purse; a purse makes one appear to be disorganized.
7. Women should form a pocket lobby and march on the New York garment district. Women should give men gifts of pocketless shirts and men's handbags.

#### Exercise 2 (pages 76–77)
This exercise is intended to encourage discussion and to force students to come to a better understanding of the purpose of the article. Students can potentially defend all seven items.

#### Vocabulary from Context (page 77)
1. status: position; rank; standing
2. prestige: power to command admiration; distinction based on achievement; reputation; standing in the community
3. correlation: a close or natural relation; a correspondence
4. purse: a handbag, pocketbook; a bag in which money and personal belongings are carried
5. to attain: to gain through effort; to achieve; to come to, arrive at; to reach; to get

#### Dictionary Study (page 78)
1. match: (*n.* 1*a.*) a person, group, or thing able to cope with or oppose another as an equal in power, size, etc.
2. tip: (second entry, *n.* 2.) a piece of information given secretly or confidentially in an attempt to be helpful: as, he gave me a *tip* on the race. also: (*n.* 3.) a suggestion, hint, warning, etc.
3. lobbyist: (*n.*) a person who tries to get legislators to introduce or vote for measures favorable to a special interest that he represents. [a person who attempts to change a group's opinions]

### Reading Selection 3: Poetry

#### Comprehension: "How to Eat a Poem"/"Unfolding Bud" (page 80)

1. a. Reading a poem is like eating because, to enjoy a poem, you bite into it; you make a poem part of you and it nourishes you. You "ingest" the poem: you pick it up, examine it closely, enjoy it, and put it inside you. You can enjoy every part of it; every part provides nourishment.
   b. The author is urging us to "get our hands dirty," to really experience and ingest the poem, to touch all parts of it.
   c. There is nothing to throw away; no part of a poem is left uneaten.
   d. Eating fruit is messier than eating bread, but it can be sweeter. Similarly, reading poetry can

require taking more chances, making more guesses, but it too can be very satisfying.

   e. This question is intended for discussion.

2.  a. Like a water-lily bud, a poem can appear at first to be closed. As we read, we open the bud, revealing the many wonderful things inside.

   b. We expect a bud to reveal a rich inner self; we forget that poems, too, reveal different colors and dimensions upon rereading.

   c. Both points of view suggest that one needs to examine poems closely, to fully appreciate them. Many differences might be mentioned. Among them is the fact that Merriam stresses the sensuous joy of consuming poetry, while Koriyama stresses the contemplation of beauty.

### Comprehension: "This is Just to Say" (page 81)

1. People who don't like the poem mention such things as the fact that it lacks poetic rhyme and rhythm, is not on a lofty topic, and it contains everyday language. People who like the poem tend to enjoy its haiku-like format, its references to nature, and the simplicity of the presentation.

2. Although the note says, "forgive me," this is not primarily an apology. The writer does not seem to fear serious punishment.

3. Most readers agree that there is a degree of intimacy between the writer and the receiver of this note. They appear to live together. Students have suggested the following relationships between the two: spouses, lovers, child and parent, siblings. This may be considered a love letter.

4. The note may have been written to ask forgiveness, but the expression of intimacy and caring seems to be its primary purpose.

5. This question is intended for discussion.

### Comprehension: "in Just-" (page 83)

1. The poem mentions spring weather (mud puddles), children's games (pirates, hop-scotch, jump-rope, marbles), and seasonal salespeople (the balloonman).

2. Eddie, Bill, Betty, and Isabel

3. mudluscious: the wonderful feeling of playing in the mud
puddle-wonderful: the fun of playing in puddles; for children, the wonder of a newly wet world

4. You can argue either that the poem evokes a happy springtime or suggests a sadder or more sinister theme. To argue for a joyful poem you can point to the use of words like *mudluscious* and *puddle-wonderful*, and to the joyful games of the children. A sadder theme is suggested by the description of the physical handicap of the balloonman who is referred to as *old* and *lame*. The balloonman is also described as *queer* and *goat-footed* (like the devil). If we change the title from "in Just-" to *injust*, it suggests that some injustice has or will occur. Is our view of the balloonman unjust, or will he perpetrate an injustice upon the children?

5. This question is intended for discussion.

### Comprehension: "Spring and Fall: To a Young Child" (page 84)

1.  a. Can you with your fresh thoughts care for leaves like the things of man?

   b. Neither the mouth nor the heart had expressed what heart heard of, ghost guessed.

2. *Goldengrove:* The initial capital letter indicates that this is the name of an imaginary place where a group of trees have turned golden during the fall season.
*unleaving:* The trees are losing their leaves.
*wanwood:* Wan is a colorless, sick color. The term suggests colorless, dead stems and branches.
*leafmeal:* In this context, meal refers to any substance with a powdered, grainy quality, e.g., corn meal. Leafmeal suggests a ground substance made of leaves. The leafmeal also apparently contains colorless, dead stems and branches.

3. Margaret is grieving for herself: like all living things she, too, will one day die.

### Reading Selection 4: Short Story "The Chaser"

#### Comprehension (pages 87–88)

1. F
2. F
3. a glove-cleaner or a life-cleaner
4. poison
5. T
6. She is sociable, fond of parties, and not interested in Alan.
7. Diana will want nothing but solitude and Alan; she will be jealous; Alan will be her sole interest in life; she will want to know all that he does; she will forgive him anything but will never divorce him.
8. T
9. The first drink is the love potion; the unpleasant "taste" is the fact that Diana will be so possessive; the chaser will be the poison (the glove-cleaner).
10. People who bought the love potion always came back for the $5,000 mixture.

#### Drawing Inferences (page 88)

1. Alan thinks the old man is describing love. The old man knows he is describing a terrible situation.

2. Alan thinks it is wonderful that his wife will never divorce him. The old man knows that some day Alan may want his wife to give him a divorce and she will refuse.

3. Alan thinks customers come back, as they do to any store, because they have found something there before that they needed; they come back of their own free will. The old man knows that if he "obliges" his customers with the love potion, they *must* come back.

4. Alan thinks the old man means goodbye. The old man means, "until I see you again"; he knows that Alan will return.

#### Vocabulary from Context

##### Exercise 1 (page 89)

1. poison: a substance, usually a drug, causing death or severe injury
2. imperceptible: not able to be perceived; unnoticeable
3. sufficient: enough
4. confidential: trusting; entrusted with private or secret matters
5. to oblige: to satisfy, please, help someone; to do a favor for; to perform a service
6. solitude: to be alone; isolation
7. jealous: demanding exclusive loyalty; resentfully suspicious of competitors; envious; distrustful; suspicious

**Exercise 2 (page 90)**

1. dim          3. apprehensively     5. sirens
2. stock        4. oblige             6. grounds

**Exercise 3 (page 90)**

1. peered: looked at closely and searchingly in order to see more clearly
2. potion: a drink, especially a medicine or poison
3. slip a little: make a mistake; fall into error; be unfaithful to his wife
4. dear: expensive
5. better off: wealthier; richer

## Unit 5

### Nonprose Reading: Road Map

**Introduction**

**Exercise 1 (pages 91–92)**

2. a. L-10
3. W. Trinity Lane and Whites Creek Pike
4. a. Bowling Green is about 25 miles/40 kilometers from the Ky.-Tenn. border.
   b. Route 31W is a Federal highway while route 65 is an Interstate highway.
   [All Interstate highways are multilane, divided, controlled access roads. In contrast, Federal highways have widely varying characteristics. For instance, although some Federal highways are divided, 31W is not.]
5. 66 miles (106 kilometers)

**Exercise 2 (pages 92–93)**

1. e          3. a          5. d
2. b          4. c          6. c

**Map Reading**

**Exercise 1 (page 93)**

1. T     3. T     5. T     7. T     9. T     11. F
2. F     4. F     6. T     8. F    10. T

**Exercise 2 (page 94)**

1. yes; 50 miles per hour/80 kilometers per hour
2. Answers might include such routes as the following:
   31W or 65 → 101 → 259 → 70
   or (31W) → 65 → 70
   You can spend the night at the Park.
3. Answers might include such routes as the following:
   56 (E. E. State Park) → 40
                         → 70 → 96 → 266

   231 (C. L. State Park) → 40 or 41 (Nashville)

### Word Study: Context Clues

**Exercise 1 (page 98)**

1. precariously: dangerously; uncertainly
2. to trudge: to walk tiredly, slowly
3. turmoil: confusion
4. grooming: personal cleaning; the act of making neat and tidy
5. matrimony: marriage
6. probe: a long slender instrument used for delicate exploration
7. to convene: to call together; to start
8. to ingest; to eat; to take inside
9. autocratic: dictatorial; undemocratic; tyrannical; domineering
10. limnology: fresh water biology

**Exercise 2 (page 99)**

genetic/genes: referring to biological inheritance; the elements by which parents biologically transmit characteristics to their children
rearing/reared: referring to the process of raising children, bringing them up. In this article nurture (child rearing) is contrasted to nature (genetics).
findings: discoveries; conclusions
shatter: disprove; destroy
primacy: being first in importance; supremacy
heredity: the biological process of passing on characteristics from parent to child
nurture: the act of raising, rearing; all the environmental factors that affect individuals as distinguished from their nature or heredity

### Sentence Study: Restatement and Inference (pages 100–103)

1. d          5. c          9. b
2. a, b       6. a, c      10. a, d
3. a, b, c, e 7. b, c, d, e
4. a          8. d, e

### Paragraph Analysis: Reading for Full Understanding (pages 104–9)

**Paragraph 1**
1. a     4. c
2. b     5. c
3. a

**Paragraph 2**
1. c     3. b
2. b     4. d

**Paragraph 3**
1. b     4. b
2. c     5. d
3. c

**Paragraph 4**
1. b     3. c
2. c     4. b

**Paragraph 5**
1. c     5. a
2. b     6. c
3. a     7. b
4. c

### Discourse Focus: Prediction (pages 110–12)

There are no single correct responses to the items in this exercise. Students should work interactively: interacting with each other and the text in order to form predictions, then reading to see if these are confirmed. The answers, therefore, are available by further reading.

1. This article is about changes in the family. You might expect to read about changes in such things as the size of families, the roles of family members, the role of families in society, or even the definition of the family. There are many other possible responses.
2–3. These questions require a personal response.
4. b, d, i
5–6. There are many possible answers. Based on the mention of family members and the reference to definition, you might have listed such things as the roles of family members, the definition of the family, perhaps the size of the family.
7. Because the opening sentence discusses changes in the historical view of family size and definition, you might expect to find historical data that speaks to these issues.
8. This question requires a personal response.
9. b, d, e, g, h, i, j

## Unit 6

### Reading Selection 1: Textbook
### "The Sacred 'Rac' "

#### Comprehension (pages 116–17)

1. the Asu
2. They live on the American continent north of the Tarahumara of Mexico.
3. T
4. The cost is so high because of the long period of training the specialist must undergo and the difficulty of obtaining the right selection of magic charms.
5. T
6. It may be used as a beast of burden.
7. The Asu must build more paths for the rac; the Asu must pay high taxes; some Asu must move their homes.
8. F
9. The rac kills thousands of the Asu a year.
10. T
11. car

#### Drawing Inferences (page 117)

She feels that individuals and societies are foolish to sacrifice so much for cars. People often notice problems of other cultures more easily than those of their own culture. The author hopes that people in the United States will be able to examine the effect of the car on their society more realistically if they do not realize immediately that they are reading about themselves.

#### Vocabulary from Context (page 118)

1. preoccupied: absorbed in one's thoughts; unable to concentrate
2. temperament: disposition; emotional or psychological characteristics; frame of mind
3. prestigious: admired; important; distinguished; of a high rank
4. to treat: to give medical care to
5. ailing: sick
6. puberty rites: ceremonies that mark adulthood
7. to petition: to make a formal request; to ask; to beg
8. detrimental: damaging; harmful; injurious
9. to regard: to consider or think of as being something

### Reading Selection 2: Essay
### "The City"

#### Comprehension

#### Exercise 1 (page 122)
1, 2, 3, 6, 8, 10

#### Exercise 2 (page 123)

| | |
|---|---|
| 1. F | 8. F |
| 2. O author | 9. F |
| 3. F | 10. O generations of American |
| 4. O Frenchman | theory; those responsible |
| 5. O others | for the Homestead Act |
| 6. F | 11. F |
| 7. O Jefferson | 12. O rural Americans |

#### Vocabulary from Context

#### Exercise 1 (page 124)
1. suspect: viewed with mistrust; believed to be bad, wrong, harmful, questionable

2. priority: value, rank; the right to come first; precedence
3. absurd: ridiculous; silly
4. to subsidize: to grant money to, as the government granting money to a private enterprise; to support
5. predicament: a troublesome or difficult situation
6. integral: essential; basic; necessary for completeness
7. corrupt: spoiled; evil; bad; morally unsound; departing from the normal standard
8. despot: oppressor; dictator; tyrant; autocrat

#### Exercise 2 (page 125)
1. dispersion
2. fend (for)
3. renovation

#### Exercise 3 (page 125)
1. to trace: to find the source of something by following its development from the latest to the earliest time
2. flocking: coming in large numbers
3. antipathy: a definite dislike
4. pastoral: rural
5. charting: planning; plotting; mapping
6. waves: arrivals of large groups of people
7. ethnic: of or pertaining to nationalities
8. to bar: to stop; to prevent
9. fled: left; ran away from
10. subtle: indirect; difficult to understand, solve, or detect; clever; skillful

### Selection 3A: Family Narrative
### "An Attack on the Family"

#### Comprehension

#### Exercise 1 (pages 128–29)
1. F
2. T
3. When he switched on the torch, they would walk away. Also, the family would not allow him to bring scorpions into the house to study.
4. T
5. The babies clung to the mother's back.
6. F
7. when Larry went to light a match after dinner
8. Margo was trying to throw water on the scorpions but missed.
9. F
10. F
11. T
12. The author carried them outside on a saucer.
13. T

#### Exercise 2 (pages 129–30)
1. Roger is a dog.
2. Lugaretzia is not a member of the family; she is probably a servant.
3. five: Mother (f), Larry (m), author (m), Leslie (m), Margo (f)
4. Leslie
5. Larry          7. Mother
6. Margo          8. the author
9. This question is intended for discussion.

#### Vocabulary from Context

#### Exercise 1 (pages 130–31)
1. glimpses: brief, quick views; passing looks
2. enraptured (with/by): fascinated; enchanted; entranced; filled with pleasure
3. rage: extreme anger

4. bewildered: confused
5. plea: a request; appeal; statement of begging
6. courtship: the process or period of time during which one person attempts to win the love of another
7. to crouch: to bow low with the arms and legs drawn close to the body; to bend low; to squat
8. in vain: without effect; fruitlessly

*Exercise 2 (page 131)*

1. trial
2. to smuggle
3. doom
4. chaos, pandemonium
5. order

*Exercise 3 (page 131)*

1. assaults: attacks; invasions
2. clinging: holding on to
3. manoeuvred: managed or planned skillfully; manipulated; moved
4. maintain: argue; affirm; declare to be true
5. hoisted: pulled; lifted
6. scuttled: ran or moved quickly, as away from danger
7. peered: looked closely and searchingly, as in order to see more clearly
8. hurled: threw
9. drenched: made wet all over; saturated with water
10. swarmed: moved around in large numbers; completely covered something
11. screeching: screaming
12. reluctance: hesitation; unwillingness; a feeling of not wanting to do something

### Selection 3B: Family Narrative
### Adaptation from Cheaper by the Dozen

**Comprehension (pages 137–38)**

| | | | | |
|---|---|---|---|---|
| 1. F | 5. T | 9. T | 13. F | 17. F |
| 2. T | 6. F | 10. T | 14. F | 18. T |
| 3. F | 7. T | 11. F | 15. F | 19. T |
| 4. T | 8. T | 12. F | 16. T | 20. T |

**Vocabulary from Context**

*Exercise 1 (page 139)*

1. litter: the total number of animals born at one time of one mother
2. whistle: a shrill musical sound made by forcing air through the teeth
3. regimentation: rigid organization by which tasks are assigned
4. aptitude: special ability, talent; quickness to learn
5. (on the) verge: on the edge; about to do something
6. hysterical: wild; emotionally uncontrolled
7. nuisance: a bother; an act, condition, thing, or person causing trouble
8. incentive: encouragement; reward that makes one work or achieve; motive; stimulus
9. voluntary: of one's own will; without being forced to do something
10. ludicrous: extremely funny; ridiculous; silly; absurd

*Exercise 2 (page 140)*

1. offspring: children
2. tender: young
3. slashed: cut
4. sweep: clean (a floor with a broom)
5. mimicked: copied; imitated
6. abstained: didn't vote

**Figurative Language and Idioms (page 140)**

1. "practiced what he preached"
2. "no telling"
3. "eat (me) out of house and home"
4. "fits (her) like a glove"
5. "deal him in"
6. "pulled (my) leg"

**Dictionary Study (page 141)**

1. off: (*adj.* 6.) not up to the usual level, standard, etc.: as, an *off* season
2. bedlam: (*n.* 4.) noise and confusion; uproar also: (*n.* 3.) any noisy, confused place or situation
3. allowances: (*n.* 3.) an amount of money, food, etc. given regularly to a child, dependent, soldier, etc.
4. to tickle: (*v.t.* 2.) to amuse; delight: as, the story *tickled* him.
5. straight face: [from the adjective straight-faced] showing no amusement or emotion
6. spit and image: [Colloq.] perfect likeness; exact image
7. offhand: (*adv.*) without prior preparation or study; at once; extemporaneously

## Unit 7

### Longer Reading: Psychology
### "The Milgram Experiment"

**Comprehension**

*Exercise 1 (pages 149–50)*

| | | |
|---|---|---|
| 1. F | 4. T | 7. F |
| 2. F | 5. F | 8. F |
| 3. T | 6. T | 9. F |

10. The quotation marks around "subject" indicate that the man strapped into the chair is not the real subject. The real subject is the person who administers the shocks.

11–12. These items are intended to provoke discussion. There is no single correct answer.

*Exercise 2 (page 153)*

1. Milgram wanted to determine the extent to which people would obey an experimenter's commands to administer painful electric shocks to another person.
2. T
3. F
4. F
5. This item is intended for discussion.
6. F
7. The answer depends on your view of human nature. You might agree with Milgram, who believed that few people have the resources needed to resist authority. On the other hand, you might believe that people are sadistic and that they want to hurt other people.
8. a. T or F. You might answer true if you believe that the subjects were simply obedient and gave positive evaluations. On the other hand, you might answer false if you believe that the subjects rated the experiment positive for another reason—if, for example, they felt that they learned something.
   b. T or F. Your answer might be either true or false depending on your answer to 8a. If obedient subjects merely continued to respond obediently to the follow-up study, the answers would not reflect their true feelings.
9. T or F. You might answer true if you consider Stanley Milgram to be an ordinary person subject to the same pressures as the rest of us. On the other hand, you might answer false if you consider

Milgram to have special knowledge about the experiment that he authored.

## Vocabulary from Context

### Exercise 1 (page 154)

1. rationalizations: excuses; explanations that are based on logical reasoning, but are essentially false
2. simulation: imitation; artificial situation created to resemble a real situation.
3. banality: commonness; ordinariness
4. controversial: full of controversy; causing argument or disagreement
5. ethical: having ethics; acting according to moral principles or beliefs

### Exercise 2 (pages 154–55)

1. atrocities
2. ingenious
3. administer
4. subject
5. contrived
6. virtually
7. sadistic
8. debriefing

## Figurative Language and Idioms (page 155)

1. "by lot"
2. "a cross section"
3. "chilling"
4. "fringe of society"
5. "has raged"

# Unit 8

## Longer Reading: Anthropology "In the Shadow of Man"

## Comprehension

### Exercise 1 (page 161)

1. T
2. F
3. F
4. F
5. T
6. T
7. F
8. F
9. T
10. F
11. T
12. T
13. F
14. T

### Exercise 2 (pages 161–62)

1, 2, 3, 5, 6

## Vocabulary from Context (pages 162–63)

1. sophisticated: complex; complicated
2. innate: possessed from birth; inborn; not learned
3. posture: the position of the body; carriage; bearing
4. to hurl: to throw with force; to move vigorously
5. to stroke: to caress; to rub lightly with the hand
6. gesture: movement of the body or part of the body to express ideas, emotions, etc.
7. inevitable: something that cannot be avoided or prevented
8. altruistic: unselfishly concerned for another person
9. to derive: to get or receive (from a source); to trace from or to a source; to originate
10. submissive: humble; compliant; yielding to others
11. spontaneously: naturally; voluntarily; freely
12. to probe: to search; to explore with an instrument; to investigate with great thoroughness

## Stems and Affixes (page 163)

1. c
2. e
3. f
4. a
5. g
6. d
7. h
8. j
9. i
10. b

## Figurative Language and Idioms (pages 163–64)

1. "spontaneously"
2. "to burst into tears"
3. "flew into a tantrum"
4. "told (him) off"
5. "to draw parallels"
6. "bowled over"

## Vocabulary Review (pages 165–66)

1. sophisticated
2. gestured
3. inevitable
4. innate
5. hurled
6. burst into tears
7. Altruism
8. submissive
9. flew into a tantrum
10. probes
11. posture
12. spontaneously
13. draw parallels
14. stroking
15. derived